GETTING
* INTO *
GUINNESS

GETTING *INTO* GUINNESS

One Man's Longest, Fastest,
Highest Journey Inside the World's
Most Famous Record Book

LARRY
OLMSTED

COLLINS
An Imprint of HarperCollins *Publishers*

GETTING INTO GUINESS. Copyright © 2008 by Larry Olmsted. All rights reserved. Printed in the United States of America. No part of this book may be used or reproduced in any manner whatsoever without written permission except in the case of brief quotations embodied in critical articles and reviews. For information, address HarperCollins Publishers, 10 East 53rd Street, New York, NY 10022.

HarperCollins books may be purchased for educational, business, or sales promotional use. For information, please write: Special Markets Department, HarperCollins Publishers, 10 East 53rd Street, New York, NY 10022.

FIRST U.S. EDITION

Designed by Renato Stanisic

Library of Congress Cataloging-in-Publication Data has been applied for.
ISBN 978-0-06-137348-0

08 09 10 11 12 OV/RRD 10 9 8 7 6 5 4 3 2 1

For Allison, Armstrong, Stretch, and Sundance
Many reasons, many years, much love

Adrian Hilton recited the Complete Works of Shakespeare *nonstop, going five days without sleep to earn his Guinness recognition. At a difficult point in his life, Hilton said a friend told him: "Adrian, if you give up now, you weren't made of the right stuff in the first place."*

INVESTOR'S BUSINESS DAILY, MARCH 30, 2007

Contents

Author's Note

*G*uinness World Records is the current name of the book that has become the biggest international best seller of all time, and it is published by Guinness World Records Ltd., a London-based company. However, both the book's title and ownership have changed several times throughout its history, so to make things less confusing, I offer the following brief explanation.

The book was originally titled *The Guinness Book of Records* and published in 1955 by Superlatives Ltd., a wholly owned subsidiary of Arthur Guinness & Sons, the huge brewing company that also made Guinness Stout. Superlatives Ltd. later became known as Guinness Publishing, and its parent company as Guinness PLC. Guinness PLC is now part of multinational beer, wine, and spirits conglomerate Diageo PLC. In 1999 Guinness Publishing changed to its current name, Guinness World Records Ltd., but has also been sold and resold and is no longer associated in any way with the brewery or with Diageo, except for the common use of the word "Guinness" in beer and book.

When first released in the United States, the book was briefly titled *The Guinness Book of Superlatives,* then quickly repackaged in a cover titled *Superlatives Book of World Records*, and soon became *The Guinness Book of Records* once again, and then *The Guinness Book of World Records*, which I believe is its best known and most widely used title, and what many fans still call it today. To further confuse matters, for more than twenty years the U.S. version was produced and distributed under license by Sterling Publishing in New York, but now it is fully owned and produced by Guinness World Records Ltd. In general, the U.S. and English editions will be referred to interchangeably throughout this work, though there were often minor differences between the two even in the same years, and some records were recognized only by one or the other version.

Throughout this book I use the original title, *The Guinness Book of Records*, the current title, *Guinness World Records,* and the in-between title, *The Guinness Book of World Records.* In addition, I use the simpler terms "Guinness book," "book of records," and even "The Book" when referring to the same work. Likewise, in describing the records themselves (each officially called by the plural "Guinness World Records"), I variously referred to them as Guinness Records, Guinness World Records, records, world records, the Guinness World Record, while identifying the record holders as record holders, world record holders, and Guinness World Record holders, among other possible descriptions.

Since the company, its book, and its records now have virtually the same name, I will italicize *Guinness World Records* when referring to the book and leave Guinness World Records unadorned when referring to either the records themselves or the company and its editors, staffers, policies, and other products. Similarly, the book's original creator is variously referred to as Arthur Guinness & Sons, Guinness PLC, and simply Guinness, as well as "the brewing company."

Finally, the expressions "Getting into Guinness," "Get into Guinness," or variations thereof always refer to an attempt to break or set a record in a manner recognized by Guinness World

Records Ltd. and its book *Guinness World Records*, with the intention of obtaining an official certificate and/or being published in the pages of the book or listed in the company's record database. These terms do not refer to the literal notion of getting into a beverage brewed by the company that makes Guinness Stout. While there is no longer any association between the brewer and the book, I would like to add that the stout is still excellent after all these years, and several were consumed by me, at my desk, in the writing of this work.

LSO, November 2007

In my research for *Getting into Guinness,* I reviewed countless published sources about the origins and development of Guinness World Records and interviewed many of the more astounding Guinness World Record holders. Combining this research with my own experiences as a fan since reading it as a child, and as the holder of two records, I have attempted to recount the enthralling 50-year history of the Guinness World Records from the perspective of the record holder (or aspiring record holder) looking into a company that has fascinated him from a young age. As such, this book is not an official history of Guinness World Records, nor has it been sponsored, endorsed, authorized, or in any way supported by Guinness World Records. Indeed, Guinness World Records may at some point elect to publish such a book, and, with its extensive archives, I am sure that it would be fascinating.

Introduction

JUNE 13, 2004, FOXWOODS CASINO, LEDYARD, CONNECTICUT

I knew I was in trouble when I got lost on my way back from the bathroom. Or more accurately, I should have known I was in trouble but did not immediately make the connection, for the very same reason I went astray in the first place: I was losing my mind. Getting lost in an unfamiliar place is not surprising. Getting lost in plain sight of where you want to go, just thirty yards away, when you are intimately familiar with the route, is something altogether different. Something crazy.

It was a security guard who first noticed my plight, perhaps sympathetic to my confused and vacant expression. Or more likely he was alarmed by what could only be construed as signs of madness, signs he must have surely seen before, given his place of employment. After all, this was Foxwoods, the world's largest casino, a self-contained city, a labyrinth of booze, bad behavior, and flashing lights, which never, ever closes.

"Can I help you?" he offered suspiciously.

"I'm trying to find the poker room," I stammered by way of reply, and then recognition dawned on his face.

"Oh, you're the world record guy! Sure, let me show you the way!" I followed his eager footsteps, and when we were within a few steps of the table, my friend Joe Kresse rushed toward me in a panic.

"Where have you been?"

"I got lost."

He didn't say anything. He didn't have to. Someone who could not walk in a straight line for thirty seconds to a place that had become a second home had some serious issues. At the moment, my most serious issue was sleep, or rather lack thereof. It had been nearly seventy hours since I had last closed my eyes. That might not sound like so long until you think of it as two full days, meaning days and nights, plus another half-day tacked on for good measure. Then add seven more hours. If you are reading this on Sunday evening, think about staying up until midday Wednesday. And you would still not be done. But you would be tired, confused, and probably hallucinating as well. I was.

I had begun playing poker at the Foxwoods Casino in Mashuntucket, Connecticut, at 1 PM on Thursday June 10, 2004. I had already been up for more than 6 hours when I first started playing, because I had gone into Hartford to appear on the local morning television news show. After returning to the casino I had played all day Thursday, through Thursday night, then all day Friday and Friday night, and then all day Saturday. It was now somewhere around four in the morning on Saturday night, or Sunday morning depending on your perspective, and I was tired, more tired than I could imagine anyone has ever been. I was beyond any measure of exhaustion I had ever known or even conceived of, not just physically but also mentally. To put it in the simplest terms, my brain had stopped working.

I once did a twenty-four-hour mountain bike ride, an arduous physical feat through an entire night in the woods. On many of my trips as a journalist, such as flying to and from Asia, I have been severely jet lagged and sleep deprived. On several occasions, I have flown overnight to Europe without sleep after a full day of work, and then worked through another long day and late until the following night. I pulled college all-nighters, and in those years also had a bit of practice with booze and the occasional mind-altering substance. But none of those experiences could even remotely compare to the state of disconnect I achieved at Foxwoods simply by staying awake. I avoided alcohol altogether, drank ample water, and lots of coffee, but by hour forty-eight, I started to have visual distortions, and by the time I got lost en route from the bathroom, I had progressed to full-blown hallucinations of the mirage-in-the-desert variety. That was hour seventy without sleep and hour sixty-four of poker playing, with just over eight remaining. The past twelve hours had been the worst: every time I glanced up from the table, things looked markedly different. The room itself changed size and shape with alarming frequency, the walls expanding and contracting, alternatingly creating a space so vast it seemed to go on forever and so small I seemed to be playing cards in someone's garage. Ditto for the table and its surroundings, which began morphing by the minute. At one point I became absolutely convinced that the table was set in a white gazebo elevated above all the other gaming tables on the casino floor. The players, many of whom had been by my side for eight hours or more, suddenly were unfamiliar and unrecognizable. At one point I looked around at their faces and abruptly became convinced I was at the wrong table, because everyone and everything looked so alien. Panicked, I stood up and tried to leave, desperate to get to where I felt I should be, but the dealer begged me to stay, knowing I was in the right place—or at least where I was supposed to be. The truly right place was probably a psychiatric hospital. Mentally, I did not think it could get any worse. But I had yet to hit bottom.

How did I get to this point? What madness compelled me to risk my physical and mental health? Why would I—or anyone—think playing poker for days without a break was a good idea? The answer is simple: to set a Guinness World Record.

2005, LONDON, ENGLAND, FIFTIETH BIRTHDAY OF GUINNESS WORLD RECORDS

When the Guinness record book reached its half-century mark, its editors celebrated with parties, TV specials, record-breaking events, and a special edition of the book, covered in shiny metallic gold. My name is in that book, and will be, forever. Fittingly, this was the result of a 2003 visit to Ireland, the birthplace of all things Guinness: it was an article in a local newspaper that first rekindled my boyhood interest in the record book. I knew the book, of course, everyone does, but I had no idea it had such a rich history. Most impressive was its unique status as the world's all-time number one copyrighted best seller, having sold well over 100 million copies in thirty-seven different languages. The article described a book that became a phenomenon, and spawned a global entertainment empire of television shows, literally hundreds of spin-off book titles, a widely syndicated cartoon of records, and a global collection of museums. In addition, records were plastered on paper cups, greeting cards, T-shirts, even a board game. Record mania, according to the article, showed no signs of slowing down: every single year, like clockwork, the book sells more than a million copies in the States, and 3.5 million worldwide, annually making the best-seller lists here and abroad.

Surely, I thought, as the freelance journalist inside me pondered the ramifications, there has to be something worth writing about in all this. There was, and less than two years later, I would be reading about myself in the pages of *Guinness World Records*. But I still had a lot to learn.

JUNE 2006, HANOVER, NEW HAMPSHIRE

"HE is in the *Guinness Book of World Records*!" a slightly tipsy reveler tells her date, just a bit too loudly. I'm at a dinner party and wine is flowing freely. I know what's coming next. A hush descends around the table and ignoring it will not end the silence.

I am not going to get out of this room without recounting at least one of my Guinness record-setting endeavors and answering the identical questions that inevitably follow. Did you get paid? What was the record before? How did you do that? Why did you do that? How did you think of that? Why poker? Why golf? Why Australia? Why seventy-two hours? What's next? Were you on TV? Does it have anything to do with the beer?

People of every age and background have an insatiable thirst for all things Guinness, and I've learned that once the topic of world records comes up, the genie is out of the bottle: like it or not, I become the center of undivided attention. The bottom line is that the book has a glorifying effect on all its record holders, which is why people are so eager to get into it. *Guinness World Records* is a collection of celebrities, famous and also paradoxically anonymous, promising its most dedicated readers a moment in the sun. It offers otherwise unknowns like me the opportunity to grab fifteen minutes of fame and achieve a glimmer of so-called "greatness," joining the ranks of elite athletes, scientists, world leaders, explorers, and adventurers who comprise its lengthy list of record holders. On the cocktail circuit, a Guinness World Record makes you an instant celebrity in a culture that has never been more obsessed with celebrity, and for many of us it is the only such path. I can most assuredly say that I will never be the first man on the moon, become the world's longest-serving head of state, its most syndicated columnist, or set the lifetime mark for most bones broken, highest box office take, PGA Tour earnings, career batting average, or most Tour de France titles, but I did manage to join Neil Armstrong, Fidel Castro, Ann Landers, Evel Knievel, Harrison Ford, Tiger Woods, Ty Cobb, and Lance Armstrong in the pages of Guinness. Hell, I've set more records than some of them.

My records are odd, offbeat, and arguably pointless, but compared to many of my peers they are totally mundane. When I first wrote the proposal for this book, my agent asked me to make it more colorful, specifically suggesting that I select half a dozen really outlandish records that would shock, amaze, and/or cause rib-breaking laughter among the editors considering buying my work. Surprisingly, this turned out to be the most difficult component of my proposal. Because singling out six Guinness World Records as especially absurd is like being asked to pick six famous people to illustrate the history of civilization. Is the attempt to break the elapsed time record for wearing a full suit of armor—while riding in an airplane—more illustrative of odd nuances than the creative loophole used by the mayor of a Spanish city, which, after coming up literally miles short in its attempt to create the world's largest sausage, set about convincing the book's staff to create a special category just for "largest chorizo sausage"? Is stuffing one's mouth with ten large, poisonous, and very much alive rattlesnakes more shocking than eating an entire airplane ground into metal filings? Which is more impressive: growing the world's longest beard, which took years, or growing the longest "beard of bees," done in just minutes by a sixty-eight-year-old Ohio beekeeper who used a queen in a tiny box strapped below his jaw to attract a staggering 17,500 bees onto his chin? Bringing to mind the timeless debate of quantity versus quality, did the 14,718 Japanese record holders all drinking tea together outdo the largest gathering of people dressed as gorillas, a scant 637 participants in London's Great Gorilla Fun Run? Perhaps my only easy choice was Germany's Rudy Horn, who won me over with his panache. When Horn set the record for Most Teacups Caught On Head While Unicycling, he threw six teacups and saucers—with his feet—catching and balancing them on his head and, lest we forget, all while riding a unicycle. But the stylish Horn was not done: after finishing his successful record, his toes emphatically added a teaspoon and a lump of sugar to the collection on his head. If his was the only feat involving multiple esoteric skills put together in a seemingly impossible combination, my choices would have been easy, but there are dozens, or hundreds, in each ever-changing edition of the book.

How did it ever come to this? How did the Guinness book, which started life as a stoic academic work intended to be as sexy as a dictionary or encyclopedia, suddenly become, much to the surprise of its authors, a runaway best seller and eventually THE runaway best seller of all time? How did it morph from reference almanac into an interactive cultural icon that tens of thousands of people would devote enormous amounts of energy, time, money, and sometimes even their lives to "get into"? Why did it spawn myriad television shows, museums, copycats, and spin-offs? Why is it so universally beloved, its appeal effortlessly crossing linguistic, religious, and cultural borders? Why is the world of record breaking so fascinating to readers and so obsessive for record breakers? These are the questions that fueled my journey inside the world's most famous record book, bringing me face to face with some of its greatest personalities, and I will share the answers I found in the upcoming pages.

1

Meet Ashrita, Record Breaker for God

Some things in life are best left unexplained. Ashrita Furman is one of them. This man is an athletic phenomenon whose ability is exceeded only by his imagination.

—JUST FOR THE RECORD (AUSTRALIAN TELEVISION)

I'm trying to show others that our human capacity is unlimited if we can believe in ourselves. I hope that after reading this you are inspired to attempt some feat of your own. The particular event is unimportant as long as it gives you the opportunity to dance on the edge of your capacity. But be prepared—the benefits could be both illuminating and far reaching.

—ASHRITA FURMAN, IN HIS ONLINE BLOG

For proof of the old adage "truth is stranger than fiction," one need look no farther than Ashrita Furman. If Ashrita did not exist, the marketing folks at Guinness World Records would have to invent him—but even the most imaginative ad person could not conjure up a character like Ashrita, who has now been intimately involved with the book for far longer than any of its staff. In the thirty years since he began breaking Guinness World Records, the men who invented the book have all passed away, its editors have come and gone, the book itself has been bought and sold and sold again, and throughout all of these changes, during the Age of Ashrita it has become the bestselling copyrighted book in world history, and by some accounts the second most widely read book of all time—behind only the Bible.

Fortunately for the more than 110 million readers who have purchased a copy of the *Guinness World Records*, Ashrita does exist, and no one in the book's half century has had the kind of impact on its pages that he has or has done more to spread its gospel. Furman was once just like the millions of other preteens who buy the book every year and have made it an annual *New York Times* best seller for decades. Like his peers, Ashrita studied its pages, and pored over images that are now iconic to generations of readers: pictures of the tallest and shortest and fattest men and women, those with the longest beards, mustaches, and fingernails. Like most kids, Ashrita dreamed of being in its pages, but unlike most kids he has lived out that dream to epic proportions. After a life-changing revelation, Ashrita got his own picture into the book in 1979 and has never slowed down since, continuing to get into Guinness at a frenetic pace with increasingly bizarre feats of stamina, strength, and creativity. Ashrita Furman is "The Book" taken to its logical, if such a word can used in the same breath as *Guinness World Records*, extreme, the mother of all record breakers. Paradoxically, he began as a contemporary reflection of the book, part of its target audience, and thirty years later, the book has become a contemporary reflection of Ashrita: its focus has dramatically turned toward him and his kin, featuring more and more self-invented records, which in many cases seem as difficult to think up as to execute. More than anyone else, Ashrita helped turn the *Guinness World Records* book from something people simply read to something tens of thousands of people each year strive to get into, and he has done so with his own unique and appealing style. By taking every child's fascination with the book and marrying this passion to the fervor of a religious zealot, then sprinkling in his sense of humor and showmanship, this soft-spoken man from Queens, New York, has become nothing less than the greatest Guinness record holder of all time.

Yet despite all his success, he remains a humble servant of God. "*People* magazine called me to be on their fifty most eligible bachelors' list," Ashrita, who has taken a pledge of celibacy, told the *New York Times*. "I told them, 'There's only one problem: I don't date.'" The celibate vegetarian has also never driven a car (though he holds a record for pushing one). He has lived in the same apartment, with few possessions, for most of the last thirty years. Even his stack of Guinness World Records certificates, the largest such collection outside of the company's headquarters, sits on the floor of his closet in a modest pile. The only one he has on display is his 100th, a special certificate the book made him to honor the accomplishment, the only one of its kind ever printed.

"Ashrita is by far the most prolific record breaker," Stewart Newport told the *New York Times*. Newport is the book's longtime Keeper of the Records, the lofty title the English concern bestows upon its top rules official. As of January 2008, Furman held seventy-two current records, his most recent being part of a group effort: he and an international team with members from fifteen different countries, all motivated by their extreme religious devotion, spent two weeks constructing the world's largest pencil. They shaped 8,000 board feet of wood and 4,500 pounds of graphite into a seventy-five-foot-long, ten-and-a-half-ton writing instrument, an anachronism in this increasingly digital age. "It wasn't easy," Ashrita wrote, not on a giant legal pad but on his blog. "We had to make the pencil to scale, it had to look precisely like a normal pencil and it had to be made out of the same materials . . . we even manufactured a 250-pound eraser." Those seventy-two records are just the ones he still claims, but overall Ashrita has set or broken 177 Guinness World Records in his lifetime, far more than anyone in history. More than twice as many, in fact: in 2003 he reached one of his many Guinness milestones when he passed legendary Russian weight lifter Vasily Alekseyev, the previous champion of champions, who had set eighty records in his vaunted career. To match Alekseyev's lifelong tally, Ashrita demonstrated patience, stamina, and above all, stability, when he stood balanced on an inflatable exercise ball for two hours, sixteen minutes, and two seconds at England's mystic Stonehenge. Shortly thereafter, he moved into uncharted territory with his eighty-first world record, this one for the fastest full marathon ever completed by someone skipping the entire way, covering the 26.2-mile course in five hours and fifty-five minutes—and in decidedly childlike fashion. For the five years since he passed Alekseyev, Ashrita has stood alone atop the record world.

Like his many incredible feats, Ashrita himself defies generalization. On one level he is reminiscent of a ski bum, except that he gets his adrenaline rush from breaking and setting records. Like the ski bum, Ashrita has structured his life and work in large part around breaking and setting Guinness World Records, and this enthusiasm has taken him not just to Stonehenge but to all corners of the globe.

On another level, one could argue quite seriously that Ashrita is among the world's greatest athletes. Among Olympians, the decathlon is viewed as the premier athletic event, and the best decathlete is widely touted as the world's greatest athlete. If excelling in just ten disciplines warrants such respect, why not give credit to a man who is the very best in dozens of them? Ashrita has been called many things in his illustrious career, but the one nickname that has stuck is Mr. Versatility, the superhero alter ego that many fans know him by (yes, he does have fans). Even if you throw out some of Ashrita's more ridiculous specialties, like finger snapping, frog hopping, or egg balancing, he has more than enough records that are truly astonishing feats of strength, speed, and endurance to put the best decathlete to shame. Ashrita sternly maintains that while some of his records may draw more laughter than respect, each and every one requires a commitment to excellence and a great deal of determination, concentration, and fitness. At age fifty-four, when almost all competitive athletes are retired, Ashrita is at the height of his game, still breaking records at a staggering pace: he bagged more than three dozen in 2006 alone, his best year ever. Despite his frenetic pace over the past two years, averaging one record every ten days, Ashrita's passion has never waned, and he says, "What I love about the Guinness Book is that I can just go through it and choose something that I've never done before, train for it, and become the best in the world at that event."

By any standards, Ashrita Furman is an incredible man. But unless he is wearing one of his many tank tops in the midst of a record attempt, you wouldn't notice his taut muscles. Nondescript, he is of average height and average build, with short hair and glasses, not thin or fat but rather solid, and if you had to guess what kind of an athlete he was, gymnast would come to mind. He certainly does not look like the best in the world at anything, but in fact he is the best in the world at many things; he has come to define the upper limits of what *Guinness World Records* has made possible. He is living proof of the American Dream version of the Guinness story, the one often mouthed by the book's staffers: if you try hard enough and dedicate yourself, anything is possible. He has also demonstrated the media side of record breaking, that if you do it enough you will get on TV and in magazines, over and over again. After all of this, his most prized paraphernalia are not the official certificates that sit on his closet floor, but rather his scrapbooks, with a page for each and every record attempt he has ever made, illustrated with his own snapshots, alongside the occasional postcard and local news clipping. These are more like photo albums of a summer trip to Europe than the main documentation of a life's purpose, and as he eagerly flips the pages, holding the book upside down to show me, the memories of various attempts and places come flooding back. It is a journey that has now spanned almost thirty years.

The story of almost every serial record breaker and Guinness devotee begins with a childhood spent thumbing the book's pages until well worn, and Furman is no exception. Born Keith Furman in New York City's Brooklyn, he grew up in a Jewish household of extreme religious devotion. His father was the president of a

Zionist organization, and young Keith attended synagogue regularly and was educated at a yeshiva, where he described himself as "bookwormish," becoming valedictorian. In between his studies, he found time to fall in love with *The Guinness Book of World Records*, at least vicariously. "I had this fascination about the book," he told me, "but it was totally theoretical. I had no interest or ability in any sport." That changed, and in the years since he has given the matter a lot of reflection.

> The target audience of the Guinness book is, I think, eight-
> to twelve-year-old boys, and there are different theories
> as to why that is. Boys of that age group are trying to find
> their place in the world, or something like that, and what-
> ever it is, I kind of fit into that pattern. Around that age
> I was just fascinated with the book. I used to scour it, I
> remember having it in camp and reading it under the covers
> with a flashlight. It's not only the records, but the exotic
> places, like seeing the Taj Mahal and the Pyramids, because
> they are interspersed throughout the book, and that also
> became part of it, sort of fulfilling a dream of not only
> breaking records but doing it in exotic places.

Like Stonehenge.

The young Keith Furman may have been a successful student, but he was neither an athlete nor content with his place in the world. In high school, Furman considered sports "a complete waste of time," and recalls getting "beaten up my first day of high school for being such a nerd." Sports were not the only aspect of his youth that left him feeling alienated. Despite his upbringing, Furman never felt comfortable within the bounds of Judaism, and his continued search for meaning in his life led him to examine Eastern philosophy and begin studying yoga. This, in turn, led the teenager to attend a meditation class with guru Sri Chinmoy that forever changed his life.

Until his death in late 2007, Sri Chinmoy was the spiritual leader

to thousands of devoted followers worldwide, espousing not an organized religion but rather a set of beliefs, an examination of the inner
spirit, and paradigms for living a just life. He was based in an enclave
in Jamaica, Queens, where he basically had his own neighborhood,
a miniature kingdom of reflective followers much like a faith-based
Chinatown or Little Italy. I met Ashrita here, at one of many vegetarian restaurants run by and for Chinmoy's followers, since eating
meat is prohibited. Several other Chinmoy-associated businesses,
including a florist and the health food store Furman manages, give
these few square blocks a surreal pervasive spirituality.

Chinmoy's way is not a religion per se, but rather a philosophy that emphasizes love for God, daily meditation, and public
service, with a broad religious tolerance and the Vedantic view that
all faiths reflect divinity. An author, artist, and athlete, Chinmoy
gained fame for organizing vast public events, including concerts
and races, to showcase inner peace and world harmony. Born Chinmoy Kumar Ghose in 1931 in what is now Bangladesh, he studied
for twenty years at the Sri Aurobindo Ashram, a spiritual community in India where he meditated, exercised, wrote, and painted. In
1964 he moved to New York, and according to his official biography, Chinmoy "sees aspiration—the heart's ceaseless yearning for
ever higher and deeper realities—as the spiritual force behind all
great advances in religion, culture, sports and science." Chinmoy
said, "Our goal is to go from bright to brighter to brightest, from
high to higher to highest. And even in the highest, there is no end
to our progress, for God Himself is inside each of us and God at
every moment is transcending His own Reality."

Chinmoy had a colorful athletic past of his own, and to demonstrate what the heart's ceaseless yearning could achieve, he em-
barked on a series of Guinnessesque feats throughout his lifetime,
minus the certificates and official recognition. An avid runner and
weight lifter, he completed numerous marathons and ultramara-
thons, and in 2004, at age seventy-three, bettered his personal record
by lifting 146,931 pounds in one day. In 2002 he lifted 1,000 lambs
over his head during six days in New Zealand, and the follow-

ing week hoisted 100 cows. In 1988 he launched a program called "Lifting Up the World with a Oneness-Heart," to honor people he felt had made a notable contribution to the world or humanity. For the next six years he took the program's name quite literally, and lifted 7,027 such honored individuals over his head—always with one arm. It is easy to see where Ashrita gets his inspiration from, not just spiritually but also for creating wacky feats of strength. His teacher also organized a biannual World Harmony Run to promote peace, a relay that spanned some 11,000 miles and eighty nations, undertaken to create goodwill between the people of the earth. Chinmoy's torch has been passed on during the run by the likes of Sting, Carl Lewis, Muhammad Ali, Mikhail Gorbachev, Nelson Mandela, Mother Teresa, and Pope John Paul II.

Chinmoy was equally earnest about art and writing, and claimed to have completed more than 100,000 paintings in less than a year, including more than 16,000 in one day. Likewise, he is responsible for countless volumes of poems, essays, and plays. To spread his message, Chinmoy hosted concerts, lectures, and public meditation sessions, like the one Ashrita first attended, all free of charge.

Sri Chinmoy's affect on Ashrita was profound, and even today, thirty years after his first taste of limitless physical and spiritual prowess, Furman prefaces almost every comment with "my teacher believes," "my teacher showed me," or "to honor my teacher." In fact, the serial pursuit of Guinness World Records has been Ashrita's platform to publicly promote Chinmoy's spirituality and draw attention to his cause—and he has been very successful at it. He wears a Sri Chinmoy T-shirt or tank top for every record breaking attempt and rarely fails to give credit to his teacher. For this reason, his job is as a manager of a health food store in Chinmoy's domain, where he is given exceeding flexibility. For years he has moonlighted as the travel manager of his guru's orchestra, organizing concert tours and traveling the world with them, slipping in record breaking feats along the way, often at the same exotic locations he dreamed of as a young boy.

Shortly after attending that first meditation with Chinmoy, Furman became a devoted follower, eventually dropping out of both Judaism and Columbia University to pursue spiritual ful- fillment. On his Web site, Ashrita recalls his early experiences. "Sri Chinmoy radically altered the way I looked at things. . . . My teacher's philosophy of self-transcendence, of overcoming your limits and making daily progress spiritually, creatively and physi- cally using the power of meditation, really thrilled me! However, I was a bit unsure about the physical part in my case due to my lifelong commitment to nerdiness!" Sensing Furman's reluctance to use his mind to expand the limits of his body, in 1978 Chinmoy told him to enter a twenty-four-hour bicycle race through New York's Central Park. As Furman told me, "It was basically 'just participate, you don't have to do great.' I was in my early twenties and I had never been athletic my entire life, so I figured okay, I'll participate." At 5'10" and 165 pounds, and practicing no physical activity, he had low expectations. Little did he know that fueled by an inner spirit discovered during the race, he would complete a stunning 405 miles, with no training, far more than most avid ama- teur cyclists could accomplish even with preparation and today's much better equipment. In fact, while Ashrita had no idea, he had actually made a pretty impressive run at the 1978 Guinness World Record for all-day cycling, at just under 476 miles.

> My whole discovery of this revolved around that bicycle
> race. It was really a life changing time for me, and I learned
> that it had nothing to do with my body. I learned that I
> could use the body as an instrument, as a way to express
> my spirit and also to make spiritual progress. The idea of
> using the spirituality to make progress at another level
> was just totally foreign to me, so this was a major break-
> through. That was the moment, when I kind of stumbled
> off the bicycle after being on the road for twenty-four
> hours, and I just remember making a commitment that I
> was going to break Guinness records, because it had always

been a goal of mine as a kid but I never thought it was possible to do that. Not for my own ego, but to tell people about meditation, and that's where it all started.

It did not take Ashrita long to make his mark on the book: with just his eleventh record, set in 1987, he earned a special and unique spot in the 1988 edition, a title he still holds that no one else ever has. His website reprints the original telegram from the book's first editor, Norris McWhirter, congratulating him. It reads "ASHRITA FURMAN OF JAMAICA, NY HAS ESTABLISHED A VERSATILITY RECORD BY SIMULTANEOUSLY HOLDING GUINNESS RECORDS IN TEN UNRELATED CATEGORIES. WARM CONGRATULA-TIONS ON YOUR ELEVENTH RECORD." This was his decathlon, a feat not lost on the media. In an article titled "In pursuit of excellence, sort of," Canada's *Globe and Mail* newspaper recognized the feat but noted, "On the other hand, we hear the nitpickers say queru-lously, this could turn out to be the dumbest decathlon of all time. Admittedly, it is difficult to think of any situation calling for any more than two of Mr. Furman's accomplishments at one time."

Most of Ashrita's copious press since has been more flattering. The *Toronto Star* called him the "King of World Records." The *New York Times* dubbed him Guinness's "King of Strange Feats, All for Inner Peace." It was the *Christian Science Monitor* that chose "Mr. Versatility," the nickname that has stuck and continues to grow ever more accurate year after year.

If there is one thing the book's weird history has demonstrated time and again, it is that no matter how flaky the intent, getting into Guinness is never as easy as it sounds, even for Ashrita, who despite clearly being the best at it, still fails now and again. Like the time a shark crashed into him while he was attempting to break his own underwater juggling record—in full scuba gear. Cracking the pages of Guinness certainly was not easy at the outset, and de-spite his middle of the night inner-reflection while cycling and the ah-hah moment when he realized his calling, the book, for a time, would elude even his best efforts.

It wasn't that easy. It took a few trials and errors before I actually got in. The first thing I tried was pogo stick jumping because it was the one thing I was good at as a kid. But it was crazy because I had that incredible experience with the bicycle and figured "okay I can do that again with no training." So a few months later I had found out the rules for pogo stick jumping and got a bunch of pogo sticks and called the media and went out there with no training. The record was 100,000 jumps. It was crazy but I had so much faith in the system, the chanting, the visualization, all these things I had done on the bicycle, so I just went out there, and after three hours everything was hurting. I had decided to do twenty-four hours of pogo stick jumping because my teacher had done a twenty-four-hour painting marathon and I wanted to honor that. It just shows you my faith, that I was going to go out there for twenty-four hours with no training. It worked. I did it, the record was 100,000 jumps in fifteen hours and I passed that in just thirteen-and-a-half hours, and then I kept going, because at exactly the moment I broke the record, I started hearing these screams, very weird noises in the park. It turned out they were peacocks in the Central Park Zoo, and it was very eerie because in Indian mythology peacocks represent victory and at the exact moment I broke it they started. The peacocks weren't anywhere near us, there is no way they could have heard us. It was like a cosmic moment. I was in a lot of pain but I kept going.

He did 131,000 jumps in those twenty-four hours, but afterward record officials disallowed his attempt on a technicality. As with many marathon endeavors, rules stipulated that Ashrita was allowed a five-minute rest break after each hour. "Since I accomplished the record in an hour and half less than [the] guy before me, because I was jumping a lot faster, I took too much time off after I passed the record. I wasn't aware of the way the rules were applied."

His next attempt also met with rule-induced failure. "Then

I did juggling. Sri Chinmoy had done 100,000 paintings and I wanted to juggle a 100,000 throws to honor him so I went to Grand Central Station and just started juggling, went all night and did 100,000 throws." It was only after he submitted proof of the feat that Ashrita learned there was no category for continuous juggling—and Guinness didn't want one. "I still had no idea about the whole process, getting approval in advance, and in those days especially, they were very much less open about new categories. If you wanted to get in the book you kind of had to pick something that was already in there."

The third time proved to be the charm, when Ashrita tried jumping jacks. "By that time I'd realized that 'okay, you've got to pick something that's in the book, you've got to train for it, find out all the rules and then do it.' So I did." In 1979 he completed 27,000 jumps. "I knew right away I was going to continue to do them. It gave me so much joy and I really saw it as such a positive experience. You've got to remember that for me, using my body to accomplish things was new. My whole childhood I grew up not doing sports so this was incredible like 'I'm actually an athlete, I can do stuff.' It was like a journey and basically there are no limits—pretty much anything that anyone else can do you can do if you have enough determination and spirituality." It was his third attempt at a Guinness record, his first success, and from then on, he was totally hooked.

"I think most people once they get one record, or two, or whatever, they are pretty satisfied. There are people who are serial Guinness record holders, but for the most part people are satisfied with that one and the fifteen minutes of fame or whatever. But for me it was a totally different reason, because I am really doing it as a way to sort of live out this philosophy of transcendence that Sri Chinmoy teaches. That's the key and the whole reason I kept doing it." But even Furman concedes there is more to it than inner peace. "I have to admit, when I first saw my photo in the Guinness book, right next to the awesome gymnast Nadia Comaneci, I got pretty excited."

For the next few years he was lulled into a false sense of record-setting security by a series of feats that are now among his most mundane: team stretcher carrying, hand clapping, creating the most expensive floral wreath, and bettering his own jumping jack mark (33,000). He was off to a good start, but it was not until 1983 and his seventh world record that his amazing athletic prowess would shine and the Golden Age of Ashrita began.

Milk bottle balancing does not sound as sexy as say, the javelin throw. But like many Guinness World Records, when the reader understands and appreciates the rules, the true difficulty begins to sink in. Milk bottle balancing, according to Ashrita, requires use of an old-fashioned glass milk bottle, full of milk, balanced on your head while you walk continuously. As with most marathon-style endurance records, there are prescribed rest breaks, but while you can stop walking to rest or eat, the bottle can never leave your head, although you are allowed to adjust it twice an hour. For Ashrita's seventh record, he kept that bottle on his head for twenty-four miles of endless loops on a high school track, wearing, as he always does for record attempts, a Sri Chinmoy tank top, while never letting the full glass bottle slip from his head. Ashrita himself concedes that the record, one of his all-time favorites, looks funny, but actually doing it for all those miles is no laughable accomplishment. With this, he raised the bar for weird endurance Guinness feats, both for himself and others. His record was soon surpassed, and like many of his specialties, milk bottle balancing would go through a hotly contested period. As a result, he has held this particular record at ever increasing distances no less than seven different times. When competitors take on Ashrita's records, they merely awaken a sleeping giant, often causing him to eventually take the standard to a point where no one can match it and thus giving it an air of permanence. At first this back-and-forth tug of wills moved in small increments, with Ashrita claiming a marathon-length, 26.2-mile milk bottle balance three years later, and 32.9 miles two years after that. But in 1998 he took milk bottle balancing to an entirely new level, one that has remained uncontested for a decade, when he walked 80.95 miles with that glass bottle on his head. The vast majority of people, even fit recreational athletes, cannot walk that many miles, period. "When I started, some clown [literally, a circus clown] had done it. This clown had done 18 miles, and I did 24, then 26, then someone did 30 and someone did 33 and it just kept going back and forth, 40, 44, up and up until I did almost 81 and no one has done it since. It is a major commitment and it is a gradual process. You don't just go out and do twenty-three hours of milk bottle balancing. It would be a pretty big jump for someone to go out and break that record." Milk bottle balancing is one of his favorite records, and one of mine as well, because it is every bit as absurdly difficult as it is absurd. It is also one of the oldest of the more than seventy records Ashrita currently holds, having stood for ten years.

The gradual competitive process he describes has become standard fare for Ashrita, especially as his growing fame has made his records more and more coveted by *Guinness World Records* devotees. The twenty-four-miler marked the point at which Ashrita went from spur-of-the-moment, would-be record holder to serious athlete. He began a well-rounded fitness routine of aerobics, running, and strength training, but has since come to realize that his specialties require event-specific training. To be good at things like long-distance milk bottle balancing you have to practice them— often more complicated than it sounds—and this is one of the reasons he does much of his work on a local high school track, free of traffic and outside interference. He recounts the difficulty of training for the milk bottle record on his website:

> The reactions I get while walking through the streets practicing for this record are precious. In Japan, people politely pretend that nothing is wrong, but once I pass them I often hear muffled giggling. In New York, bystanders openly laugh, cheer, jeer, or even throw rocks to try to knock the bottle off my head. One kid even used a slingshot! The most unique reactions were in Cancun, Mexico, as I walked along the main boulevard in the tourist district. Onlook-

ers would frequently try to startle me into dropping the bottle . . . teenagers would drive by in their cars screaming and honking their horns. One imaginative fellow snuck up behind me and barked like a dog in my ear! But the best was the city bus driver who crossed over to my side of the road, charged his vehicle through a huge puddle and drenched me in a shower of warm muddy water.

None of this fazes Ashrita, because faith is on his side. He laughs such incidents off, and occasionally it takes such an encounter to make him remember that his lifelong passion is still odd to others. One of his many unusual records involves pushing an orange one mile with his nose, which at a world record pace requires swatting it with your face so that it rolls as far as possible, and then scrambling after it and doing this again and again. This record is one that is almost harder to practice than to actually break, especially since when he broke the record, a long passageway in New York's JFK airport had been cordoned off for his attempt, while his practice sessions took place in city parks. Over lunch he told me, "It sort of epitomizes the Guinness records: it's nuts and if someone looked at you during it they'd think you really lost it. I remember when I went to the park to practice I'd look at everyone having picnics and think to myself 'do I really have the guts to do this? To get down on my hands and knees and start smacking an orange with my nose?' When you're part of the regular world you see how crazy it must seem."

The year 1983 began a watershed period for Ashrita, who would string together five defining records over a three-year period, beginning with the milk bottle balancing, taking his quest into the realm of the extreme. As evidenced even in the twenty-four-hour pogo stick failure, his unique ability to ignore pain and do things for very long periods of time would become the backbone of many of his greatest achievements. He also carved out a niche with a handful of specialties that when combined, account for the bulk of his records, which he describes under the umbrella category "childlike pursuits."

Many of the records involve childlike activities such as juggling, hopscotch, unicycling, pogo stick jumping, somersaulting, yodeling and balancing objects on my head or chin. You know how children are so close to their parents? That's how my teacher Sri Chinmoy says we should be to God; you should feel like a child with affection and sweetness toward God. That fits in with the childlike nature. I like doing these things. When people ask me how I choose what record to do, I always say choose something that you love to do, something that gives you joy, because you are going to have to practice it for hours and hours. There's a record for eating an onion. I'm good at it, I'm a fast eater and I am within a few seconds but I can't stand doing it. I tried it and I'm not getting any joy, so forget it, I'm not going to deal with it. There are so many other things I can do.

Like peeling and eating a whole lemon, which he must like better than onions, since he set the record in 2007, for the second time, at under eleven seconds.

Another thing Furman has become famous for is the locations he chooses to set records. His first seven, including milk bottle balancing, were all done in New York City on a high school track or in Central Park. But his eighth was the start of something new in his spiritual and record quest. Despite having been thwarted in his initial attempt at getting into the record book, he tried the pogo stick route again and became the very first person to jump up and down Japan's Mount Fuji, on a rough hiking trail to and from its summit. This feat inspired him to begin choosing his record-setting locations carefully, but in one memorable case, perhaps not carefully enough. Following the Mount Fuji stint, his newfound focus on spiritually or historically significant settings would lead him to his longest-standing Guinness World Record and, in his mind, the most difficult ever. This record will almost surely never fall, since

Guinness "retired" it, in part due to the danger it entails. For his landmark tenth record, Ashrita took somersaults, or forward rolls as they're known in Guinness-speak, to the extreme.

At the time, Ashrita still was not obsessed with record-specific training the way he is today.

> Now I have a much better idea of how much I have to train for a record. In those days I really didn't train a lot. I was basing it a lot more on my faith. Now I am pretty demanding as far my training and I won't try a record until I feel like my body is there. In those days it wasn't like that. I was planning on breaking the somersault record somehow. *People* magazine called and they wanted to cover the somersault thing, and there was no time to train, and I had only trained up to a few miles. I just went out and did it, and that all contributed to the difficulty. Plus, I never even looked at the course. It was a terrible course. I had only trained on a flat path and it was all up and down. I just said, "I'll go out and do Paul Revere's ride."

This, of course, refers to the historic Revolutionary War route Paul Revere rode on horseback at midnight between Charlestown and Lexington, Massachusetts, to famously warn the populace that "the redcoats are coming!" As Furman recalled, "I sort of always had this idea of making the records more creative and more interesting. It started with Paul Revere's ride, the somersaults. That was the first one where I picked a place, and that just happened spur of the moment." In the case of the Mount Fuji run, Furman was in Japan for Chinmoy-related business, and once there, decided to try to set a record but had not traveled for that specific reason. Paul Revere's ride came about because, as he puts it, after his *People* magazine interview, "I was just kind of stuck." Paul Revere's route spans some twelve miles and 390 yards, much of it on dirty city streets. It took Ashrita ten and a half hours.

Even in his colorful litany of records, ten and a half hours of somersaulting stands out. Furman has since covered many miles by pogo sticking, sack jumping, unicycling backward, juggling, stilt walking, carrying a person on his back, and crawling while pushing an orange with his nose. But somersaulting Paul Revere's ride seems the most impossible: the length is comparable to a hilly half-marathon, exacerbated by rolling over and over on your head—on pavement. He had to throw up several times along the way. "It is really like banging your head against the wall," Ashrita said, grimacing and clearly not fond of the memory. "I find that when I train my brain is always dull for a day or two after. The Paul Revere somersault thing was the hardest one. The somersault thing was brutal." Strong words from the eternally nonplussed meditation fan.

It took decades for the memory of the agony of the somersaults to wane enough so he would consider trying to break his own record; even in the hypercompetitive world of Guinness, with Ashrita's records the most coveted, no one else bothered in the more than twenty years since. But when he submitted an application to try it again, Guinness refused.

I got this inquiry back saying "when you did it the first time, was it truly continuous?" and I had to say no, there were a few times I stopped to throw up. I don't think you could literally do it continuously, because you do have to throw up. So they said "by the strict rules it wasn't consecutive so if you want to do it now, it has to be the most somersaults in 12 hours." So they are allowing what I did to stand, but if I want to break it, they redefined it and it has to be a new category. So I said "fine, let's do that." But then they must have had a meeting or something because they got back to me and sent me an e-mail saying "we don't want to do that, we don't want to have a category like that." I think they thought it was too dangerous. I'm stuck. But that's okay because there are so many other things I can do. I'm not going to go crazy about it because there are so many other challenges.

Like pogo sticking up Mount Fuji, somersaulting Paul Revere's ride taught him the importance of location, and how a superlative setting could make a Guinness superlative even more so, and thus attract more publicity for his spiritual cause. This historic route endeared him to the media, and his nonstop record-breaking pace has made him the closest thing to a mainstream celebrity ever produced through purely Guinness World Records feats. Besides having the most records, he has many colorful, if sometimes bizarre ones, set in exotic places. His record breaking also travels well to the television studio, where he can break records live and on demand. For these reasons he has become a media darling, using his prominence to spread the word of Sri Chinmoy. Ashrita has been the subject of hundreds of newspaper and magazine stories, and a guest on numerous television shows, including those of David Letterman, Oprah Winfrey, Joan Rivers, and Bill Cosby. As recently as late 2007, he was featured on *20/20*. He has frequently appeared on the various Guinness-related shows in the United States and England, and these days is contacted at least weekly by radio, television, and newspapers from around the world. Television crews from Japan have come to film him at his house in Queens, and he appeared on a show whose host he described as "The Jay Leno of Bulgaria"—during which he leapt onto the host's desk and began doing deep knee bends.

Ashrita's résumé of records has grown far too long to list, but it includes numerous odd combinations of and variations on his "childlike pursuits," such as jumping rope while on stilts or pogo stick jumping underwater (he calls this variation "aqua pogo"). He has crafted a whole genre of juggling records: while pogo stick jumping, hanging upside down, even underwater. One of the more demanding combos is "joggling"—juggling while jogging—and Furman says he trained harder for his first joggling marathon record (an impressive 3:22) than any other attempt. He still holds the ultramarathon fifty-mile joggling record. Like so many of his feats, it sounds wacky but passes the test of "if you think you can do better you should try it."

Another now-common approach to Guinness record setting that Ashrita helped popularize is to take some existing feat and do it backward. He has claimed backward records in unicycling and bowling, scoring a very respectable 199 with his back to the pins. Likewise, he takes old-fashioned exercises such as jumping jacks, squats, crunches, and sit-ups, and adds a twist. He's done them in the baskets of hot air balloons, while balancing on exercise balls, even on the backs of elephants. "I love elephants, so naturally, it's been my lifelong dream to do a Guinness record on the back of an elephant," he said, as if any explanation were necessary.

For the past two years he has averaged more than three records per month, which is logistically extremely difficult. To do so, Ashrita has piled up certificates not only with odd combinations of skills but also by doing the same activities for varying lengths. He has revisited his unassailable skill at milk bottle balancing by substituting the fastest mile for endurance. Besides pogo sticking up Mount Fuji (twice), he set records for the pogo stick 10K, the pogo stick mile (on the same Oxford University track where Roger Bannister first broke the four-minute mile AND at Australia's iconic landmark, Ayers Rock AND near the South Pole), and the vertical record for pogo stick jumping up the stairs of the world's tallest structure, the CN Tower in Toronto (twice), "climbing" all 1,899 steps in under an hour. The first attempt was captured on film for *Record Breakers*, a popular British Broadcasting Corporation show based on the Guinness Book. Longtime *Record Breakers* producer Greg Childs recalls the shoot.

> One of the nicest guys, but crazy, is Ashrita Furman. The terrible dilemma of being a record-breaking producer is not knowing the outcome. But with Ashrita you sort of know: if he says he can do it, he does. We had him on at least a half a dozen times during my time at the show. He is part of a sort of cult, and we never would have dealt with

him if he didn't seem so nice and above board. He stays with people from the cult wherever he goes, so it really kept the costs down, which BBC loved. He did a fantastic thing where he pogo sticked up the stairs of the CN Tower in Toronto, the world's tallest free standing building. We filmed the whole thing. He went so fast the crews couldn't stay with him. Then we tried to get him to forward roll the entire course of the London Marathon, but there was no way we could get permission.

Furman's use of wondrous settings has taken him from that humble start at Mount Fuji to numerous landmarks and all seven continents. The most difficult trip, logistically, was the time he hitched a free ride on an Argentinean Air Force cargo plane for a brief landing in Antarctica, where he barely had time to rush out, measure off a mile with a surveyor's tape, and then pogo stick the frozen distance in record time. He did his somersault mile on the Mall in Washington, DC (prompting random passerby and renowned campaign strategist James Carville to tell him, "You're not crazy. Kidnapping a school bus, that's crazy. You're not crazy. Maybe half a quart low . . ."). He has detoured from the Middle East to Iceland to break a record there, and his most memorable record-breaking sites include Stonehenge, the Great Wall of China, the Eiffel Tower, the Parthenon, the Pantheon, the ruins of Tikal in Guatemala, Yellowstone's Old Faithful geyser, the Amazon (underwater pogo stick jumping), the Great Pyramids, St. Basil's Cathedral in Moscow, Ayer's Rock, and Cambodia's Angkor Wat and Indonesia's Borobudur, Asia's two preeminent ancient temple complexes.

"I'm always trying to be creative and come up with interesting places and ideas, but a lot of times it is a struggle. One thing here and in a lot of Western countries is the insurance issue, places don't want to take the risk and they don't see a benefit from the publicity. They are totally worried about the risk. Radio City I thought was a cool idea [he wanted to break a high-kick record on the Rockettes' famous stage but they turned him down]. The sit-up record I wanted to do at the Atlas statue with the famous abs in Rockefeller Center but they said no." Even Ashrita's fabled pogo stick assault on Canada's CN Tower was the result of the Empire State Building, World Trade Center, and Eiffel Tower all turning down his request. Yet foreigners, even Canadians, seem to get it. "In some other countries they are eager. The book's pretty well known and widespread here, but in some of the Asian countries," he rolled his eyes in amazement.

> Like I was in Malaysia last year, and they are totally into records, it's just incredible. I was a celebrity in Malaysia and I didn't even know until I got there. That juggling with the sharks thing I did? There were like forty people from the media there. For me it was great because I had my pick of wherever I wanted to do the records. They were like "sure, so what if there are sharks and you might not come out alive? That's fine, go ahead. You want the convention center? City Hall? Sure." Pretty much anywhere I wanted. In India it is really big, and some of these other Asian countries, like Singapore. I saw this article in India about how Guinness World Records there are like Olympic medals. They don't do well in the Olympics for some reason but they take their Guinness records to that level. In the article this guy, who had done some impressive athletic feats, and he was, I think, a mountain climber, he said "yeah, I want to break that Ashrita Furman orange record and then maybe I'll get some respect." It's kind of funny because here you don't get much respect for it here.

Perhaps the oddest choice of landmarks on Ashrita's scenic record world tour was in front of the locally famous dog statue of Greyfriar's Bobby, in Edinburgh, Scotland. This reflects another of Furman's deep and heartfelt passions, animals. "I love animals. I set the record in New Zealand with the shark [underwater juggling, forty-eight minutes, the record he was later attempting to better when a different shark collided with him]. The one on the elephant. Last year in Malaysia I did a record for hopping on one leg and I hopped with an owl. The dog one is one of my very favorites. Guinness came out with a new record, they invented it, not me, the most jumps on a pogo stick in one minute. I knew I could do it, so to make it even more challenging I decided to hold a dog in one hand. It was so exciting! I had to have a vet on hand. That was my hundred and first."

If exotic locales and animals are good for record setting, then it only stands to reason that exotic animals are even better. "So, a few days before I was scheduled to go to Mongolia," Ashrita blogged, "I began thinking about what kind of exotic animal I could meet in Genghis Khan's homeland. And then I remembered reading that Mongolia has the second largest population of yaks in the world, after Tibet. Now you can't get more exotic than a yak! I don't think I had ever even seen a yak in a zoo. So with yaks on my mind, I boarded the plane to Ulaan Bataar, and somewhere over the Pacific Ocean, the idea came to me. I had been practicing for the sack racing record—why not race a mile against a yak in a sack?" The actual record attempt was for the fastest mile jumping in a sack, so it didn't really matter if he beat the yak or not, yet Ashrita's competitive streak came out and he edged the animal at the finish line. But his fun with Mongolian animals did not stop there. Having already run the fastest mile on a conventional pair of stilts, he had been planning to conquer the same distance on stilts made entirely of cans and string, the kind children make from empty cans, its own separate Guinness record category. Inspired by his yak victory, he impulsively lashed the cans to his feet and returned to the mile course, this time leaving a Mongolian camel in the dust.

On one occasion, Ashrita's fondness for animal records led to questionable decision making. He decided to try to break the 5K skipping mark at the Wat Pa Luangta Yanasampanno Forest Monastery in Thailand, where Buddhist monks care for injured and orphaned tigers. His plan was to skip the first twenty-five meters with a full-grown tiger on a leash, despite the handlers' worries

that he might get mauled. He ended up breaking the record unscathed, but Sri Chinmoy was very unhappy with his pupil because of his strong belief that a life is valuable and should not be
risked unnecessarily.

While Sri Chinmoy supported most of Ashrita's non-tiger
record attempts, even he drew a line somewhere between sublime
and absurd. According to the *New York Times* in 2003, several
years earlier Ashrita had begun eating a large birch tree near his
home in Queens after he learned that someone else had set the
world record for tree eating. He was trimming branches and grinding them up in a kitchen blender, when his teacher found out. "He
heard about it and said: 'That's absurd. Tell him to stop.'"

In the case of the tiger, Ashrita may have gotten carried away
by his own name. In Sanskrit, Ashrita means "protected by God."
The name, given to him by Sri Chinmoy years ago, has served him
pretty well, both with animals and his thirty years of breaking
records. His only two significant injuries have been in training: he
cut his hand seriously with broken glass while practicing balancing a huge stack of pint glasses on his chin, severing a nerve and
requiring hand surgery. Later, he broke a rib while training with a
giant, aluminum hula hoop (another niche in which he holds several records). "Sri Chinmoy, when he looks at a person, rather than
seeing the outer form he gets the feeling of their inner quality. Everybody has a soul and they are all different and express different
inner qualities, so after you've been a student for a while he'll give
you a name that is descriptive of your inner qualities. Most people,
their name doesn't mean anything, it's just something their parents
gave them. It reminds you of your soul's mission, because everyone
has a mission in life. So he gave me that name, and of course, I'd
much rather use that name, so I made it my legal name. My father
wasn't that happy about it."

That was not the first time. The deeply religious elder Furman
was very upset when his son abandoned Judaism for what he saw as
a cult, and the two did not talk, on and off, for years. Interestingly,
Ashrita thinks that it was his pursuit of Guinness World Records

that ultimately led him to reconcile with his father. "The Guinness thing actually helped because it was something he could relate to. He couldn't relate to my joining this group, and he thought I was giving up my religion, even though I had already become totally disillusioned. When I started getting media attention, it was something he could understand and it really helped a lot. He came when I set a jumping jack record, but then he said it was too painful to watch and that was the only one he came to."

Over the years, Furman has amassed an impressive list of record-breaking locales, but like the ski bum, he has worked out a lifestyle to do it on the cheap. "The travel sounds better than it is. My teacher holds these free concerts and I organize the trips and get a tour conductor's ticket, and I also get miles. There are times when I specifically go to a place, like Egypt, because I wanted to set a record at the Pyramids and I use miles, but most of the time, it's wherever I am traveling with the band. Last year we went to Turkey, Bulgaria, and Thailand and I didn't have to pay. Also you always need witnesses and that can be hard in other countries but on our concert trips we have all these people who are credible witnesses for Guinness, like professors and doctors, so I'll use them."

The last few years have been especially intense, since his record-breaking velocity has picked up. In 2006 he set thirty-nine different records, and then added thirty-six more in 2007, a pace that shows no sign of slowing down. In historical perspective, it took him eighteen years to notch his first fifty records; just eight years for the next fifty; and in the two years since he has added seventy-seven more. Part of this has been the self-fulfilling prophecy of his success: the more he does, the better he gets at logistics and fitness, and the more he can do. But structural changes at the book have also made it easier. Whereas early on he scoured the pages for existing records he could break, in recent years Guinness World Records management has gotten much more permissive about new, invented records. Twenty years ago, in all likelihood, the existence of pool cue balancing would have precluded the acceptance of his baseball bat balancing, and Hula Hoop Racing While Balancing

Milk Bottle on Head, Fastest Mile, would never have been accepted, period.

Ashrita recalled how the many changes in the book over the
past three decades have affected him and his spiritual quest.

> The Guinness book was a reference book, an encyclopedia,
> a place where you could ask "what's the most push-ups
> anybody has ever done?" and then open it up and it would
> be there. It was like that for years and years and years,
> until maybe 1996. Around then it changes. It stopped
> becoming a reference book and it became just a list of
> fascinating facts. That affected me in a number of ways. It
> is more difficult to find records. They cut out a huge chunk
> of records and everything is in a database that the public
> does not have access to and that's a problem because you
> really are in the dark, you don't know if there is a record.
> There is a tiny percentage of all the records, something like
> 2 percent [actually, about 8 percent of all official Guinness
> World Records are published in the book each year]. That
> allowed them to expand the categories and changed the
> philosophy from having to do something that was already
> in the book to get in, and I think that was a good thing,
> because now they are much more open minded about new
> categories. It's a tremendous opportunity for me and I am
> having a great adventure, but there is some feeling of loss,
> because it's no longer a book where you can go through
> it and say "wow, let me try that, or that would be great to
> break." That's the major change. But I still go through the
> new book as soon as it comes out. I devour every new edi-
> tion and I think I've already broken eight or nine records
> from the 2007 book.

He told me this in March 2007, just six months after the book
had hit shelves.

The other change for me personally is that because all the records aren't published in the book anymore, each record is not as competitive. Someone could do a record, like one I just saw for throwing the Guinness book the furthest distance. I would never have known about that if I hadn't read an article about it. That guy threw the book, and it was accepted. Okay, so you are supposed to have media coverage, but let's say his local paper covers it and it never shows up on the Internet. He's got the record, he gets the certificate, it's not in the book, I have no idea, and no one is going to try to break it so he could have that record for ten years and no one knows. I don't know what the solution is, and I'm not complaining, but it changes things. That definitely diminished the level of competitiveness and maybe the standards somewhat.

Competitiveness is a huge factor in the book's appeal and history, but most would-be record breakers are simply competing against essentially faceless opponents. They are, in fact, named, but for all purposes are anonymous to readers who do not actually know them. Not Ashrita. He is a prized target, and by virtue of his all-time Guinness champion status, his records carry more cachet, both for the onetime record breaker and for a handful of challengers who have emerged over the years to make a run at the King of World Records. "I love some of the rivalries," says Ben Sherwood, former executive producer of CBS's *Good Morning America*. Sherwood is also a longtime *Guinness World Records* fan, and author of the Guinness-inspired novel *The Man Who Ate the 747*. "Ashrita has some great rivals. There's some dude in Morocco who walks farther with a brick than he does, so one year it's him, and the next year Ashrita has to walk *five* miles farther with the brick without putting it down, and then the next year the guy in Morocco walks five more miles than that. There are those kinds of funny rivalries over who can walk the longest distance with a certain kind of brick without putting it down. But in Ashrita's case it has a lot to do with his faith, and that's an unusual thing and he is not typical."

Ashrita admits that records can become somewhat personal possessions, and losing them hurts, but at the same time he makes himself an easy target. Knowing that records actually published in the book are much more likely to be broken, as public knowledge makes them easy targets, Furman could keep the bulk of his 170-plus records, nearly half of which are current, out of the public eye simply by not mentioning them. Perhaps five to ten of his records are printed in the book itself each year. But his regularly updated website offers a detailed chronological list of his feats—along with advice on how to go about being a record breaker. This supports what he claims is the real purpose of his mission, to inspire others, and he cannot do that by hiding his records.

> When my records are broken there is a part of me that says "oh no," especially if it is one of the longer ones that takes weeks or months of training, but it doesn't really bother me, I've really come to a good place about it. Now I really see it as an opportunity. Because for some reason I don't have the same motivation to break a record if I still have it. I think there is an innate push inside of everyone to make progress and I think this is progress. Why do people climb mountains or race cars? I think there is an urge to transcend. That is a lot of the motivation, to be the best and push past the limits. I'm not going against any person, but against the ideal. When someone breaks one of my records, I'm happy because he's just raised the bar and, in some way, increased the level of progress of humanity.

He insists it never gets personal—at least for him. "It's not about competing with someone else, it is about finding the talent within yourself, the inner strength, doing the best you can and making spiritual progress. But over the years there have been a few people who wanted a rivalry."

Like Steve the Grape Guy, whose record for catching thrown grapes in his mouth Furman recently broke. Ashrita says the Grape Guy's agent called, trying to set up a high-profile grape record showdown in New York. Ashrita passed. "I wished him the best of luck, but I'm not breaking his record. I'm not going against the person but against the record." He says Suresh Joachim has also challenged him. Joachim is the closest thing in the world of Guinness to Ashrita, both in terms of numbers of records, types of records, and stunning physical endurance feats. Despite still being far behind Ashrita in total records, Joachim is another leading example of the extreme of serial Guinness record setting. His website refers to him as "Suresh Joachim, The Multiple Guinness World Record Holder," and he claims to have broken more than thirty different records, some of them mundane (riding escalators), some romantic (most bridesmaids and groomsmen at a wedding, his own), some mind-numbingly difficult (standing on one leg for over seventy-six hours). Ashrita recalled looking at Joachim's website and reading about his intention to become the man with the record for having the most Guinness World Records, Furman's most important "possession." Nonetheless, Ashrita has deep admiration for his fellow record holder, especially since Joachim excels at phenomenal feats of endurance, such as running for one thousand hours. "He's been doing records for years and he does more long-term ones, some of them are incredible. Some of the things overlap, like he had a crawling mile record and I broke it and he broke it back and I broke it. I think in his mind he would like to be the guy with the most records so obviously that's a rivalry, but for me I am really trying to keep it at a different level, to inspire other people." In speaking with Ashrita, it becomes obvious that he is pulled in opposite directions by his devotion to his religion and the understandable pride he has in his feats. "I don't want to be the king of Guinness, that's not my goal," he insists. "I want to transcend my physical and spiritual boundaries. In that way, the Guinness book is part of my spiritual quest."

Ashrita's record curriculum is a microcosm of the book itself:

it is impossible to say one record is necessarily better than another, but some are stunning in their apparent difficulty, while others seem like technicalities that somehow snuck by the Guinness staffers, or were cheap shots at easy marks, like finger snapping. Both the eighty-one-mile milk bottle balance and the twelve-mile somersault over Paul Revere's route stand out as unfathomable—and untouchable—the kind of feats Norris McWhirter, the book's creator, liked to call, "Almost very nearly impossible." But the record I will always associate with Ashrita Furman is the one journalist Ben Sherwood spoke of: brick carrying. Even thinking about it hurts. Imagine picking up a standard construction brick. It weighs nine pounds. Hold it in your fingers, palm down, as rules stipulate. As soon as you have a good grip, begin walking. The goal is to keep going, brick in hand, for as long as possible. If you stop walking, or drop the brick, the event is over. You cannot change hands, touch the brick to your body, or in any way rest the brick on anything, ever. If you need to adjust your grip, you have to do so nimbly, without using the other hand or any outside agency. How long could you walk? At first I thought a few minutes, and on further reflection, maybe I could go half an hour. Maybe. No one I know who has pondered this question has answered more than two hours. The forearm cramps from imagining it. Ashrita has held this record many times, but like his great advancement in milk bottle balancing, I doubt his best will ever be challenged. He carried the brick for thirty-one hours. To make matters worse, as if things could get worse, he did it on a cinder track and pebbles got in his shoes. He got terrible raw blisters. Then it rained. He never faltered. Looking back, even the unshakable Ashrita cannot believe what he did. "Afterward I had these blisters, all infected, and I went to a podiatrist. He said it was the third worst case he had ever seen in his life." It is probably the only time Ashrita Furman will ever finish a mere third in anything.

Not long after our lunch, Ashrita was back to his usual antics, breaking the rope jumping on stilts record in Mongolia's Gobi Desert. Never one to waste a trip, Furman also broke records in baseball bat balancing, along with his can-and-string-and-sack-jumping-with-animals miles while in Mongolia. Along the way, he stopped in Key Largo, Florida, to set the duration record for underwater hula hooping, then in Norway for a (different) can-and-string record. His scuba hula hoop record, set in May 2007, was his landmark 150th, and by year's end he had added twenty-seven additional records to his total—more than most serial record breakers accumulate in a lifetime.

2

The Greatest Record of All: Birds, Beaver, Beer, and Sir Hugh's Impossible Question

The next best thing to knowing something is knowing where to find it.

—SAMUEL JOHNSON

The original edition has an introduction by the chairman of Arthur Guinness & Co, Ltd., the Earl of Iveagh. What his Lordship wrote in October 1956 is very interesting, more interesting perhaps now than it was then.

Wherever people congregate to talk, they will argue, and sometimes the joy lies in the arguing and would be lost if there were any definite answer. But more often the argument takes place on a dispute of fact, and it can be very exasperating if there is no immediate means of settling the argument. Who was the first to swim the Channel? Where is England's deepest well, or Scotland's highest tree, Ireland's oldest church? How many died in history's worst rail crash? Who gained the biggest

*majority in Parliament? What is the greatest weight a man has ever
lifted? How much heat these innocent questions can raise!*

*Guinness hopes that it may assist in resolving many such disputes,
and may, we hope, turn heat into light.*

—*THE INDEPENDENT* (LONDON)

ince its inception more than fifty years ago, the *Guinness
World Records* book and its readers have always had an in-
fatuation with animals. The very first edition applauded the exploits of a terrier named Jacko, a canine rodent-killing machine
whose prodigious "ratting" skills made him a record holder. Years
later, Ashrita got into the book on the back of an elephant, skipping
with a tiger, and pogo stick jumping with a dog in his hand. Jackie
"the Texas Snakeman" Bibby became one of the book's all-time
icons by sharing a bathtub with poisonous rattlesnakes and dangling them from his mouth. It is only fitting that animal-related records have been such a mainstay of Guinness, since the book itself
is the direct result of the chance interaction between two animal
species, bird and man. The birds in this historic case were a grouse
and golden plover, and the man Sir Hugh Beaver, a corporate titan
whose improbable animal name was a perfect one for the father of
the *Guinness Book of Records*.

The original 1955 edition of the book has a notable entry for
another business genius associated with animals, Walt Disney,
whose claim to fame was for having won the most Oscars, some
two dozen of them. After achieving unparalleled success in creating one of the world's best-known brands and a diverse entertainment empire worth billions, Walt Disney was famously quoted as
saying, "My only hope is that we never lose sight of one thing, that
it was all started by a mouse."

It is easy to forget such humble beginnings when a brand goes
global and becomes a household name transcending borders and
languages. Walt's surname, Disney, is just such an iconic name, one
instantly recognizable in all corners of the earth. Whether it is em-

ployed to refer to a man, a company, a library of cartoons, a film studio, or a collection of theme parks, everyone knows Disney. Very few brands have achieved this level of universal pervasiveness and *The Guinness Book of Records* is one, enjoying Disneyesque global recognition—and for good reason: it is the best-selling copyrighted book in the history of mankind and is available in the native languages of most citizens of the world. Amazingly, it may have even surpassed the brand recognition of the famous brewery and stout for which it was named. One would be hard-pressed to find anyone, anywhere, who does not recognize Guinness records, yet at the same time, the famed collection of superlatives and astonishing feats remains cloaked in mystery and misinformation. Everyone knows what The Book is, but almost no one knows much about it. While Walt Disney's hope remains fulfilled, and everyone understands that "it was all started by a mouse," who recalls that the *Guinness Book of Records* was all started by a pair of birds?

The mid-fifties were the dawn of the Golden Age of Trivia on both sides of the Atlantic, represented in the United Kingdom by the explosion of interest in pub trivia, and in the United States by the many "quiz shows," beginning with *The $64,000 Question*, first aired by CBS in 1955. The show's popularity has never since been equaled on network television. "It was the first and only pre–Regis Philbin game show ever to be the nation's top rated television program," according to Ken Jennings, the all-time winningest player in *Jeopardy!* game show history, and the author of *Brainiac*, a history of trivia. Jennings goes on to state that "America's crime rate, telephone usage and theater and restaurant attendance would all drop measurably on Tuesday nights, as an astounding 82 percent of viewers were tuned to CBS."

In 1955, $64,000 was a lot of money by any standards, and especially for answering a question, proving, as Jennings loves to point out, that not all trivia is trivial. In recent years television game shows attempting to re-create the drama of this original hit have had to up the ante considerably, offering million-dollar prizes just to get viewers to tune in. Certainly the chance to answer a question worth this much money does not come along every day. But even these riches pale in comparison to the payoff Sir Hugh Beaver got in 1954, when he innocently inquired of a hunting companion, which was the fastest game bird in Europe, the golden plover or the grouse? Sir Beaver had no way of knowing that his would be the most significant trivia question ever asked.

Born in Johannesburg in 1890, Hugh Beaver moved around quite a bit in the first half of his life, and his professional career began with a twelve-year stint in India on the national police force. He then relocated to London, where he joined the engineering firm of Alexander Gibb & Co., becoming a partner in the firm in 1932. Shortly thereafter, Gibb was selected to construct a large new brewery in Park Royal, on the outskirts of London, for Arthur Guinness & Sons, then the world's largest brewer. Beaver was put in charge of the huge project, and for several years worked closely with C. J. Newbold, Guinness's managing director. Newbold formed a very favorable impression of his younger colleague, and in 1945, almost certainly at his urging, Rupert Guinness, better known in England as Lord Iveagh, tapped Beaver to become the assistant managing director of the company. Beaver accepted, and when Newbold died suddenly a year later, Beaver succeeded him as managing director, a position he would hold for fourteen years, until his retirement in 1960. During and after his stint at Guinness, Beaver assumed many other important positions, including chairman of the British Institute of Management, chairman of the Advisory Council of the Department of Scientific and Industrial Research, chairman of the Industrial Fund for the Advancement of Scientific Education in Schools, and chairman of the Board of Governors of Ashridge Management College. He was also president of the Federation of British Industry and of the Sino-British Trade Council, treasurer of the University of Sussex, and served on the board of the Ministry of Works as well as on many other boards and several charities. In his scant spare time, the tireless Hugh Beaver led official trade missions to China and East Germany.

Hugh Beaver was the kind of classical, colonially inspired child of the British Empire, hard to imagine in this day and age, one for whom the world was almost too small a place and whose talents and achievements in so many fields seem more the stuff of novels than reality. He was indisputably the father of the far-reaching Guinness World Records empire, yet this remains just a small entry on his resume. In addition to running the world's largest brewery and chairing or serving on the boards of numerous government and nonprofit entities, Sir Hugh was passionate about causes, especially air pollution and social reform. He considered his duty as chair of the Committee on Air Pollution among his most significant roles, and was quite passionate and vocal on the topic, writing letters to the editors and giving speeches as a sort of proto-environmentalist. Likewise, he was a champion of racial equality in the workplace and used his position to advance the cause of minorities both within Guinness and in the greater society. One of his personal files is devoted to clippings about this topic in which he was quoted, alongside his many letters to the editors where he made his position crystal clear. At the time, his brewery did not just supply beer to bars; it was one of the U.K.'s largest landlords, leasing many pubs to the those who operated them. Sir Hugh was not shy about wielding Guinness's power for what he considered the greater good, and one of his treasured newspaper clippings is an article about the giant brewery's revocation of a publican's London lease for refusing to serve "colored customers." The same file contains hate mail in the form of snumerous bigoted letters attacking him for his progressive positions, some exceptionally vicious, violent, and disturbing.

His accomplishments were certainly impressive, and if anyone deserved a knighthood, it was Sir Hugh Beaver, KBE. Most of his credentials as a business leader, social progressive, and man of charitable works are beyond doubt, as was his tireless approach to juggling the many responsibilities he undertook. Perhaps the only remaining unanswered question about the life of Beaver was how good his aim was.

Depending on who tells the almost apocryphal story of Sir

Hugh's "Guinness Book hunting moment," he is either a very good shot or a lousy one, and it remains uncertain whether his question about which bird was faster, the golden plover or grouse (in some accounts it is the closely related teal or snipe), was brought on by his success at bird hunting that day—or his frustrating stream of misses. According to his 1967 obituary in *Guinness Time*, the brewing company's in-house newsletter, "He was a particularly fine shot," and this one, like other accounts, has him pondering the speed of flight issue over a collection of downed birds of both types after a day of shooting in County Wexford, Ireland. But the most accurate account seems to come from Norris McWhirter, the editor of the very first edition of *The Guinness Book of Records*, recalling a conversation at which he was actually present. It is his retelling of the story in *Ross*, the biography of his twin brother Ross McWhirter, which rings truest.

> [W]hen a golden plover had come high overhead and he had missed it. Later, in the home of his host, conversation turned to whether or not the plover, of which the eight members of the shooting party had bagged 20 that day, was indeed the fastest game bird in Europe as someone there had claimed. When various expensive encyclopedias in the library failed to really settle the point whether or not teal were as fast, an irritated Sir Hugh announced that "books as expensive as these ought to provide the answer to so simple a question." Another member of the party . . . remarked that encyclopedias did not necessarily give that sort of information. Sir Hugh retorted that records were just the things that started pub and bar arguments and it was about time somebody produced a book full of records to settle this kind of dispute.

Not a man to mince words or delay action, Sir Hugh took it upon himself to do just that after returning to England and discussing the matter with his colleagues. At the time, Guinness was on tap in some 84,400 pubs throughout the British Isles, and Sir Hugh saw this market alone as big enough for a book of records, one that would also be a branding opportunity, clad in the green of Ireland and sporting the Guinness logo, not much different than the bar mats or signage the brewery supplied to pubs as part of its marketing efforts.

In addition to the question of Sir Hugh's shooting aptitude, a further mystery surrounds the date of the shoot itself. It is known that the shoot occurred at Castlebridge House, the country estate of a friend in County Wexford, in the southeast of Ireland, where the issue was passionately discussed over port that evening. Although Guinness began in Dublin, where scion Arthur Guinness had started making stout at the now world famous St. James Gate brewery in 1759, Sir Hugh lived and worked in London, where Arthur Guinness & Sons was publicly traded on the London Stock Exchange. Most histories, including the "official" one listed today on the *Guinness World Records* website and in promotional materials, date the shoot to 1951, but this makes little sense in light of other evidence. All accounts describe Sir Hugh acting quickly on his intuition, and most versions of the story have the debate continuing into the libraries of London upon Beaver's return from the shooting excursion, this research unfolding over a period of just weeks or months. The conversations and actions leading to the hasty production of the first Guinness book, which was a rush job (the first edition was written in just sixteen weeks), all took place in early 1955, with no justification to explain a four-year hiatus from Beaver's grouse vs. plover frustration. For what it's worth, both the *New York Times* and the *Scotsman* attribute the genesis of Sir Beaver's idea to 1954, which seems much more plausible. In Beaver's meticulously detailed personal appointment diaries, in which his days were constantly jammed with meetings and business travel, from 1951 to 1953 there is not one mention of shooting. However, on Wednesday, September 8, 1954, Sir Hugh wrote, in his perfect penmanship, the single word *SHOOT* across two full pages of the diary, representing an entire week. The absence of previous trips and the timing of this one suggest that it was in mid-September

1954 that Sir Hugh's moment of world record enlightenment struck like a lightning bolt. The diaries also support the contention that he couldn't have been that fine a shot, unless he made do without practice for years at a time. Given that he had so many business responsibilities, it is hard to imagine him keeping sharp with the shotgun. Leisure in any form was largely unknown to Sir Hugh, and over the first half of the decade his sole shooting trip equals the length of his only other weeklong break, a voyage to Italy, the only vacation with Mrs. Beaver recorded in his diaries. Aside from these two trips, in five years he seemingly satisfied himself in the way of leisure with a single night at the theater with his wife, a few games of lawn bowls, and a lone round of golf every few years.

Having conceived the need for such an argument settling record compendium, Sir Beaver will forever be known as the father of what was originally titled *The Guinness Book of Records*. But oddly, his interest in the project seems to have ended almost as soon as it started, as if commissioning the creation of a product to fill a void he saw in the market was just another one of the myriad business decisions he faced daily, no more important to him personally than the color of the cap on a bottle of beer. In the twelve boxes of his personal papers now stored in the archives of the London School of Economics, including an early draft of a life memoir, there are almost no mentions of the book, and it is clear that Sir Hugh was more intent on focusing his energies on his public service than book selling. This is made clear in a letter dated November 23, 1964, three years before Sir Hugh's death, handwritten on the personal Park Royal Brewery letterhead of Viscount Boyd, the head of Arthur Guinness & Sons. It reads:

My dear Hugh
I am very sorry you cannot come to the dinner on Friday,
13th November to commemorate the millionth copy of the
Guinness Book of Records. *As you were the prime mover*
of all this it is very sad not to have you there, but we quite
understand as it coincides with the University of Sussex

events. Everyone will be thinking of you and will certainly drink to your health.

His preference for attending an event at a university where he served as treasurer—rather than a party for what was already an astonishing feat in publishing—may have shown what Sir Beaver thought about the historic enterprise he had started. Or perhaps it merely reflected his workaholic nature. Maybe he just did not like parties. Whatever the reason, his connection to what would become the best-selling copyrighted book of all time essentially ended with the hiring of editors Ross and Norris McWhirter. Like everything else Sir Beaver undertook, this moment was recorded in precise pencil-written letters, in an understated tone. On May 3, 1955, eight months after his shooting trip, his diary reads simply *Mr. McWhirter and Mr. Horst lunching,* amid several other appointments that day. While Sir Hugh fathered "The Book," as its fans would come to call it with near biblical reverence, Ross and especially Norris McWhirter were its nannies, or perhaps even its adoptive parents.

Ross and Norris Dewar McWhirter were identical twins, born just twenty minutes apart at Winchmore Hill, North London, on August 12, 1925. From that moment they were destined, it seems, to create the *Guinness Book of Records*. Everything the McWhirters did from their earliest age set them on a path toward The Book from their father's journalism background to their childhood hobbies to their schooling and athletic pursuits, even their inherited photographic memories. Far more than mere editors, the twins would become television stars, political figures, and first-rate promoters. Without a doubt, the odd pair played the largest role in the epic's history.

The twins' father, William McWhirter, was a successful journalist who managed three national Fleet Street newspapers and would become the managing director of Associated Newspapers and the Northcliffe Newspaper Group. Innovation and a thirst for knowledge seemed to run in the family's DNA, as the twins' grandfather, also William McWhirter, was the famed inventor of the voltmeter and ammeter. Their father, in turn, was said to bring home some 150 different newspapers a week, which his young sons, who always had a fascination with facts, figures, sports, and superlatives, would devour cover to cover, keeping an extensive catalog of clippings of interest. "From an early age my twin brother, Ross, and I collected facts and figures just as some children collected tram tickets," Norris later recalled. Likewise, in an interview with the *Harvard Crimson*, Ross explained that they had been interested in facts from an early age and clipped interesting items from newspapers, which they then committed to what would prove to be an amazingly prodigious pair of memories. "We kept lists of the largest buildings, that sort of thing." This was no fleeting childhood hobby; it was a passion the inseparable siblings would continue to practice throughout their time together at Marlborough prep school, Oxford, and in the British Royal Navy. Decades later, David Boehm, founder of Sterling Press, the longtime U.S. publisher of the Guinness books, was still in awe of the twins' penchant for facts. "They memorized every important date in world history, rivers and mountain ranges, and every world capital—and later every record in the Guinness book."

The twins' most emphatic area of passion was sports, and they were no mere armchair quarterbacks. They were standout athletes who competed at the national and international level in track, and also excelled at rugby. Both attended Oxford's Trinity College, where they ran the 100-yard dash, and Norris was good enough to race against (and lose to) Trinidadian Emmanuel MacDonald Bailey, then the U.K. record holder in the event. He was selected as a "possible" in the 200 meters for the 1948 British Olympic team but strained a hamstring before securing a spot on the squad. Their success on the track was all the more notable given the stiff competition: Ross and Norris were on the same Oxford team as the legendary Roger Bannister, who became a lifelong friend before he became famous as the first human to run a mile in under four minutes. Also on the track team was Chris Chataway, another friend who would later pace Bannister's epic mile and become the world record holder at the 5,000 meters. Completing their education after an interruption for military service, all four were part of a twenty-man team chosen to represent Oxford in its first postwar foreign athletic tour, a group that turned out to be quite a distinguished bunch. As Norris wrote, "It would have taken a clairvoyant rather than an acute observer to predict that among that carefree band there were members who were to become a prime minister [Ratu Kamisese Mara, Fiji], Europe's fastest sprinter, history's first four-minute miler, a leading headmaster and [in the case of Ross] the first editor ever to sell 25,000,000 copies of a book in a lifetime."

Aside from a brief stint serving on separate ships during the war, the twins were rarely far from each other's side, and as a result, graduation steered them down an unusual path together. "It never occurred to either of us that we would do anything separately or that we would be employees of some great company. It was always tacitly assumed that whatever career we had, it would be together and it would be as private enterprisers," Norris wrote matter-of-factly. In 1949, drawing on their lifelong passion for sports, facts, and statistics, as well as their childhood experience on the periphery of Fleet Street's journalistic hub, the twins formulated a plan to set up their own business supplying facts and figures to newspapers, yearbooks, encyclopedias, and advertisers. Knowing the specialty business would take time to research, launch, and build, they simultaneously began writing their first book, *Get to Your Marks*, subtitled *A Short History of World, Commonwealth, European and British Athletics*, to provide some income. That book was published in 1951, and two decades later *The Guide to British Track and Field Literature from 1275–1968* would call their debut "a landmark in athletics literature. The text is distinguished by a degree of precision and thoroughness which no athletics historian had achieved before. In Britain the McWhirters spearheaded the emphasis on statistical data which is a feature of modern athletics writing."

Research showing that no other fact business of its kind existed did not worry the brothers, who instead found this void encouraging, and on March 2, 1951, McWhirter Twins Ltd. was formally registered as a business. They immediately began cold-calling newspapers, trying to sell them their fact-finding services. Due to fluke timing, one such sales call quickly led not to the sale of facts but to the offer of a full-time job for Ross with London's *Star* as the lawn tennis and rugby correspondent, as well as part-time seasonal freelance coverage of other sports for Norris. Thinking it over, the McWhirters concluded that Ross's income would give them some stability, while Norris would still have enough time to run the upstart fact-finding firm. Before long, their rising stars in sports and sportswriting led Norris to begin doing part-time event commentary on radio for the BBC as well. Then, in an eerie Guinness precursor, one of the first substantive pieces of business landed by McWhirter Twins Ltd. was a contract to produce "interesting information" to be printed on boxes of Shredded Wheat breakfast cereal. The twins clinched the deal and won the bid only when they suggested using "superlative objects and people," accompanied by artist's renderings, for the cereal box factoids.

Things progressed smoothly for the twins for a few years, with Ross covering major events such as Wimbledon and his twin researching quirky cereal box facts and growing his reputation as a sportscaster. Norris also took a position editing *Athletics World* magazine in 1952, which he would continue to do through the amazingly busy next four years in the twins' lives. They seemed to be cut from the same cloth as Sir Beaver, keeping their hands in an ever-growing number of enterprises. Norris's work with BBC radio also took a major step forward with his broadcasts from the 1956 Melbourne Olympics, which in turn led to a job on television as part of the BBC's commentary team for the next four Olympic Games: Rome (1960), Tokyo (1964), Mexico (1968), and Munich (1972). Before long, this on-camera experience would prove instrumental in promoting the Guinness brand.

The McWhirters' growing success came to a head in 1954, the year Norris dubbed "Annus Mirabilis" in his book *Ross*, an amalgam autobiography and biography of his brother. The miracles referred to were the breaking of the four-minute mile by their friend Roger Bannister and the grouse vs. golden plover question by Sir Hugh Beaver. The first occurred on May 6 at the familiar Oxford University track where Norris, Ross, and Roger had run for so many years (and where Ashrita Furman would later make a record-breaking pilgrimage, albeit on a pogo stick). Norris was hired to provide the track commentary through the public address system, and knowing how much closer his friend Roger was to the mark than many observers suspected, he took great pains the night before the race to rehearse a "spontaneous" announcement, should Bannister indeed deliver the historic benchmark. By a meager six-tenths of a second he did just that, and slowly and without emotion Norris announced, "Ladies and Gentlemen. Here is the result of event number nine, the one mile. First, number 41, R. G. Bannister, Amateur Athletic Association, and formerly of Exeter and Merton colleges, with a time that is a new meeting and track record, and which, subject to ratification will be a new English native, British Empire and World's record: the time three minutes. . . . " The rest of his announcement, "fifty-nine point four seconds," was forever obscured by the loud and riotous reaction of the crowd, some 1,200 strong. So important was this event in sports history that Norris later said, "The total crowd was estimated at 1,200 and I have met all 10,000 of them since!"

As the world famous record book by the twins would prove dramatically for the next six decades, records are meant to be broken, but firsts are forever. Bannister's new mark stood for just forty-six days, and it would be the next holder, Australian John Landy, whose 3:57.9 would grace the mile entry in the first edition of *The Guinness Book of Records*, though Bannister would long secure a place in its pages alongside the likes of Neil Armstrong and Sir Edmund Hillary for historic firsts. The twins were not yet done with mile records: later that year Landy's success set the stage for a hugely anticipated showdown between the two sprinters at the 1954 Commonwealth Games in Vancouver, where Norris reported that scalpers were getting upward of $100 Canadian, a stunning amount at the time, for the event, dubbed "The Miracle Mile" by the press. The McWhirters were once again on hand to witness track and field history when Bannister won in 3:58.8 with Landy less than a second behind him, making it history's first double sub-four-minute mile.

Around the time the twins were reveling in Vancouver, Sir Hugh Beaver was bird hunting in Ireland. Connecting these dots was the job of another employee of the famous brewery, Oxford track standout and world record sprinter Chris Chataway, teammate of the McWhirters. Chataway had just given up full-time athletics and taken a position as an underbrewer at Guinness's Park Royal Brewery in London, the facility Sir Beaver himself had helped build in his previous career in engineering. After returning from his shooting vacation, Sir Beaver immediately began bouncing his idea for a book to settle bar disputes off Guinness executives, and fellow managing director Norman Smiley (who had also been a miler at Oxford) was very enthusiastic. Smiley re-raised the issue with Beaver several times in the ensuing months until one morning, Sir Beaver and Smiley began chatting with Chataway over breakfast about the concept. Eventually, the pair asked Chataway if he knew anyone appropriate for taking on such a project, and without hesitation he recommended the McWhirters. At his bosses' request, Chataway rang up his old friends and asked them, in a manner Norris recalled as quite mysterious and secretive, if they could come to the brewery for a meeting to discuss "a project." Chataway refused to give any more details and informed them that he would not personally be present at the luncheon meeting. Norris would recall later that "It seemed that Sir Hugh had an instinct for confidentiality which has always been an unfortunate but necessary part of the publishing profession."

When the twins arrived at the London brewery, they were led to the board's private dining room, where they found a large group of company directors and no other outside guests. As Norris recalled the fateful meeting:

After the usual conversation, Sir Hugh led round to the subject of records and record breaking. Ross and I were asked the records for a number of what to us were fairly simple categories, such as filibustering (Senator Wayne Morse of Oregon, over 22 hours) and pole squatting (a man in Portland also in Oregon called Howard who stayed up for 196 days). Lord Moyne was more interested in how one found out, rather than if we knew the answer, and posed the question how, for instance, would one discover the identity of the widest river that had ever frozen? Ross replied, before I could, that this particular problem was really quite simple because it could only lie between three contenders, namely the three Russian rivers, the Ob', Yenisey and the Lena which flowed into the Arctic, adding that the Antarctic of course did not have any rivers.

Sir Hugh then began talking about his experiences as a civil engineer in building harbors in Turkey three or four years before the war, and mentioned that the problem was in getting the specifications translated from English into Turkish. I interposed that I could not see why Turkish should be a particular problem since the language had only one irregular verb. Sir Hugh stopped dead and said "Which is the irregular verb?" I replied "imek, to be." "Do you speak Turkish?" he asked, so I admitted I didn't. "Then how on earth do you know that?" he queried. "Because records of all kinds interest me and I had learnt that fact in trying to discover which language had fewest irregular verbs, compared with the 180 or so in English."

Sir Hugh seemed to decide that he had discovered people with the right kind of mind for producing the book, which he now resolved should be published under the Guinness imprint, to settle arguments in the 84,400 pubs in the country. Quite suddenly he said "We are going to set up a publishing subsidiary. Which one of you is to be Managing Director?" Ross explained that he had a staff job in

Fleet Street and that I would be better suited to take on the assignment. Sir Hugh, who was now anxious to get off to another appointment, merely added: "Before you leave go up and see the accountant and tell them how much money you need."

The twins soon formed Superlatives Limited, a subsidiary of and financed by Arthur Guinness & Sons, with offices in the fifth floor of Ludgate House in Fleet Street, just blocks from where their father had first introduced them to journalism. They had only sixteen weeks—until July 1955—to complete the first edition of *The Guinness Book of Records*, and to do so, the pair worked ninety-hour weeks, long into the early morning hours nearly every night. According to Norris, "The work on the book could be summed up as extracting '-ests' (i.e., highests, oldests, richests, heaviests, fastests, etc.) from 'ists' (dendrochronologists, helminthologists, paleontologists, and volcanologists, etc.)." To get these -ests from the -ists they fired off hundreds of letters to experts around the globe. When the first edition came out, the acknowledgments page thanked ninety-five different entities, ranging from major Detroit automobile manufacturers to the German Diplomatic Mission and Japanese Embassy, the U.S. Coast Guard and the BBC, and such specialty groups as the British Mycological Society and British Speleological Association.

In the course of letter writing, the twins quickly learned the ground rules of the record research business. They discovered that they consistently had more success when they found what they thought was the right answer through their own research and then asked experts for verification, rather than if they simply asked for the answer straight out. "People who have a total resistance to giving information often have an irresistible desire to correct other people's impressions," Norris wryly commented. Likewise, they found that enthusiastic amateurs were more forthcoming than jaded professionals, and that foreigners would answer inquiries from abroad when they wouldn't give the time of day to their fellow countrymen. French experts would not respond to letters in English, while German experts became irate if the Brits translated letters into German. At the end of this frantic search for superlatives, Norris concluded that "Compiling a reference book thus is something which we discovered entails not only an expenditure of energy far beyond that called for by any fiction writer, but also the deployment of some measure of psychology."

On August 27, 1955, the McWhirter's office manager walked into the Superlatives Limited headquarters with the very first bound copy of the book, bearing a plain green linen cover and the words *The Guinness Book of Records*, along with the brewery's trademark harp logo, all embossed in gold. (The harp is a popular image in Ireland, appearing in the Republic's coat of arms, on coins, and as the symbol of Trinity College, Dublin. The image appears on the Guinness label, and in addition to its namesake stout, the company also brews one of the world's great lagers, fittingly named Harp.) It also included a moving foreword by the Earl of Iveagh, the Guinness chairman, implying that more than mere ink and paper, the book was something that could turn the heat of an argument into the light of knowledge. For those familiar with editions printed in the last forty years, the dignified original bears only a vague resemblance to what *The Guinness Book of Records* has evolved into. It was, after all, inspired by encyclopedias, and it is very much a research book, conservative in appearance and something to be put on the bookshelf alongside the World Almanac and dictionary. Amazingly, despite its tiny editorial and research staff, and the incredible time pressure to produce it, the original book contained some 8,000 records, far more than today's volume, reaching a level of comprehensiveness that would consistently decline over time even as the book got thicker and larger. The decision was made to price the 198-page book, complete with illustrations and a full-color frontispiece (a luxury at the time), at just five shillings (£0.25, or about fifty U.S. cents today). Opening the cover today, the original book remains as dramatic as it must have been to the first readers more than half a century ago, who were confronted with two almost totally blank white pages, bearing just a few words on the lower right-hand corner:

MOUNT EVEREST (29,160 FEET)
The highest mountain in the world

Wonderfully bereft of punctuation, it summed up so much of what the book would become known for, including an "-est," in this case highest, and an "in the world," representative of the name by which the book would later become known, one of not just records but world records. Readers flipping this page were then greeted by a rarity in 1955, a full-color picture of the mountain itself, wrapped in clouds, a suitably massive image for the collection of superlatives they held in their hands.

The first copy was sent to the man who had commissioned the work. Sir Beaver promptly wrote back to the twins:

On arrival home last Sunday I found your letter of 27th August and the first bound copy of The Guinness Book of Records. *I did greatly appreciate your sending me this. I have read through the greater part of it and am amazed at the skill with which you have put it together. As value for the money I think there is not likely to be anything like it on the book market this year.*

The first print run was 50,000 copies, which would have been quite optimistic were it not for the huge base of pubs already affiliated with Guinness. Commercial sales started quite slowly, and the Superlatives team was crestfallen when W. H. Smith, the nation's leading book retailer, ordered a scant six copies—and insisted on the option to return them. Ross, Norris, and their small staff tried to reason this unexpected resistance out in their offices, but within two hours of having returned from their personal call on Smith, the bookseller, presumably after having begun to actually read the fascinating work, rang back and increased the quantity to

100. Later that afternoon Smith again changed its tune, ordering a thousand copies. By the week's end this one account had ordered a full fifth of the entire print run. "The realization dawned on us quite quickly that the book which had been produced to settle arguments in pubs . . . was about to become a best seller. Ross and I had long had the suspicion that our own fascination for records and superlatives might not have been as quirkish as some of our closer friends had thought, but until now there had been no confirmation that it would arouse such a widespread enthusiasm among others."

According to Ken Jennings in *Brainiac*, the McWhirters had a ripe market for their project because the English had long been enthusiasts of odd facts. "The earliest roots of trivia, in the sense of miscellaneous-and-not-entirely-useful-facts, date back to the 'commonplace book' of ye olde England . . . at the dawn of the Victorian age, a commonplace book was becoming something a little less commonplace: a miscellany of random facts the writer happened to find interesting. A book like Sir Richard Phillips's 1830 *A Million of Facts* is half almanac (listing eclipses, weights and measures, and so on) but half trivia book as well. Tradesmen and farmers of the time had no practical need to know that 'The oldest known painting in England is a portrait of Chaucer, painted in panel in 1390.'" Phillips's language from over a century earlier is quite similar to entries in the early Guinness books, as Stephen Moss, a reporter for Britain's *Guardian* newspaper confirms. "It is also historically misleading to think of the GBR as a pioneer. The late nineteenth century was awash with almanacs and annuals—a reflection of the Victorian age's fetish for collection and its faith in fact." Regardless, there was nothing on the market like *The Guinness Book of Records* when it debuted in 1955, and whether it broke new ground or rekindled old desires, everyone wanted one. Its timing may well have contributed to yet another U.K. trivia outbreak that Jennings describes: "Pub trivia, like 1960s rock and roll, is a British invasion, and just like the Beatles, it can be traced to Liverpool, circa 1959."

"It makes sense that it started in the pubs, because we have such a unique pub culture in this country," Mark Frary, author and correspondent for London's *Times*, told me. "People think nothing of spending a few hours every night in their pub; it is a very social aspect of life, and that was where people gathered and the book gained an audience. It was just the British eccentricity of it all that fascinated people, and people loved it."

Norris was right about the realization inspired by W. H. Smith's huge order. By December the book had become a best seller, beginning a tradition that would continue every single year in which a new volume was released. It had never been envisioned as an annual, and it would be more than a decade before dates began appearing on the cover of the book. The first edition simply became known as the "green" one, and it had to be reprinted three times to meet demand. The holiday season came and went, but the book's popularity showed no signs of waning. When the fourth printing of January 1956 was exhausted and sales of the bargain-priced volume had reached 187,000, the brewery decided to call a halt and regroup. The decision was made that an updated and more realistically (higher) priced edition would be published later that year. The McWhirters went back to work, and released the fifth edition (known in the U.S. as the second edition) in October 1956. This book, known as "the blue," was only the second version, meaning the first with any changes to the original contents; it was virtually identical in appearance except for a blue linen cover. Enjoying similar success, the blue became a best seller and was reprinted just two months later. There was no 1957 edition, as the management at Superlatives would spend much of the year trying to break the Guinness book into the larger American market. In 1958 there was a red version, followed by two more biannual editions. In 1964 the book became a recurring annual fixture, and a new version has been released every year since. The editions changed color annually and remained dateless through 1969, after which the book would undergo its first radical transformation in 1970—still under the guidance of Ross and Norris McWhirter.

The twins were apparently tireless; they continued to update the book, fulfill their other writing and editing assignments, travel extensively, and broadcast. Yet somehow they found time for annual vacations. Shortly after the breakout success of the original *Guinness Book of Records*, both McWhirters married women they met on ski trips, first Ross in 1956 to Rosemary Grice, and then Norris in 1957 to Carole Eckert. Still, from the reader's perspective, they remained far more anonymous than the characters they immortalized. The green, blue, and red editions all were authorless except for the mysterious "compilers," as the McWhirters were called. Always ones to give credit to others, the twins began to pepper the acknowledgments page with names of their office staff and secretaries as early as 1958, but it was not until the black volume in 1960 that the twins themselves got their due, when the facsimile signatures of Ross and Norris began to appear regularly. It became the twins' practice to thank every single person in the Superlatives office who had assisted in the book's frenetic production.

Within a few months, what had begun as a bird-hunting lark and pub marketing scheme had turned into a serious business, and the unexpected success quickly led the Guinness executives to expand into the larger and more lucrative U.S. market. Norris was dispatched to the States to do what he did best—conduct a fact-finding mission and research an expansion strategy. The pressure from above to rush out a U.S. version quickly proved troublesome: 50,000 (green) copies (titled *The Guinness Book of Superlatives*) were published speculatively for American readers, the name changed out of misguided concerns that Americans would confuse "records" of the sporting type with phonograph records. Working out of cramped quarters in the brewery giant's New York sales office, Norris managed to hawk a mere 29,000 copies. While not a bad showing for the average new book, it paled before the runaway success at home. The United States had no pub culture of the type Mark Frary described, and on top of that, the twins' very limited book publishing and marketing experience was with their home market, where advertising was not only unnecessary but somewhat frowned upon. Norris concluded that on the other side of the Atlantic quite the opposite was true, and that "In the United States people will not buy anything unless it is advertised because they think that the manufacturer cannot really believe in the product unless he spends a lot of money pushing it. In New York we were not prepared to advertise our pioneer edition which was unwisely entitled *The Guinness Book of Superlatives*, and in addition, we had no distribution set-up." A presumably disappointed Norris McWhirter left the U.S. operations of Superlatives Limited in the sole hands of Miss Dorothy Nelson, an office manager charged with marketing, selling, shipping, billing, and handling returns for the company and its book. Little did Norris know that while it would take a few tough years and the fortuitous intervention of American book publisher David Boehm, his record book would soon become even more popular in the United States than at home—and something fans were obsessed with getting themselves into it, not merely reading it.

The sixties and early seventies were golden years for the McWhirters and the Guinness records franchise. Having already become a best seller on both sides of the Atlantic by the early 1960s, the world was at their feet, and record mania quickly spawned editions in French, *Le Livre des Extremes*, and German, *Rekorde Rekorde Rekorde*. By 1966 a million and half copies had sold, and Japanese and Danish editions were added. By the following year, consumers had snapped up another million copies, and the book was translated into Spanish and Norwegian. Another year and another million and a half copies later, *The Guinness Book of Records* was translated into Finnish, Italian, Danish, and Swedish, and the book began running full-color photos throughout its pages, not just as the frontispiece. The sixties closed in dramatic fashion, not just with the addition of Czech and Dutch versions but with one of the greatest Guinness records of all time when Neil Armstrong helped to create an important new category—Lunar Conquest.

By the time the 1970s dawned, the McWhirters had become celebrities at home, but their book needed a bigger venue. Television came knocking, the McWhirters answered, and pop culture would never be the same.

OBITUARY OF SIR HUGH BEAVER, K.B.E (1890–1967)

(EXCERPTED FROM *GUINNESS TIME*, THE NEWSLETTER
OF ARTHUR GUINNESS & SON)

. . . the slender leisure which he had for hobbies of archaeology, local and natural history, poetry and that omnivorous appetite for reading. He was a particularly fine shot. It was after a shoot by the estuary of the River Slaney in County Wexford, that he was frustrated in an attempt to find out whether the snipe [grouse] or golden plover, which he had shot, was the faster game bird. He had at that moment the inspiration which determined him to commission the *Guinness Book of Records*. This title has ever since remained a source of irritation to professional publishers who have watched its number of foreign editions grow to the point where it is now available in the first language of 790 million people.

(The same edition of *Guinness Time* contains a detailed story about and recipe for the world's largest cake.)

3

Getting into Guinness
Gets Personal

Jack Nicklaus. Bobby Jones. Tiger Woods. Annika Sorenstam. Ben Hogan. Larry Olmsted..

What do these golf luminaries have in common? Except for one, they are household names, the world's most accomplished players and in (or headed for) the Hall of Fame. As you might have already guessed, the one exception is me, Larry Olmsted. How do I fit in this Who's Who of golf greats, this pantheon of smooth swings? I hate to boast, but Annika, the boys and I are all current holders of Guinness World Records for our accomplishments on the course.

—*GOLF MAGAZINE*, MAY 2004

While some records can only be attained by people who have dedicated their lives to acquiring expertise we are also very keen to include records to which people of no particular brilliance can contribute.

—PETER MATTHEWS, EDITOR, *GUINNESS WORLD RECORDS*, 1997

In the spring of 2003, I was like most other people in America: I knew what the *Guinness World Records* book was, had grown up reading it as a child, had seen it on television, but that was it. I did not really know anything more about the book itself. But my curiosity was suddenly piqued by a newspaper article I had read while on a golf trip to Ireland and Scotland, all about the upcoming fiftieth anniversary of the book. I found this milestone and the many other factoids the article recounted very curious, and it stuck in my memory.

A few months later, I was in New York City, having breakfast with Evan Rothman, the new managing editor of *Golf Magazine*, the nation's largest and most influential golf publication. Over bagels, we discussed how golf is often perceived as a rather staid and unsexy sport, and *Golf Magazine* as an equally staid publication, written for an older, plaid-pants-wearing audience, despite the current boom in youth interest by the sudden dominance of superstar Tiger Woods. Rothman did not want to miss out on this emerging market and was looking for offbeat stories with interesting, humorous, and more unique slants in an attempt to court younger readers. I had heard this tale many times before: it is editor-speak for "we want something different from what we are used to and since it is different we don't know what it is and cannot really describe it." Like Supreme Court Justice Potter Stewart's famous nondefinition of pornography, "I know it when I see it," editors often go on these vague mission quests for new direction.

Making golf sexy is no easy chore. Lots of people can write magazine articles, but new and interesting topics are hard to come by month in and month out. For a freelancer, good story ideas are the coin of the realm, and soon I was put on the spot when Rothman asked me what kind of "radical, different, edgy" ideas I had for this new format, which I had known about for all of five minutes. As I pondered what exactly could make golf suddenly quirky, sexy, or at least entertaining reading, something in my synapses fired and connected with the newspaper story.

"How about . . . ," I stammered, trying to choose my words even as my thoughts were still forming, " . . . I try to break a Guinness World Record in golf, and write a funny first-person piece about my efforts? Even if I don't succeed, it should be entertaining." I began speaking faster, spitting out words before he could say no, pouring out what I recalled of the facts and figures I had read, about the huge sales figures and the global popularity, relating it all to the book's upcoming anniversary. "We could pepper the story with funny records and even," I added on the spur of the moment, "run a sidebar on how to go about breaking Guinness Records, about getting into Guinness." I had nothing else to add, because at the moment, that was the sum total of my Guinness knowledge.

Like Justice Potter, Rothman knew quirky when he saw it. My proposal was quickly approved and we figuratively shook on it, pending my research and more formal proposal explaining just what I intended to do to get into Guinness, which was an awfully good question. I still knew virtually nothing about the book, about how to go about breaking records, or even about what kind of golf records it covered. So my first tentative steps into the world of *Guinness World Records* began when I walked into a nearby bookstore to pick up a copy of a book I had not read in more than twenty years.

I went home and began imagining what kind of record I might break. I toyed with an idea for hitting balls on the practice range until I saw that such a record already existed—and was insurmountable. The record at the time was for most balls hit in an hour, and to avoid the cop-out of tapping them in rapid fire succession just a few inches from the tee, the rules required that each shot travel at least 100 yards to count. Clearly, Guinness had already thought of every shortcut readers might try to use to sneak into its pages. The current record was 2,146, or one ball struck every 1.67 seconds. For me, it was out of the question. Ditto for most holes played in a week (1,706, or thirteen and a half full rounds each day!), most holes played in a year (10,550 or just over 27 a day), and even most golf balls stacked and balanced on top of each other without adhesive (nine . . . but how?). It was far too late for me to start collecting golf balls: fellow American Ted Loz already had 70,718, each with a different logo. I quickly scanned the golf records in the book and checked out the *Guinness World Records* website but found surprisingly little to go on. Only about one-tenth of 1 percent of the published entries pertained to golf; to make matters worse, most were not in the book at all. Up to that point, I had assumed the book was comprehensive and contained *all* the Guinness World Records, but I quickly discovered that less than a tenth of all certified records were actually printed and bound, so I had no real way of knowing what the slate of existing golf records was. In addition, there is virtually no description of how records are set or under what rules, just the results themselves. I did learn from the website, under the flashy headline "Become a Record Breaker!" that I could essentially make one up and try to set a new record. If approved, the bar would presumably be much lower, as I would be the first to try it. Since I was primarily a travel writer, I focused on travel and came up with a few ideas for new records. One was either the most countries or most states played in during the same day, figuring that in either case I could manage three, possibly four, rounds including border crossings. Alternatively, in what I saw as a clever twist on the Guinness classic of the most people jammed in a Volkswagen Beetle routine, I could try to convince record keeping authorities of the wisdom of a record for the most people to ride in a single golf cart while playing eighteen holes, thus sharing my soon-to-be Guinness fame with a select group of golf buddies. But when I called my editor to discuss these possibilities, he quickly dismissed them, explaining that he thought setting a new record was lame compared with breaking one that already existed. To make the story more colorful, he wanted me to beat someone. This mandate sent me back to the pages of Guinness, and severely narrowed my choices.

Given the small amount of space the book devoted to golf, there was not a lot to work with. Existing records included the Most British Open titles (six, Harry Vardon); Most U.S. Open titles (four, a four-way tie including Jack Nicklaus); Lowest Score (59, a three-way tie including Annika Sorenstam); and Highest Career Earnings (over $41 million, Tiger Woods). Obviously, I had no chance at any of these—or any skill-based golf record. I'm just not very good. Given a year and a lot of funding, I am pretty sure I could break the 27-hole-a-day average, but the downside was that my wife would leave me. I was getting desperate and contemplating calling my editor back to beg for permission to create a new record when I saw it, near the end of the golf record section: the Greatest Distance Traveled Between Two Rounds of Golf Played on the Same Day. A wordy title if ever there was one, I had to read it three times just to be sure what it meant. The current record was held by one Nobby Orens of the United States, who in 1999 had played twice on the same day, first in London, England, and then Tarzana, California, spanning a distance of 5,954-miles between the two rounds. Bells went off in my head. If a professional travel and golf writer couldn't find some way to better Orens's mark, I certainly did not deserve to get into Guinness.

I immediately filed my request to break the record through the Guinness World Records website, the only way to do it in this information age. Just as quickly, I began to learn of the organization's plodding mechanics and penchant for red tape. To register, first you file a request online, whether you want to break an existing record or petition them to set a new one. Several weeks later, they send you a form to sign, mainly a legal document giving them all sorts of rights to publicize your record without compensation and so forth, down to limiting your ability to call yourself a "Guinness World Record Holder" for commercial purposes, should you succeed. You then sign and fax or mail this form back, to which they respond in four or more weeks with either a thumbs up or down on your record attempt, and if the answer is positive, they also send a lot of rules. The website says to expect four to six weeks for the entire process, but six to eight weeks or even longer is more common in my experience.

The frustrating bottom line is that it takes two to four months from start to finish to get an answer, and if the answer is no, you have to start all over again. This is why pros like Ashrita Furman send in proposals regularly and always have multiple record attempts in the pipeline, rather than just trying their luck one at a time and wasting months in between. To further confuse matters, if you do try for a new record, like my idea for the most countries golfed in one day, there is the very strong possibility that it is in fact not new at all, since more than 90 percent of all records aren't available to the public, in which case one of two things will happen. They might give you approval, but you were hoping to play in four countries and you find out that the current record is already up to seven or something totally preposterous that you cannot match. Or there might be a similar record, in which case they could come back and inform you that you cannot set the record for most countries golfed in a day, but you can have a go at breaking the one for the most continents golfed in a week, or some such derivation.

I also learned some other important truths about the application process. First of all, Guinness World Records is a marketing -driven company, and they like seeing their records broken on television and in print. That means that if you contact their public relations people (they have both in-house staff and an outside agency) and tell them you are trying to write a high-profile feature for the nation's largest golf magazine but things are moving too slowly, things suddenly begin to move faster. This is not to suggest they are any less lenient about the actual standards of achievement for media, but they were able to expedite both the application process before—and the approval process after—my attempt. I have since confirmed this habit with several other media outlets, but I also know that while they do respond faster, they still sometimes say no, even when it means losing a lot of publicity, which is reassuring in a purist or egalitarian sense. If you are not involved with the media, there is still a way to get quick and easy service when it comes to applying for records. Every would-be record breaker has the option of paying an expediting fee for what Guinness World Records calls Fast Track service. This guarantees you a response to your query in no more than three days versus somewhere around six weeks, a tempting convenience. The catch is that as of this writing, the Fast Track fee was £300 per record request, well over $500, and while they reply faster, they might well still say no. If that happens, any further requests you want expedited, even in the same category or record setting vein, require additional Fast Track fees. An unprepared or unlucky record seeker could run up thousands of dollars in fees before getting permission to try a single sanctioned attempt. I cannot imagine this route appeals to any but those most desperate to be in the book and to be in it quickly.

One more optional expense is to pay for a Guinness adjudicator to attend your attempt and certify your record on the spot, if successful, saving you another slow and detailed paperwork (and often video) process. Like expediting record proposals, having an official verify your feat is another expense large media outlets, such as the *Today Show*, will get for free but that regular record breakers have to pony up for. Prices vary but are substantial because you will have to transport, feed, and house the official. Thus, if you go first class all the way, rushing your application, and having the event witnessed by Guinness World Records, even a no-cost record like juggling in your living room can end up costing thousands of dollars to break. The company is a for-profit enterprise, after all, as current editor Craig Glenday reminded the *Wall Street Journal*: "We get seen sometimes as a public service, as if the tax payers expect it from us."

However you choose to apply, things are easier when you go after an existing record, since it is hard to justify refusing you when somebody else has already gotten approval for exactly the same thing. But a final complication is that the record may have already been broken one or more times since the mark you just figured out how to break was set—or worse, after you break it but before the book comes out. This happened in 1978 to a frustrated 1,223 Notre Dame college students who played what they thought was the world's largest game of musical chairs, to the tune of Jackson Browne's *Running on Empty*, only to find out when the new edition came out that they had been upstaged by a Salt Lake City high school that had turned out 1,789 students, music unknown, causing one Notre Dame student to lament, "We thought we were in the book for sure." In a similar vein, Ashrita Furman told me, "I saw a picture of the orange pushing with your nose mile in the book, and it was 70 minutes for the mile so I trained for it, was ready to break it, and I was going to do 60 minutes when I found out some other guy had broke it and did 44 minutes. Right before you do the record you have to check again, like a week before, to make sure someone else hasn't already bettered it. So my training got much more intense, I was really hitting it with my nose, jumping up and running after it, much more intense. So I got ready again and was going to break it in Barcelona when I found out someone else did it in 29 minutes. While I was training for it, the record got broken all the way from 70 minutes down to 29. So I got really intense, starting to work on technique and oranges and I finally did it in 24 or 26 minutes." His secret was switching to a green, unripe orange, which is harder and rolls better.

Fortunately, golf is not as popular as pushing an orange with your nose for a mile, so no one else had decided to go after Orens's record. After giving me the go-ahead to try and chase it down, the record management team sent me lengthy rules and instructions detailing what I could do (complete my two rounds in the same calendar day) and what I could not do (utilize private jets). I also had to play both rounds with credible witnesses, who had to sign my scorecards and supply signed, original written statements describing having played eighteen holes with me, under the official rules of golf. I also had to turn in copies of my airline tickets, boarding passes, hotel receipts, and anything else Guinness could think of that would substantiate my actual trip. This is one of the reasons Guinness heavily suggests record breakers get local media coverage, as well as video or photos, as they consider clippings or newscasts of your feat credible evidence.

Now for the hard part. After more than a month of paperwork, I still had to figure out how to break the record. Studying Nobby's feat, I realized that he had used the time change to his advantage, playing in London in the morning and then traveling eight hours back in time en route to California, negating most of the flight time. But it was still a very tight schedule, and I couldn't go any farther west than California. Hawaii, the next stop, was too far to arrive and still have light to play. Whatever route I chose, the basic limitations were clear: I needed to play somewhere close to a major airport, where I could tee off first thing in the morning and catch a flight by around noon, one that would arrive at my final destination early enough in the day for me to get to another course near that airport and still have time to play eighteen before dark. Nobby had already pushed the limits of what mere time zones could do to help, but I realized I could do him one better if I also crossed the international date line and gained back an entire day. The rules stipulated only that my record must not exceed a single calendar day and thus did not limit me to twenty-four hours. To use the dateline to my advantage, I'd have to go west to east, and I wanted a nonstop flight to reduce the chances of missed connections or airline delays. Sunrise, sunset, flight times, and the distances between golf courses and airports and the airports themselves were my limiting factors. I began studying dozens of routes and long-haul flights from Australia to the Western Hemisphere. Tempting routes, like Singapore to New York, one of the longest nonstops, were tossed aside because they landed at night, when golf courses are closed. I eventually hit upon the Sydney to Los Angeles Qantas flight, which met all my criteria. If I was going to break my very first Guinness World Record, I would do it in as much style as possible. The finest course in greater Sydney is the New South Wales Golf Club, one of the most famous in the game and perennially ranked in the World's Top 50. What better place to start? Likewise, the highest-ranked public layout around Los Angeles was the North Course at Pelican Hill in Newport Beach, a perennial U.S. Top 100 course, and not too shabby a finishing venue. It did mean a longer drive, about an hour from LAX, instead of a nondescript course just fifteen minutes away, which would have given me more of a cushion, but if you are going for a world record, you might as well go big. These were two world-class courses most golfers would be lucky to play in a lifetime, much less a single day.

I honestly expected my first foray into the Guinness book to be easy. There was no human endurance factor, no fitness or co-ordination requirements in this goal. It was a record of logistics, with jet lag being the only physical challenge, and I was used to traveling. On paper, my plan was easy: play, fly, play, get certificate. I had already played thirty-six holes dozens of times in my life, so the golf itself was of no concern, and my friends at Qantas were good enough to bump me up to business class for the high-profile record attempt, so I could recover between rounds in the airborne equivalent of a La-Z-Boy recliner while drinking whisky, eating fresh lamb chops, and watching movies, maybe even napping. It would be easier than my normal recreational thirty-six, which does not allow for a fourteen-hour rest break and lavish meals between rounds. In my naive eyes the only thing that lay between me and fleeting fame was the on-time performance of Qantas Airlines, which was statistically reliable. If my flight was on time or even close, and barring an earthquake or a carjacking on the LA freeways, the record was mine. But I quickly learned that in the high-pressure world of Guinness, things do not always go as planned. The day of my record attempt, things immediately got off to a rocky start when the car service driver taking me from downtown Sydney to the golf club turned out not to know where the unmarked course in the suburbs was, and while driving around frantically trying to locate it, I nearly missed my 7:30 AM tee time, which had been specially arranged as the first of the day so I could hurry along with no one ahead of me. Immediately after me was a member's tournament, so I simply had to be on the tee on time—which, in the end, I accomplished only by sprinting from the pro shop.

When I finished the hurried round and signed the card with my playing partner, the club pro, I found unexpected guests waiting for me in the clubhouse. A well-known reporter and television crew from Sydney's *Channel Nine News* had shown up for an un-scheduled interview, drawing a crowd of onlookers. To this day I have no idea how they found out about my record attempt. After the interview, they insisted on filming me walking into the Qantas international departures terminal, so they would have an artistic closing shot for their piece, setting up the second half of my journey. What this meant in practical terms was that I waited for about ten minutes at the golf club while the news team went ahead in their van to set up, and then I was driven to the airport. By the time I arrived curbside in a black Mercedes sedan with smoked windows, a large crowd had gathered alongside the satellite truck and news crew, obviously expecting Russell Crowe or Nicole Kidman. When I got out, there was a collective exasperated exhale of disappointment, and the onlookers might as well have been holding signs reading "Thanks for wasting our time." Minutes later, hurrying through the terminal, I overheard a woman muttering to her friend, "I don't know. It was just some American."

My next challenge was at the Qantas check-in counter. Despite flying business class and traveling very lightly, and having decided to leave my clubs home and rent in order to forego checked luggage and the wait it would mean upon arrival, the airline's representative steadfastly insisted that I check my carry-on bag. Since I cover aviation and travel, I knew with absolute certainty that my bag was smaller than the maximum dimensions for an allowed carry-on. But despite my most polite entreaties, the agent refused to give me my boarding pass until I turned over my tiny piece of luggage, containing just golf shoes, a glove, a toilet kit (in the days when you could still carry those), and a change of socks, underwear, and golf shirt. Now I'd be faced with an additional, unplanned wait at the other end, and given my tight schedule, I decided that if my bag did not emerge promptly, I would simply leave the airport and abandon it. This is the kind of price you have to be willing to pay to join Neil Armstrong and company as a world record breaker.

The reception was not much warmer on my side of the Pacific, as I landed at LAX in an unexpected and uncharacteristic downpour. People don't go to Southern California for the rain, and, at least in my case, they also do not bring raingear. At least my bag came out fast and I had my shoes. My playing partner, the general manager of the course, took pity on me and lent me a rain suit to wear, commenting that in six years he hadn't played in weather like this. So we slogged around the sloppy but beautiful Tom Fazio–designed layout. Instead of begrudging the horrid weather, the Aussie lynch mob, the luggage debacle, or the clueless sedan driver, I took these setbacks in stride, realizing that world records, even esoteric and possibly foolish ones, were records nonetheless and thus deserved some drama. If it was truly easy, what would be the point?

So it was that on February 18, 2004, I shattered Nobby Orens's record by about 1,500 miles, playing in Australia in the morning and California in the afternoon, covering a distance of 7,496 miles. In the process I earned myself a coveted spot in the 2005 gold-covered, special fiftieth anniversary edition of *Guinness World Records*, proving yet another piece of advice I had been given: breaking records already printed makes it far more likely that you too will be among the less than 10 percent of record breakers to appear in the book (historically, about three-quarters of the published records typically repeat from one year to the next). To cap a memorable feat, I even birdied eighteen at Pelican Hill, the thirty-sixth hole of my very long day, to seal the record in memorable fashion.

Several days later, and much to my surprise, Nobby Orens himself sent me a heartfelt congratulatory e-mail, having seen my feat on the evening news. I found this inspiring, and it added to my growing fandom and respect for the *Guinness World Records* tradition, derived from the book's British roots and faux Anglo formality. The elaborate yet vaguely democratic rules (no private jets, lest records become the sole province of eccentric billionaires) and quirky titles like Keeper of the Records (what the company calls its top rules official), made the whole undertaking somehow seem more noble. Orens's gesture fit this model of a gentleman's game. This was one of the things that would later inspire me to write in my article for *Golf Magazine,* "For nearly half a decade his record stood as a testament to the iron will of the avid traveling golfer. Having devoted a large portion of my life to promoting golf travel, I hope Mr. Orens realizes I had no malice in my epic journey, which I consider good for the game itself. Similarly, I expect to one day find my own name stripped from the pages of Guinness by another thrill-seeker who admits that a long plane ride between rounds is far more practical than shooting 58." Later, when I interviewed him by phone, Orens, now a senior citizen who has given up record breaking, explained his motivation to me, "Why? Ego. It makes me feel good to have the certificate on the wall. I'm looking at the certificate right now, as we talk. But I wasn't upset when it was broken because I didn't expect it to last forever. If I had expected it would never be broken I would have been upset. The day after I set it I was talking to my wife and said 'someone will break it one of these days.'" In this same spirit, I regularly told my friends and my wife the same thing, that I expected my record to fall and that I wished the next long-distance golfer good luck.

I lied. When my record was usurped a year later, I was not happy about it at all. I questioned the integrity of the record breaker and the book, since I know a thing or two about the limits of this record, and the new mark, given its particular terminus points, seemed implausible at best. It had been broken by an Australian not long after my try, proving that everything I would later learn about printed records and more publicized records being much more tempting and vulnerable marks was true. I imagine the Aussie watched it on Sydney's *Channel Nine News* the morning of my greatest day and immediately began making his plans to erase me from the record book.

What had started less than year before with a random newspaper article had brought me into the limelight of Guinness, and was about to draw me further into the whirlpool of madness that I would soon see in many other record holders. They say it is better to have loved and lost than never to have loved at all, but for me there was another alternative. Having tasted world recordom, and having lost it, I could get it back and taste it again. And I would.

Why couldn't I just go quietly into the night with the same good grace as Nobby Orens? Because breaking the record had become a much bigger deal than I ever expected. I knew it would be fun, and

I knew it would make a good story for *Golf Magazine*, and I knew it was something none of my fellow golf writers had ever done. What I did not know was that I would become the center of more attention than I had ever gotten in my life. This started before I even left the golf course at Pelican Hill that day. As I sank my birdie putt in the waning daylight, a film crew from ESPN was on hand to record it, possibly tipped off by their peers Down Under. My trophy case is not exactly overflowing with sports awards, but I was a Top Ten Play of the Day on ESPN's *SportsCenter* that night. As soon as I walked off the green, I was interviewed by an ABC crew and numerous radio stations. I was on ABC evening news nationwide and on *Good Morning America* the next day. Friends I had not spoken to in ages called to congratulate me, having seen me on the tube. In the next few weeks I got incessant calls from many more radio stations and newspapers, and was filmed for the local news on NBC. All this attention slowed down, but for months I got phone calls at home from radio stations asking for interviews. An NBC news crew came to my house to film me. My local paper, the award-winning *Valley News*, made me the featured cover story above the fold on page one. The crazy part of all this is that my record was not especially impressive or shocking, and it lacked the visual drama of say, holding rattlesnakes in your mouth or pulling a 747 down the runway. On top of its specificity and difficult to understand title (The Greatest Distance Between Two Rounds of Golf Played on the Same Day), it was just one of hundreds of records broken or set that year and not even the only one that day (incredibly, somebody else set the record for lifting the most copies of the new edition of the Guinness book itself). I'm still sane enough to know that the record never warranted the level of attention it received, which begged the question, how far could someone promote a really fun record? My Guinness World Records certificate, signed by the Keeper of the Records himself, soon arrived in the mail, and I promptly had it expensively framed. It is now proudly displayed in my home. To this day, every time I attend a party or function and someone I know tells someone else about my records, people want to know everything. My fifteen minutes of fame waned but never really ended: more than three years later, after my record had been broken and is no longer in the book, I still get the occasional call for a newspaper or radio interview.

I never confused myself with a celebrity, and no one ever recognized me because of my record or my television appearances. I knew that it was all only interesting to myself, my family, and my friends, yet Guinness fever still set in. The thing that made me step back and look at the Guinness phenomenon in a new light is that I had already had the chance to be in the public eye. I had been an expert guest on numerous television and radio shows before, had spent time with numerous celebrities, had been made up for the cameras in the green room. My name had bylined more than 3,000 articles, and during my travels I had repeatedly met readers of my columns who did not know my face but knew my name. My wife used to joke that her husband was one of the few men who had his picture taken for *Playboy*, as my mug appeared a couple of times on its contributors page. If a Guinness World Record for something so stupid as playing golf with a break for movies and cocktails could become so personally important to me, what would be the effect of this attention on someone who had never before been in the public eye? What was so powerful in the book's allure? I would soon find out.

4

Guinnessport: Getting into Guinness Goes Prime Time

The thing about these people is that they are crazy, but they are doing stuff, that as Norris McWhirter would say, "was at the edge of possibility." We never laughed at them. Even if they were flipping beer mats [coasters], we'd say "you go try it." These guys had taken the time to learn how to do something that no one else can do, and that's amazing. I had an enormous amount of respect for them. It's not the same as being an Olympic Gold medalist or concert pianist, but they do something better than anybody else. Ultimately the only difference is in the "quality" of what they do.

—Greg Childs, longtime producer of BBC's *record breakers*

If you want to settle a pub argument in 2004, you'd be crazy to go to Guinness World Records. *Actually, you'd be crazy to go to it at all, unless you wanted to know who has the largest ice-lolly stick collection in the world, or the most Pepsi cans from around the world. But I have never been in a pub conversation in which someone said: "I wonder*

who has got the most yo-yos in a private collection," or "What's the most
Smarties eaten by someone using a chopstick in three minutes?"

—MILES KINGTON, *THE INDEPENDENT* (LONDON)

It is no coincidence that the *Guinness Book of Records* sold more copies and gained popularity as it added more and more pictures to its pages. Likewise, it would increase sales and become even more popular when it put its images on the airwaves. It didn't hurt that the book had no competition, was part of a famous brand, and filled a void in the marketplace. But the book's rapid evolution from a bet-settling device and barroom curiosity into mainstream reading was driven not by a global need to locate the highest point in Ireland, but rather by the nearly universal appeal of its human element. Almost from the beginning, readers formed bonds with the likes of the world's oldest, fattest, tallest, and shortest people, alongside those sporting the longest beards, mustaches, and finger-nails. All of these were cases where a picture was worth a thousand words. While no photo will ever bring the world's largest boiler to vivid life, a picture of the obese McCrary twins on side-by-side motorcycles creates an indelible impression for the reader that no simple textual description of their weights could achieve. When the original staid book failed to sell nearly as well in the States as it had in England, and Norris McWhirter was at a loss to comprehend the new market, he let U.S. distributor David Boehm, chief of Sterling Publishing, carry the ball. A savvy marketer, Boehm wrapped the plain green cloth in a glossy cover, printed front and back with images and bold print espousing superlatives, including a picture of the most people riding a single bicycle along with illustrations of a man eating an ox and a lion tamer at work. Fully three-quarters of the images on Sterling's "new" cover were of actual people set-ting records, despite their minuscule representation in the pages of the book, whose content leaned toward mountains and machines. This skewed ratio would immediately begin changing, and with nearly every subsequent issue, more and more pages and photos were devoted to humans. No matter how odd a cross section of humanity they were, readers could relate to them as fellow human beings, and this, it would seem, was part of the key to the public fascination with Guinness.

In the course of research for this book, I interviewed dozens of people, many of whom had read the book as children, a rite of passage in the United States, and then not picked it up in the years or decades since. At the mere mention of its title, the *Guinness Book of Records*, nearly everyone I spoke to between the ages of twenty and fifty conjured up the same exact memories, recalling a handful of iconic images: the guy with the long twisting fingernails, the McCrary twins on their matching motorcycles, the original Siamese twins, the man with the "beard" of honey bees, and Robert Earl Hughes, holder of the lofty title, Heaviest Human of All Time. All were remembered more for their shocking pictures than the accompanying text.

"I'm sure you have interviewed countless people who have said the same, not especially original or profound thing, that there was something very relatable about everyday people doing incredible things," explained journalist Ben Sherwood, a lifelong fan of the book and until recently the executive producer of *Good Morning America*. Sherwood recalled how his childhood memories of the book helped shape a novel he had written.

> I was the number two producer on the *Nightly News with Tom Brokaw* at the time, and when I was working on that there was the impeachment of President Clinton and the war in Kosovo and other interesting stories, but there was so much media focus on certain things, and I wanted to find a way to talk about important truths, without writing a book about a network television producer or magazine. *The Guinness Book of World Records* popped up, because I had always loved it and Robert Earl Hughes and all those guys were floating around in my head.

These universal recollections led to Sherwood's Guinness-inspired romantic comedy, *The Man Who Ate the 747*, the vehicle he used to talk about the important truths of human existence.

> Like every boy, I just loved the pictures and the people.
> My 1974 edition of the book, it was shaped like a brick in
> those days, and it was my most coveted possession. I read
> it so many times that I literally had to keep it in a shoebox
> because it was falling apart. The principal characters in my
> novel, many of them were inspired by characters of my
> childhood imagination, from the book, and they became
> sort of imaginary friends. I stared at their pictures and
> wanted to know what the world's tallest man was like,
> what the world's heaviest man was like.

The journalist in Sherwood added, referring to Robert Hughes, "He was buried in a coffin the size of a piano, but not actually a piano, a distinction which is often misunderstood."

"What's the world's best-selling copyrighted book?" Ken Jennings asks rhetorically. Of course Jennings knows the answer, just as he remembers more trivia factoids than most of will forget in our lifetimes. In his book *Brainiac*, documenting the history of trivia, he recalls eagerly reading the Guinness book on family car trips at age seven or eight and trying to impress his parents with its esoteric facts. "These are a particular favorite of young boys who have just received a copy of the world's best-selling copyrighted book, the *Guinness Book of World Records*, and want to quiz you on that book's semi-famous superlatives—the crazy guy in Nepal with four-foot fingernails, for instance, or those fat twins on the motorcycles." Jennings's book gives no specific details about these people, because he rightly assumes that for his audience, no further explanation is necessary: everybody everywhere knows exactly what fingernails and fat twins he is talking about. As he told me, "When I think about the Guinness records that I remember as a kid, there's got to be some element of the nineteenth-century carnival freak show about it. It's freaks . . . those are the people that everyone remembers. So there is certainly something about ogling the oddball as well, which is a less inspiring answer as to why people like it than the limits of human achievement or whatever."

The book's embrace of the human element in both photo and print began almost immediately. While the content is nearly identical, the first U.S. version, printed less than a year after the book's debut and still bearing the original green cover, rearranged the order, opening with the Human Being, which had been relegated to the fourth chapter in the original British edition, behind the Universe, Natural World, and Animal Kingdom. In just one year, the emphasis had already shifted, and readers' first glance at the *Guinness Book of Records* would be one of amazing humans for decades to come. This section focused on anatomical and biological records, oldest, tallest, fattest, and the like, rather than on the "human achievements," such as juggling and sword swallowing, which had their own chapter farther back in the book. The very first truly updated edition, the blue book of late 1956, had several times as many pictures as the original, published just a year earlier, and specifically, many more photos of people. But these early volumes still focused on famed athletes, explorers, and adventurers, rather than images of the individuals whose claim to fame was quirky or unintentional. This omission did not last long: photos of the longest mustache appeared in the light blue 1964 edition, along with Britain's ("and possibly the world's") longest married couple. The light blue also included, alongside its scientists and Olympians, an eerie image of Ms. Henrietta Howland Green, the world's most miserly millionaire, who despite amassing a fortune of $95 million, delayed necessary surgery on her son while searching for a free clinic, resulting in the amputation of his leg. By the maroon edition of 1966, giants, dwarves, and Britain's most prolific murderer were appearing in the greatly expanded photo sections. The following year's turquoise edition was a watershed for human record holders: for the first time photos moved onto the pages of the book itself, accompanying the text, rather than on special photo insert pages, a change that caused the human element to multiply even more quickly in both image and word. By the cerise edition of 1969, which marked the final year of the book's original size and format, these images had become the precursor to today's visually driven editions, showing readers the world's fattest man standing on a scale, the shortest dwarf standing next to a kilted "normal height" human, and most important, the first ever image (albeit a drawing rather than photo) of the man who, since the very first *Guinness Book of Records* in 1955, came to epitomize all things Guinness—the tallest man in the history of the world.

Born in Alton, Indiana, on February 22, 1918, Robert Pershing Wadlow looked like a normal infant, and there was nothing to suggest the stature he would go on to achieve. When his parents, Addie and Harold Wadlow, first held their son, he was a slightly-above-average eight-pound, eight-ounce baby, born into a family of five healthy children, with two brothers and two sisters, all remarkably average in physique and appearance. But not Robert: at the age of two, he underwent a double hernia operation, and from that point on began to grow at a rate still unprecedented in human history. By age five he stood 5'4". He was over six feet tall by the age of eight, while at nine he could carry his 5'11" father up the stairs of the family home on his back. Although he remained enviably slim, his weight would reach almost a quarter of a ton by age twenty-one (491 pounds) and he grew to an ultimate height of 8' 11.1". Despite having died a decade and a half before Sir Beaver's inspired idea for the record book (from a foot infection directly related to his size and poor circulation), Wadlow became a revered fixture of *The Guinness Book of Records*. He was codified in the very first edition as the tallest human being of all time and still holds the title, one of just a meager handful of original records that have never been broken. In fact, while Wadlow belongs to an elite club that includes the Best Selling Record of all time (Irving Berlin's "White Christmas"), the world's Largest Dam (Hoover), and the Largest Office Building (the Pentagon), Robert P. Wadlow's record is likely the only remaining human record from 1955, excepting firsts, such as Hillary's ascent of Everest, which can never be broken. Someone could theoretically grow taller than Wadlow, but no one has done so or even come close. His height is nearly a full foot taller than that of media darling Bao Xi Shun, the towering Mongolian sheep herder who frequently made headlines during his recent reign as the tallest living human being, and still five inches taller than the new record holder, Ukraine's Leonid Stadnyck (a veterinary surgeon standing 8'5.5"), who took the mantle from Bao with the 2008 edition. Wadlow's place in biological history seems secure, while his place in *Guinness World Records* history is unparalleled: by the fiftieth anniversary 2005 edition, his enduring popularity warranted an entire sub-chapter, a two-page spread complete with half a dozen photos, a detailed biography, and a table listing his height benchmarks by age. No other individual or object or invention is awarded such extensive coverage in the book, and the authority on superlatives calls Wadlow's record a "true classic" and "one of the most popular and memorable in the 50-year history." While he never lived to see it, Wadlow became one of the most famous record holders of all time, his likeness replicated in statue form for Guinness World Record museums, where his popularity lives on. When the company opened its flagship museum in London's Trocadero, the synthetic Wadlow was given an honored position as the very first exhibit visitors saw. A critic for the London *Times* happily reported that, "Given that many people find a macabre fascination in looking at 'freaks,' I was heartened by the reactions of the children and adults I observed, all of whom expressed not only amazement but sympathy for this gentle giant."

Amazingly, Wadlow was still growing fast right up until his untimely death at the age of twenty-two and a half, and had added nearly three full inches just since his twenty-first birthday, having actually broken the world record by age eighteen. Even without the book, he was a celebrity, and reporters would stand on stepladders to interview him face to face. After his death, Wadlow's brother Howard recalled that life was far from rosy for the giant and that "he couldn't go anywhere without drawing a crowd." Echoing this sentiment, Chris Sheedy, Guinness World Records's representative in Australia, told a Melbourne paper the tallest-person record is both the book's greatest and its most tragic. "They are very sad people who have been thrown the world's most vicious curve ball. They are going to die earlier than anyone else and they are stared and pointed at everywhere. They are such grand creatures, but they all have sadness in their eyes." Howard Wadlow's recollections of his brother support this. "He had to duck to go through all doorways. No room on a bus, no room on a train, no seats on an airplane. Everything was made for a person six feet tall or under. He probably wished that he wasn't as tall as he was and wanted a normal life, which he couldn't possibly live."

Wadlow's staggering height helped create a lasting fascination with tallness as a record, the record Sheedy called the book's greatest. Considering how difficult Wadlow's mark is to break, the book has been driven to add categories for the tallest *living* man and woman, and has awarded a record for Europe's tallest man as well. Guinness World Records recently went so far as to hold an uncharacteristic search, proactively seeking out the tallest men in the U.K., Canada, and the United States respectively, fostering an entire record industry in tallness. Given that he also held the records for having the world's largest hands and feet, with hands that stretched more than a foot from his wrist to the tip of his middle finger, and he wore size 37 extrawide footwear over his eighteen-and-a-half-inch feet, Wadlow truly had big shoes to fill. He paved the way for the likes of Sandy Allen, the world's tallest woman (7' 7.25"), who is also re-created in life size at Guinness museums, and whose fame (derived from the book) led the renowned Italian director Federico Fellini to cast her in the film *Casanova*. The *New York Times* devoted a lengthy feature article to the simple event of Ms. Allen meeting Chris Greener, at the time Europe's tallest man. More recently, Chinese giant Bao Xi Shun, who held the record as tallest living man until 2007, was in the news on a regular basis. The *New York Times* reported that Bao saved the lives of two dolphins at the Beijing aquarium when he used his 41.7" extra-long arms to reach his hand down their throats and remove the plastic that they had swallowed after it fell into their pool. "Attempts to remove the plastic surgically failed," the paper reported, and for Plan B, somewhat astonishingly, "veterinarians decided to ask for help from Mr. Bao," who saved the dolphins like a cartoon superhero. Likewise, Bao's marriage three months later was widely covered by international media outlets such as CNN, which cheekily noted that "After searching high and low, the world's tallest man has married a woman two-thirds his height." This unceasing media interest in human height proves that society's fascination with Wadlow and company, which made the Guinness book an instant hit, remains undiminished today.

Things came full circle for Bao when he leveraged his newfound stature as a Guinness World Record holder to be granted permission to travel outside of China for the first time—where else but to London and the offices of the Guinness World Records? Current editor Craig Glenday reported that the visit went fine, with the notable exception that Bao could not fit into the airplane's lavatory during the long trip, just the kind of annoyance Wadlow's brother had described that historic giant as having to endure. "The best part of the job for me is getting to meet these people. I mean where else are you going to meet a giant?" Glenday asked. Where else indeed?

"The World's Tallest Man has been in it since the beginning," Stuart Claxton, U.S. head of business development for Guinness World Records, and a frequent spokesperson for the book, told me. In trying to explain the book's unique appeal, he noted that

> the fascination I think is in all of us as human beings. Learning what the limits are in all these fields, the tallest, biggest, etc. is always going to be interesting. A record is a report documenting change. If you have an awareness of the limits, the smallest and the largest, then you can place yourself, or the tree in your garden into that spectrum and

it gives you context. You know where you stand, how your tree compares to the world's tallest tree. If that's the fastest someone can run 100 yards, how can I do? It gives you a place in the world.

Craig Glenday agreed, telling an interviewer that, "Everyone wants to know what their place in the world is. The book provides an image of the world and shows you where you stand." Michael Roberts, executive editor of *Outside* magazine, has spent years documenting, debunking, and often just shaking his head over people's obsession with records and record breaking and superlatives, something his magazine covers regularly in the fields of athletics, mountaineering, and exploration. Roberts believes "It's something innate in our culture. It's a way to compare yourself to others. If life is a race, then how am I doing?" Jason Daley was also an editor at *Outside*, where he specifically covered record attempts for the magazine's "Dispatches" column, and later wrote a similar column called "For the Record" for *Men's Journal* magazine. "After years of going through this, I saw that the bottom line is just people's fascination with the E.S.T: Fastest, longest, tallest." The book and many of its most enduring records do provide something of a framework of our realities, no matter how extreme. Regardless of your own height or weight, the two Roberts of Guinness fame, Wadlow and Hughes, will put you in your place, at least perspective-wise.

In many cases, a Guinness record comes to define the person who holds it and becomes the most important thing about them. As readers, we don't know Sridhar Chillal, we know the guy with the really long fingernails. This may not be true for celebrity record holders such as Tom Hanks or Sir Richard Branson, but it clearly is for the guy who lifts weights with his eyelids and for most of his fellow human record holders. Among these, there are a handful of record holders who have become truly iconic, usually for their images, such as the obese McCrary twins on motorcycles or Jackie "the Texas Snakeman" Bibby with his swarm of poisonous rattlesnakes dangling from his mouth, but even among this exalted group, Wadlow stands out. He needed no props to improve the audacity of his appearance, nor did he attempt to get into the book. He was the first new human hero the book introduced to its readers, and he immediately changed the way people viewed the book. While images of Mount Everest and the lunar landing came and went, Wadlow's photo would return year after year.

Obesity became another favorite reader obsession, not only with Wadlow's counterpart Robert Earl Hughes, who so inspired Ben Sherwood, or the McCrary twins whose images Ken Jennings could not forget, but also with record holders for fattest man living, fattest woman living, and the fattest man and woman in Great Britain and Ireland respectively. As if readers could not get enough of weight, there were similar records for lightest categories, for greatest weight differential in a married couple, and both the greatest recorded weight gain and loss (this last quaintly called "slimming"). Alongside the tallest and heaviest were the oddest, such as Sridhar Chillal's grotesquely curling and twisted fingernails, which were left uncut for more than fifty years and proved unforgettable to anyone who saw his picture. Never ones to be accused of sexism, the editors also added the woman with the longest fingernails. In this mold, the book also featured the longest mustaches, beards, and hair. There were the potent Siamese twins, Chang and Eng, the original pair from Siam who inspired the very lexicon—and fathered twenty-two children between them. And then there was a category that would become as compelling as tallest and fattest to Guinness readers and compilers, that of longevity, or in the -est world of Guinness, oldest. While offering readers the same "framework of limits" that gave an idea of their place in the world, this record category had far more action. Wadlow has gone unchallenged for more than half a century, and living giants often hold their spot for years, but the oldest living person is one of the most regularly broken records, since its holders have the unfortunate habit of dying. In less than a one-year span between mid-2006 and mid-2007, the oldest living woman record changed hands at least four times.

"One of the marvelous things about doing this job is meeting superlative people. I have met the tallest man in the world, the tallest woman in the world, oldest man in the world—every possible kind," said Norris McWhirter. As history's ultimate arbiter of the superlative, and one who for most of his years at the book's helm actually committed every printed record to his prodigious memory, Norris's opinion of which records are most impressive cannot be taken lightly. His choice? Oldest. "The one that has made the biggest impact on me is the champion of the all-time most competitive of all records, which is staying alive. There are five and a half billion people on earth and every one is trying to stay alive and he is the supreme champion." At the time, "he" was Japan's Shigechiyo Izumi, who later died at his home in 1986 just shy of age 121. Norris continued, "The thing about him that was so amazing, and so annoys the doctors, is that he drank like a fish and smoked like a furnace. He began smoking when he was 70 years old. His wife died at what he regarded as the pathetic age of 90 and he was born a few weeks after Lincoln was assassinated in 1865." David Boehm, the publisher of the American edition, had Izumi on his television show when he was 115 and explained his secret to longevity: "He starts the day walking his dog, then sits around drinking whisky."

McWhirter was very proud of the self-proclaimed fact—or record—that he was the only person on earth to have met both living people aged 120 or older, Izumi in 1986 and then in 1997 Madame Jeanne Calment, of Arles, France, who was approaching 122. "It was very fascinating—she remembers Vincent van Gogh going into her father's shop." Calment, who finally succumbed at 122 years and 164 days, joined Wadlow in the world record Hall of Fame when she became the longest-lived confirmed person of all time, which proved to be very good news for everyone except the French notary public who tried to make a killing by buying her house. In France, they have a creepy combination of real estate investment and gambling called *viager*. The macabre transaction works like this: Find an elderly person with a desirable home, and agree to buy their house when they die. The buyer begins making the mortgage payments immediately based on the agreed sales price, but when the owner passes away, no more payments are made, and the buyer often gets the home for a fraction of its market price. The upside to the seller is that they can begin to cash out of the equity in their home without having to move out. The notary who agreed to buy Calment's home must have thought he was getting a steal when he closed the deal with her at age 90. Thirty-two years of payments later, she was still having the best of both worlds, living in her home with a long and unexpected stream of payments. Talk about bad luck: the very worst-case scenario in *viager* is making a deal with the longest-lived person in human history, exactly what Calment became, complete with a framed Guinness World Record certificate hanging in her bedroom. When explaining her amazing span, she said, "I've been forgotten by God." To this day the oldest living person record continues to fall regularly; it is described on the Guinness World Records website as among the most frequently broken of all records. Calment was an exception to the rule that the title, while desirable, is usually short lived.

Remarkably, for a period of time in 2007, both the men's and women's record were held by denizens of Kyushu, Japan. Japanese holders of this record aren't uncommon, as the nation has nearly 30,000 residents 100 years old or older, but Kyushu is a rural island some 560 miles from Tokyo, and it seems too good to be true that both Yone Minagawa and Tomoji Tanabe lived there holding the women's and men's longevity records respectively. Proving that it really does take all kinds, Tanabe uses a much different strategy than his predecessor, Izumi, and drinks a glass of milk daily, does not smoke, and credits his longevity to his temperance. "I don't drink alcohol—that is the biggest reason for my good health." Then again, the teetotaler is still a decade shy of the standard set by his hard-drinking, chain-smoking, dog-walking countryman.

Thanks to the oldest, tallest, and fattest humans, a generation of readers would not be able to put down the stories of the book's characters. No sooner had the *Guinness Book of Records* been invented than Robert Pershing Wadlow quickly became the living embodiment of the public's fascination with the book's records. He became an icon for the fascination that generations of Guinness readers have shared with the extreme limits of the human form, from the shortest to the tallest, skinniest to fattest, youngest to oldest, for both men and women. No reader could set out to break Wadlow's record, but at the same time, he helped make the very notion of being in Guinness popular, and many of his fellow real people in the first edition laid the groundwork for the search for "vulnerable" records. Just before the book came out, Roger Bannister's breakthrough sub–4-minute mile had been heralded as one of the most important events in all of sports history, yet in less than two months it had fallen in equally publicized fashion, putting Australian runner John Michael Landy in the pages of the inaugural *Guinness Book of Records*, and demonstrating that even the loftiest records could be broken, and broken quickly. Like Wadlow, Landy's record may have been out of reach of virtually every reader, but for readers encouraged by these very human heroes, it was not much of a leap to notice that the very first edition had a handful of the type of quirky records, which have since become its hallmark. When the book jumped onto the best-seller list, those fascinated by human record holders must have also been drawn to the potential in the Longest Dog Team Ever Harnessed (73 Siberian huskies); Brick-Laying (fifty-eight per minute for sixty minutes); Juggling (ten balls or eight plates); Highest Stilts (22' at the ankle); and Most Hamburgers Eaten (seventy-seven in one sitting), all tempting benchmarks of that first edition. As Ross McWhirter explained the soon-to-be-popular craze of record breaking in the United States, "Records are used there as a substitute for frontiers." The looming presence of Wadlow, Hughes, and others must have made those frontiers seem worthy of exploration, and in addition to making the book incredibly popular for decades to come, would inspire the very first readers set on joining their ranks.

The original 1955 edition of *The Guinness Book of Records* was a slight and slender reference book, written for an adult audience of legal drinking age. Austere in appearance, it had very few pictures, and human entries constituted just a small percentage of the superlatives, mostly natural, mechanical, and scientific, catalogued within. There was no website, no suitable for framing record certificates, and most significantly, not a single person had applied to be in the book.

Fifty-three years later, *Guinness World Records* is a coffee-table-sized volume, with color pictures on practically every page, many of them shocking to behold. It features glow-in-the-dark ink, and recent editions have showcased holograms, fold-out sections, and even trading cards. "The old Guinness looked more like a psalm book, or even a Bible, with a sober dark blue cover enlivened only by the discreet golden Guinness harp. The new Guinness has huge lettering on a glitzy gold cover. It's the difference between a librarian and a man with a megaphone," chided London journalist Miles Kington of the *Independent*, critiquing the fiftieth anniversary edition of 2005. No longer requiring the ID of bar patrons, today's book is aimed solidly at preadolescents, mainly male, and accordingly is filled with accounts of people skipping, unicycling, juggling, and frog hopping their way to records, and also of doing almost all these things and many more backward or upside down. Today's most photogenic record holders lift enormous weights with their ears, attach them to their beards, and even pull them with their eyelids. Nasal ejections, full-body tattooing, and speed gluttony are all surefire roads to inclusion. The number of records in the company's files has increased dramatically, and over 65,000 record-setting inquiries reach the book's offices each year, almost all via the Internet. As a result, the number of staffers (nine) employed simply to handle the paperwork of these inquiries exceeds the entire group that compiled the original book. In 1955, Sir Hugh Beaver wrote to the McWhirters after reading the first edition and was amazed at its interesting and thorough content. Were Sir Beaver to return from the grave today and pick up the 2008 version, it is reasonable to assume he'd find it almost completely unrecognizable.

What happened in the past half century? How did the book

change so dramatically that while it has remained a perennial best seller, it now has a completely different format, appearance, and audience? The short answer is an almost immediate compulsion among readers to join the ranks of record makers and breakers in the pages of Guinness, fueled by the glory of television and accomplished chiefly through the advent of "Guinnessport."

The term was coined by *Sports Illustrated* in a seminal 1979 article in which the normally tight-lipped record book staffers gave surprisingly candid interviews and access. In a lighthearted but well-researched piece by Jerry Kirshenbaum, this article remains the most thorough one ever published about the book, its creators, and its fanatic followers. Kirshenbaum summed up the fixation with getting into Guinness, and the inventiveness it can drive readers to, when he wrote:

> Nothing, however, points up the book's success more dramatically than the zeal with which people try to get their names into its pages—and of course, onto those cereal boxes and greeting cards. Fraternity boys, failed athletes, assorted crazies and maybe even some normal folk eagerly participate in what might be called Guinnessport, whose main purpose is to "get into Guinness." . . . Guinnessport flourishes because the book contains such a wealth of categories for would-be record-breakers to choose from, including many that rely less on talent than on brass and tenacity. Among these are underwater violin playing. . . . The U.S. is a hotbed of Guinnessport. There appears to be no shortage of people in this country like 17-year-old Lang Martin of Charlotte, NC, who made it his mission to crack the pages of Guinness by balancing six golf balls vertically.

According to Kirshenbaum, it took Martin weeks to perfect his special skill, working late into the night, sticking with it as stack after stack toppled because he "was wanting to get into that book real bad." He was neither the first nor last driven by such motivation.

In the simplest terms, Guinnessports are new "sports" made up just to get in the book. For instance, if breaking Lance Armstrong's record for seven consecutive victories in the Tour de France seems beyond your reach, you might instead choose to eat a bicycle. "There's not much left to do that is fastest, highest, or first, so you have to redo it with your own statistics, the youngest, shortest, first with some disease, first left handed. We're all firsts in some sense," said Jason Daley, a records expert who closely followed world records in sports and exploration as an editor at *Outside* magazine and the "For the Record" columnist at *Men's Journal* magazine. Individuals seeking recognition regularly peppered Daley with accounts of their feats, often bizarre firsts. One of the most popular outdoor magazine subjects is climbing Mount Everest, and more than a half century after Sir Edmund Hillary bagged the coveted first ascent, climbers are still claiming numerous firsts on the mountain every year, including the guy who wanted recognition for being the first to summit while wearing shorts. Really. "When it gets absurd is when it's something they made up out of whole cloth, a sport they invented so they can call themselves world champion of it, with nobody else doing it and no objective way to measure its difficulty," Daley said, perfectly describing most Guinnessports. It may be absurd, but it is a sure path to the record books, since there is no previous benchmark to beat when you make up a new category. When CNN.com ran a story about *Guinness World Records* titled "Shortcuts: How to Get into the Record Books," one of its six tips was, obviously, "Invent a record: If all else fails, think up a new category in which you can claim to be the world's best."

It is easy to see where readers got the idea for Guinnessport. Despite its reference library pretenses, the book was never exactly stoic and sober, and some of the most colorful records and seemingly made-up contests stem from long before the first edition was even published. In the premier edition, just for example, all the most important "ratting" records were claimed by Mr. J. Shaw's terrier "Jacko," who killed 1,000 rats in less than 100 minutes in

London, including a prodigious 100 rats in the first 5 minutes and 28 seconds on May 1, 1862, nearly a century before Jacko or his owner could have *intentionally* set out to achieve *Guinness World Records* immortality. In way of comparison, today the company has had to ban weight records for dogs as a record category, for fear of owners so eager to get into Guinness that they force-feed or starve their pets for a glimpse of Jacko-like immortality. Likewise, while much more limited in scope, even the earliest editions had a clear reverence for odd feats that remained outside the boundaries of traditional sports, yet were worthy of the label "human achievements." These included the "rockathon" (rocking chair marathon), pole squatting, and prodigious facial hair growth, as well as a short section on gastronomic records, with several that might be considered dangerous today, featuring mass and speed consumption of alcoholic beverages. Readers might have also been encouraged to try odd new feats by the book's tone, with an underlying emphasis on the bizarre and macabre, a flavor apparent from the very beginning with record categories like longest coma, greatest ritual murder, and most fingers (twenty-six!) sprinkled liberally throughout the book. Early Guinness books also had a rather bleak preoccupation with natural and man-made disasters, serial killers, fastest-acting poisons, and the like. Tornadoes, floods, earthquakes, and any kind of mass devastation, along with train wrecks and related accidents, soon became a popular subject for charts and tables. Each book had a chapter titled "Accidents and Disasters" that featured records for the worst pandemics (Black Death), famines, floods, earthquakes, landslides, bombings (conventional and atomic), dam failures, fires, explosions, tornadoes, and accidents of the mining, plane, train, road, and submarine variety. By the 1960 edition, such disasters were thoroughly detailed in their own page-long chart.

The earliest readers could find examples of Guinnessport they might consider imitating in the original book, even though the concept and practice had yet to be invented. The first record holder for Longest Beard had begun growing his in 1912, the Longest

Mustache had been maintained since 1949, and while longest fingernails did not appear as a record until the 1964 edition, a sign of the book's increasing reliance on oddities, the nails themselves had been grown back in the 1920s. Of course, none of these feats had been undertaken with the goal of setting Guinness records, which did not yet exist. The same can be said of various records such as marathon piano playing, talking continuously, stilt walking, walking on hands, and the ever popular skipping, all of which have record-keeping histories predating the Guinness book. But their very inclusion opened the door to new feats in similar veins.

A final encouragement to would-be Guinnessport practitioners was the chance to see hotly contested records change hands frequently, even in the earliest years of the book. While no one could go back in time and be the first to reach the poles or climb to the world's highest point, readers watched as real-life adventurers and explorers continued to grab records, often from each other, with each new edition. In the early years of *Guinness World Records*, the most frenetic and contentious record breaking occurred not in pogo sticking miles or joggling races but in areas of mechanical and transportation speeds. The books featured numerous such records, and for Atlantic crossings alone some editions listed separate entries for first, fastest, fastest roundtrip, and fastest submerged. The fastest car speed contest was a slugfest, soon becoming a back-and-forth war of burning rubber between the United States (represented by Mickey Thompson and later Craig Breedlove), and Great Britain (Donald Malcolm Campbell, CBE). Until the likes of Ashrita Furman came along, these speed junkies were the serial record holders of the book, appearing over and over in its pages. After crashing and wrecking his first-generation Bluebird, built especially for the attempt at a cost of over £1 million, Campbell achieved success in 1964. (Notably, this was the year the McWhirters switched gears, chapterwise, and moved car speed records from Human Achievement to the Mechanical World, making more room in the former for the growing number of Guinnessport "achievements"—such as haggis throwing.)

Rivals Breedlove and Campbell would exchange records for years afterward, and Campbell, who had also set the waterborne speed record in 1956 in his turbojet engined ship, not so creatively named Bluebird, at 225.63 mph on a lake in England, eventually claimed eight world speed records on land and water, and won four Seagrave trophies (awarded annually to a British subject who accomplishes the most outstanding demonstration of transportation by land, air, or water). His last Seagrave was awarded posthumously, as Campbell was killed trying to rebreak the water speed record. Breedlove, in an equal case of name fixation, christened all of his cars Spirit of America, and in the course of setting five world records, became the first to ever drive at 400, 500, and 600 mph respectively. In 2006 he finally retired and sold his latest jet-powered version of Spirit of America to adventurer, aviator, fellow Guinness World Record holder, and speed freak Steve Fossett. Fossett was killed in 2007 when the plane he was piloting crashed. He was airborne in order to scout dry lakebed locations suitable for his upcoming land speed record attempt in Spirit of America.

Unlike brick carrying and orange pushing, land, sea, and air records have long been highly competitive with or without Guinness, and have their own rewards, like the Seagrave and the coveted Blue Riband Trophy for fastest boat crossing of the Atlantic. Sir Richard Branson, the billionaire founder of the Virgin empire, including retail stores, an airline, record label, publishing house, and more, has both kinds of records. "I've been very fortunate to have lived in an era when there are still records to be broken. Scott of the Antarctic is a great, great uncle of mine or something, a distant relative, who was a very famous Englishman who tried to get to the Antarctic and actually perished on the way back. England is full of its Drakes and Raleighs and people who went out and explored the world, and as young English people we were brought up to admire them."

Branson's record-setting personality is not inherited solely from Robert F. Scott of the Antarctic: his grandmother, Dorothy Huntley-Flint, was also a Guinness record holder, as the ninety-year-old passionate golfer made a hole in one with a 7-iron from 112 yards out at her local club in Barton-on-Sea, England, making her the oldest woman to ever have done so (since surpassed). Branson himself joined such illustrious ranks in 1986, a year after capsizing in his Virgin Atlantic Challenger, when he succeeded in bringing home the Blue Riband and in getting into Guinness by crossing the Atlantic in the Virgin Atlantic Challenger II, breaking the existing speed record by two hours. The next year he made the first ever crossing of the Atlantic by hot air balloon, in the Virgin Atlantic Flyer, and in that successful attempt also broke the record for the largest hot air balloon ever flown.

Having set records in the air, on the water, and on a combination of roads and water, next on Richard Branson's agenda is outer space and an attempt to extend his family's Guinness record-breaking tradition to four straight generations. "I'll be going into space with Virgin Galactic in eighteen months' time and a few of us will be breaking records. My son will be the youngest to ever go into space, twenty-two at the time, and my parents will be the oldest, ninety-one and eighty-nine respectively. My daughter will be twenty-five and she may well be the youngest woman, I'm not sure. That trip will be taking place and will be the start of space tourism, which will be very exciting." Youngest and oldest in space may or may not fit the mold of Guinnessport, but either way, if it works it might well also set the record for the most expensive record-breaking undertaking of all time.

"I think that the actual record itself, just the two lines someone gets in the book for achieving something, is nice but it's not that important," Branson continued. "It's the actual doing and experience and accomplishment that really gives the satisfaction, but that being said, the *Guinness Book of Records* is something that has been incredibly well respected and I suspect it has encouraged people to do things which they should never have dreamt of doing. I think it has added a lot of fun to British life and world life and it has recognized people who have accomplished incredibly brave things and some incredibly stupid things as well."

My nominee for the stupid thing category is Jim Rogers of Columbus, Ohio. Rogers's claim to fame will forever be that of the man who introduced marathon drumming to the world. Other than the McWhirters, Sir Beaver, and a handful of Guinness executives who knew that the first edition was coming, no one could make an advance effort to be in the book. But given its 167,000 copies and instant popularity as a best seller, it is not surprising that readers immediately saw opportunities to overtake printed records—and invent their own. By definition, the earliest an activity created explicitly to get into the book could have appeared was in late 1956, with the release of the blue edition, which is exactly where you can find Mr. Rogers. In the very first revised version of *The Guinness Book of Records*, there were less than half a dozen new records added in the "Miscellaneous" and "Endurance" sections of the "Human Achievement" chapter, which at that point were the only parts of the book suitable for intentional acts of "getting into Guinness." Of these, several were in the works long before the book existed. For instance, while Los Angeles bartender Beverly Nina O'Malley certainly deserved her record for Most Marriages when she divorced her thirteenth husband to marry number fourteen in 1955, that marriage marathon presumably had been going on for more than a year. Not so for nonstop drumming, which requires more stamina than musical ability. A close examination of the first few editions suggests that by pounding away on his drum, Rogers was the first person ever to gain entry for a new and pointless category of human achievement, basically inventing Guinnessport, and paving the way for Ashrita Furman, Jackie Bibby, and thousands of others. This breakthrough must have prompted readers, which by that time included many in the United States, to ponder the question, "If he could get into Guinness by sitting around banging a drum, what can I do?" Watching television, playing board games, and going bar hopping were all obvious answers—and all correct ones, Guinnessport "feats" that would get countless entrants into the pantheon of world record holders. The book would never be the same.

Fifteen-year-old Roger McEwan was another early ground-breaker of Guinness lore. While the drum playing Mr. Rogers appears to be a pioneer, the first to get into the book through Guinnessport, or by inventing a new category of record, young McEwan seems to be the first to do it the more conventional way—by breaking a previously published record. Assuming that the athletes, explorers, financiers, and longevity champions had other motivations, and that disasters, either man-made or natural, were not undertaken solely to get into Guinness, one can surmise that McEwan's assault on the crisp-eating record, Brit-speak for potato chips, was done for Guinness glory alone. In November 1959 he raised the bar for most potato chips eaten in an hour without a drink, from twenty-nine bags to thirty, leaving himself a full minute to spare, making him likely the first Guinness-inspired record breaker, rather than record setter.

In 1960 another cornerstone of Guinnessport lore was laid by Felicity Ashton, Valerie Cleverton, and Patricia Frend, when they set a marathon record for forty-eight hours of nonstop knitting. While endurance knitting is clearly an example of Guinnessport, this was not their groundbreaking innovation. That would be the earliest known introduction of charity into the record-setting mix, as they knitted blankets for refugees, and in the process raised £50 in donations while casting on and casting off. Over the years, this would become an oft-repeated strategy that would make it easier to get the book's approval, as well as to help round up bodies for mass participation record-setting events, obtain sponsorship, and receive all important media coverage.

"Everyone is always interested in the biggest and the best, the most, the tallest, the highest, the largest, and the greatest. It's a book of superlatives, and media feasts on superlatives, so the book of records is made for media because they love superlatives," said longtime television news producer Ben Sherwood, explaining why record breaking gets disproportionate news coverage. "Secondly, the media loves entertainment, and the combination of superlatives in entertaining categories makes it even more perfect. So it's superlatives in an entertaining fashion, and the trifecta, the iron triangle connecting media and the *Guinness Book of Records*, is average people, ordinary people, the person next door. So it's the greatest, the most entertaining or curious or freak value, and folks like you and me doing it."

But according to Sherwood, the addition of the charity component takes media interest to a whole other level. "Most of these people have publicists now, and we get pitched all the time. Organizations have figured out that it's a sure way to get media attention, and people now definitely manipulate the book in order to get attention for their charities. Someone will say 'we're going to make the most pancakes for breast cancer awareness.' If you can break a record *and* raise money for cancer . . . if you add charity to the mix of the three keys I described, entertainment, superlatives, and the guy next door, then it's not just the trifecta, I don't even know what you call it, maybe the Final Four. Once you add charity to it, the 'we're actually going to do good,' then who can resist it? Every local television camera shows up to see 10,000 people jumping rope to fight colon cancer."

If Mr. Rogers's first use of a made-for-getting-into-Guinness activity, McEwan's 1959 assault on an existing quirky record, and the knitters' introduction of charity into record setting created a trifecta of Guinnessport pioneers, then rounding out the inspired Final Four of early Guinness World Record seekers were Gerry Germeny and David Gascoyne, students at England's Derby College of Technology. Mr. Rogers may well have invented Guinnessport with his drumathon, but these guys perfected Guinnessport through their inspired piano smashing on May 13, 1961, and it became a model for the evolution of many other bizarre records. It was not just one of the first stunts tailor-made for securing a spot in the book, but most likely the first with its own arcane rules included in the record. Almost as soon as people began making up new records to get into the book, lines had to be drawn, apples compared to apples, so that records could be fairly contested under similar circumstances. By specifying that it had to be an upright piano, the students took away the vague choice of baby grand or concert grand piano. By working in tandem they set a two-person standard, but their real coup was the invention of a device for precisely defining the meaning of "smashed." Hence their record, in a time of 14 minutes and 3 seconds, for demolishing an upright piano and passing the entire wreckage through a 9" diameter ring. This combination of senselessness and precision was perfect for Guinness, and predictably, the record became a favorite of college students everywhere. By the next edition, two years later, one college's record had been shattered by another: two members of the Delta Chi fraternity at Michigan's Wayne State University demolished a different upright piano, passing the mess through a 9" diameter ring in just 4 minutes and 51 seconds—just over a third of the original time.

Piano smashing would become a microcosm of all "intended" Guinness World Records, meaning those that people apply for, rather than those of the "first man to the moon" variety. These records tend to follow a pattern: There would be an initial hotly contested period, until the record improved to the point where it eventually became unassailable (a trend that would later be seen in Ashrita Furman's endurance feats of brick carrying and distance milk bottle balancing). At that point, the record would mutate and breed spin-off variations (fastest milk balancing mile). Such feats also challenged the editors to draft and apply standards at a formative stage in the book's history, something that would forever be a sticking point for would-be record holders. Since each record is so different, the editors and rules officials have historically relied more on a set of principles than on written code. In most cases, it seems like the first object or distance chosen becomes the standard, as when Ashrita attempted to balance a baseball bat on the palm on his hand but was told that tradition dictates a pool cue be the officially balanced object of choice for such feats. And in the mile record for pushing fruit with one's nose, history requires that an orange be used, and the underlying presumption is that the Keeper of the Records wouldn't approve an identical effort with an apple, cantaloupe, or grape. Similarly, there are records for swimming the English Channel, for walking Ireland end to end, and for reaching the poles, but not for swimming any old channel, walking any island, or reaching any remote point. At the same time, there have been enough exceptions to these time-honored principals to cause a Guinness World Records purist consternation, such as multiple records awarded for largest pies based on flavor (apple, banana, etc.) and for biggest ice cream sundaes, depending on whether they contain bananas. Fixing rules for each attempt has been an ever-evolving learning process, and while some records have pages of detailed rules, others operate under standards that seem arbitrary and capricious. Piano smashing reflects these growing pains. When a group of students from Medway College of Art and Medway College of Technology in Chatham, England, decided to wrest the coveted record back across the Atlantic from their American peers, they upped the ante, employing seven students when both previous records had only used two, and using a bigger 10" diameter ring for the wreckage—both clearly advantageous rule changes that the book still strangely allowed. A bigger ring meant the destruction did not have to be as thorough, and the extra inch and additional five bodies allowed them to take the time down to 3 minutes and 11 seconds. Notably, this was also the first time the book detailed the weapon of choice, a seven-pound sledgehammer.

By 1979 piano smashing was down to a hard-to-fathom 97 seconds, almost a tenth of the time it took the record's pioneers some eighteen years earlier. That meant smashing aficionados had to look at other alternatives. The traditional approach to variations on Guinness World Records that have worked countless times is to do the same thing but backward or underwater, but this logic couldn't be applied to piano smashing. As the standards for the original Guinnessport achievement became harder and harder to beat, two different schools of thought emerged, both removing the sledgehammer of any weight from the equation. One new tactic was successfully tried in 1971, when the fastest time for sawing an upright piano in two was first entered in the record book, at over two hours, joining the (by then) more traditional smashing method. This proved that in the fast-paced world of Guinnes-sport, rarely does the original record last or even remain the standard. Simply being the first with the vision to smash or saw an upright piano falls short of the immortality achieved in other more conventional firsts, such as walking on the moon, running a four-minute mile, or conquering Everest, feats that have remained glorious despite being surpassed. When it comes to made-for-Guinness efforts such as destroying pianos and the like, readers take a decidedly "what have you done for me lately?" approach.

In 1973 the practice of destroying an upright piano saw the abandoning of implements of destruction altogether, when yet another new approach to piano mayhem was realized. Whether inspired by an austere sense of Guinness record purism or simply years of martial arts training is unknown, but a group of karate practitioners decided to take matters into their own hands—and feet—when they smashed a piano to smithereens using no tools in just over forty minutes. While impressive, this time was quickly denounced as amateurish. Six years later, three karate instructors in Lexington, Kentucky, would attack the record in earnest and demonstrate just how defenseless a piano truly is, when they destroyed one in 2 minutes and 39 seconds—a mere 62 seconds slower than that year's mark for those using sledgehammers.

With limits on how many ways a piano could be destroyed, and other musical instruments apparently too fragile to make an impressive target, would-be smashers were forced to once again expand their horizons, and, in true Guinnessport fashion, soon looked beyond the music room at the bigger picture. Fortunately for fifteen members of an English karate club, in 1972 a vacant six-room Victorian home presented itself and in about six hours, they destroyed it using "head, foot, and hand," earning a new record for "Demolition Work." This record would stand for more than a decade, until 1984, when fifteen members of a Canadian karate club located a seven-room farmhouse ripe for the kicking in Alberta. While the same number of assailants apparently raised the bar by one room, this record also goes against the general Guinness record spirit of "oranges to oranges." Who judges which house is more difficult to karate chop to pieces? Is the seven-room house actually larger than the six-room one? Is one older, more rotted, or otherwise of flimsier construction? What if one has concrete walls, lots of pipes, or even insulation? For these kinds of reasons, almost all records are based on isolating one variable, like being fastest to do something over a standardized distance, or to cover the greatest distance in a standardized time. But with multiple uncontrolled variables, house destroying seems to be a judgment call that appealed to editors not for the usual Guinness World Records reasons, but rather for the sheer theater implicit in kicking a house to pieces. It also marks one of the first examples of made-for-Guinness record creativity coming full circle, tracing the trajectory of a single, made-up activity, piano smashing, into several different Guinnessports, including piano sawing, piano karate smashing, and whole-house karate demolition. The move from pianos to different kinds of smashing helps explain why there are well over 45,000 records in the files of Guinness World Records, and more being added all the time.

The appeal of record setting is so strong that even highly regarded adventurers and acclaimed writers aren't above a little Guinnessport. Despite his very real and risky achievements in aviation and sailing, Sir Richard Branson also has a less serious record-setting side. On the same day I was nabbing my second Guinness World Record, he was at it as well, piloting a prototype amphibious car from London to Paris over land and the English Channel—a first and probably last for that particular record, since Branson believes he owns the only existing version of that Aquaticar. "It was such a fun thing that I have never laughed and had a more enjoyable day in my life. It was a great car, a real James Bond car that turned into a boat. It drove beautifully at 125 mph on the road, and it turned into a fantastic speedboat, sort of an every boy's dream vehicle. The picture of that Aquaticar that is in the *Guinness Book of Records* I think will be the only picture people will ever see of that vehicle but it was magnificent. It is still possible that the technology will result in the car of the future, or the car boat of the future, and the good thing about people pushing technology forward is that occasionally they get fantastic breakthroughs but at other times they disappear." Branson can philosophize about the implications of scientific progress in his feat all he wants, but the made-for-Guinness aspects of the event are clear in the video, as he goes all out, indeed James Bond style, wearing a tuxedo at the wheel, arriving to a sea of popping Champagne corks. Unlike his Blue Riband, or his historic first crossings of the Atlantic and Pacific Oceans by hot air balloons, or even his failed quest to be the first to pilot a balloon around the earth, Branson had no standard to beat and no competitors dogging him for the Aquaticar record.

Like Branson, acclaimed novelist, journalist, and actor George Plimpton got into the game, further blurring the lines between mainstream sport, which he became famous writing about, and Guinnessport. Plimpton is best known for taking firsthand shots at the sports he covered, often to the point of putting himself in harm's way, such as when he played in preseason National Football League games with the Detroit Lions for his book *Paper Lion*. Likewise, he got into the ring with boxing legends Archie Moore and Sugar Ray Leonard for an article, trained with the National Hockey League's Boston Bruins for his book *Open Net*, and even pitched against the National League's All-Star team for his baseball work *Out of My League*. Regarded as a pioneer in the world of participatory journalism, the author of *Fireworks* and the honorary Fireworks Commissioner of New York took the same approach to his beloved pyrotechnics. Like Ashrita Furman or Jackie Bibby, who channel their longtime passions for childhood pursuits into world records, so did Plimpton when he lit the fuse of a 720-pound firework, Fat Man II, the largest such shell ever exploded. His sporting accomplishments are legend, but in the end, only a match could get him into the record book.

After its debut with Mr. Rogers's watershed drumathon, Guinnessport continued to creep into the book with rapidly increasing frequency. The 1960s saw more and more such entries as brick throwing, which first appeared in 1961 and quickly became a perennial favorite. Like piano smashing and many of the most interesting Guinnessport records, brick throwing would also morph and multiply quickly, spawning one of the book's largest subsets of popular records, all under the "throwing" umbrella. So popular has this catchall category become that it has spun out of control and moved from things that logically should be thrown, like Frisbees, boomerangs, and paper airplanes, to bricks and early Anglo-eccentric oddities such as gumboots and haggis to eggs and cow chips and even the *Guinness World Records* book itself. Most of these examples appeared relatively early in the book's history, but less creative record setters still prey on this category today, to the point where it seems that if one cannot think of a truly original record, one just needs to throw something that has not been thrown before. This tradition is still going strong: one brand new record making its debut in the 2008 edition, forty-seven years after the first brick was hurled 114'5", is the Guinness World Record for throwing a washing machine (11').

Other early additions that shaped the flavor of the book included seesawing, telephoning (cramming as many people into an English or American phone booth as possible), submergence in a wetsuit, riding a Big Wheel, being buried alive, spitting, slinging (using a slingshot), pram (stroller) pushing, endurance pipe smoking, coal carrying, marathon showering, car cramming (getting the most people in a Volkswagen Beetle, later expanded to a second category for Mini Coopers), and the one that would inspire Ashrita Furman a decade later—brick carrying, which debuted in 1960.

"It was in the mid-sixties when the book began to evolve," Stuart Claxton, a Guinness World Records spokesman and head of U.S. business development, explained to me. "In the space of about ten years it evolved into something people tried to get into. The look and feel of the books during this time went from a studious academic tome to something popular." In the preface to the black 1960 edition, the McWhirters wrote that "Record breaking in the 1960s is proceeding at such an exhilarating pace that even historic landmarks of human achievements are often short-lived as records. To compensate for this, some progressive tables showing records step by step along with their dates, have been put into this edition." Such tables charted not just man's race to the heavens but also endurance "marathons" in everything from bowling to playing Monopoly—everything except actual marathons.

1969 was a pivotal year for the book, the last time it would ever appear in its original almanac form. The first inside photo page, traditionally reserved for the most impressive superlatives, was once again suitably reverent, celebrating Neil Armstrong's first steps on the moon, which would become one of the book's most reprinted and beloved records, "Lunar Conquest." But change was afoot, and the sixties went out with a bang, seeing the continued explosion of Guinnessport categories including Eating Out, Apple Picking, Bag Pipe Playing, Bed Pushing, Coal Shoveling, Hairdressing, Hoop Rolling, Hop Scotch, Plate Spinning, Shaving, Tunnel of Fire, and so on. These changes, gathering steam and increasing in number annually since the 1956 drumathon, had become too much for the book's original format to bear. In 1970 an edition much closer to the one we have today was launched, measuring 12" x 8.5", with a glossy cover instead of linen cloth, covered front and back with images, both cartoon and photographic, of bed pushing, seesawing, circus weight lifting, and, reflecting its more human element, a man with a huge beard, the famously fat McCrary twins, and of course, Robert Pershing Wadlow. Perhaps the only visible connection this harpless version had with the previous sixteen editions was the small photo of a bottle of Guinness stout on its back cover.

Changes would continue to be introduced over the next thirty years, including a major design overhaul in 1996, with greatly increased reliance on color photographs. In 1997, the book officially changed its name from *The Guinness Book of Records* to *Guinness World Records* (the U.S. edition had been published under the compromise title *The Guinness Book of World Records* since the late fifties). By 1999, the *Wall Street Journal* reported that the editors' target audience had switched from ten- to fifteen-year-old to seven- to fifteen-year-old boys. Accordingly, categories were again updated and embellished, with, for instance, statistics about battle-ships moved from the humdrum section "Ships" to the new and improved "Killing Machines." According to the *Journal*, other category casualties in this seismic shift were Highest Price for a Painting, First Person to Walk on Both Poles, and Biggest Bottle Collection, replaced by Largest Sports Salary, Highest Paid Child Performer, and Biggest Social Climb. The book continues to evolve today, with increasing celebrity influence, but the fundamental shift from records about the world around us to records about us was in place by 1970. As the *Independent*'s highly critical Miles Kington lamented, recollecting the original edition and its inspir-ing foreword by the Earl of Iveagh, describing a book that could turn the heat of disputes into the light of truth:

> Except that it's not that kind of book anymore. I have been through the new, gold-plated *Guinness World Records 2005* as carefully as I can, and can find no information on who was the first to swim the Channel. Or the fastest. Or the youngest. Or anything about swimming the Channel at all. I have also been unable to find any information on the deep-est well in England, or indeed much about that sort of thing at all. . . . Nor is there anything about Scotland's highest tree. Or Ireland's oldest church. Or Parliamentary majori-ties. Or even, I think, rail crashes. With the partial exception of weight-lifting, not a single one of the questions playfully raised by Lord Iveagh in 1956 can be answered by the book known as "Guinness World Records 2005."

Lord Iveagh likely did not anticipate Guinnessport or expect it to take off with the fervor it has. The resulting change from demure reference book to in-your-face visual began in the early 1970s, driven by unrelenting twin forces: the compelling need of many readers to get into Guinness, and television.

"There was a very successful BBC TV show called *Record Breakers*," explained Stuart Claxton.

A gentleman by the name of Roy Castle and Norris McWhirter were the co-hosts. People who set records on the show often got into the book, but it was not guaranteed, still an editorial decision. At that point, the book still had its original editorial direction, the result of a massive research project. But by the mid-sixties, the book had begun to evolve, in large part due to the show, where people would come on and try to break records, and McWhirter was the face of the Guinness book. In the space of about ten years it became something people wanted—and tried— to get into. The whole thing was catapulted forward by the show, and the certification procedures for records, the guidelines, the certificates of recognition, all of that came about in the mid- [to] late 1960s. I think it's that whole 15 minutes of fame element. People out there watching and reading either have a talent, or think they can beat a record, and they want to do it because it is an accomplishment.

The show was an instant hit for BBC, running in prime time for the next thirty-two years. Roy Castle, OBE, was a sort of vaudevillian entertainer, a singer, dancer, comedian, and musician who became an incredibly popular children's entertainer and had his own eponymous variety show on BBC before achieving greater fame with *Record Breakers*. Greg Childs, producer of the show from 1988 to 1998, said of Castle, "He was sort of like the Sammy Davis Jr. of the U.K. He was the world's fastest tap dancer, played all these instruments, sang. He would set records himself as well, like when he parasailed under all the London River bridges." During his two decades as host, Castle also set records for speedy tap dancing, wingwalking on a biplane from London to Paris, and playing the same tune on forty-three different instruments in less than four minutes. He even wrote and performed the show's theme song, "Dedication," which became the mantra of many English would-be Guinness World Record holders. Here is one representative stanza:

> If you're the rarest, the fairest, grown the longest hair,
>   If you're oldest, the boldest, got the most gold,
>   If you're the newest, the fewest, largest tattoo,
> Then you're a record breaker, you're a record maker,
>   You're a record breaker.

Mark Frary, a longtime correspondent for the London *Times*, and author of books on everything from code breaking to astronomy, recalled the show's popularity and influence on his generation.

I think the British really love eccentricity. As a culture, we embrace people like Eddie the Eagle [the distance-challenged Olympic ski jumper whose heartfelt attempts against a far more talented field endeared him to a nation not known for its winter sports], champions of oddity, and that was part of the show's charms. Ross and Norris were sort of odd and odd looking themselves, and twins as well—identical twin eccentrics! And they couldn't have chosen a better host then Roy Castle: today if you went to a network and said you wanted this juggling trumpeter as the host they would never go for it, and the whole show does not fit with today's television, where the emphasis is on beautiful people, but it worked, and it became a British institution. In that sense, the Guinness book and the *Record Breakers* show are very much a part of the fabric of British Society.

Somebody would set a record for eating pies, which is also a very British thing, or jamming people in a red telephone box, and you would watch and think "wow, that guy ate a lot of pies," and it was just the British eccentricity of it all that fascinated people, and people loved it. It was something everybody knew about and talked about and understood. I'm 38 and I remember coming home from school and eagerly watching *Record Breakers*. You have to remember that at that time there was very little on TV compared to today, we had a couple of BBC channels and ITV and that was it. Everybody watched it. Today there are hundreds of channels, but there weren't in the seventies and eighties. At school, it was like the office water cooler conversations today. "Did you see what they did on *Record Breakers* yesterday?"

The show would go through a number of hosts and co-hosts over the years, and was often a stepping-stone to fame. Some of the crew included Cheryl Baker, who Childs described as a "pop star who had won Eurovision, sort of our American Idol before there was *American Idol*," Olympic medalist Kriss Akabusi, and even Ron Reagan Jr., son of the former president. "No one in the States knows about it, but he was our U.S. correspondent for three years. He had a very dry sense of humor. Ashrita did the forward roll mile with him."

If fifteen minutes of fame and inclusion in the book was the flickering flame that drew Guinnessport practitioners like moths, then television was a bucket of gasoline thrown on that flame. Not only did it greatly increase the attractiveness of and recognition for being a record holder, but as a format it was perfect for Guinnessport. The show was filmed in Europe's largest television studio, BBC One, which couldn't hold Mount Everest but did lend itself to frequent mass participation events, like the longest chorus line. Each episode included three segments: a record-breaking attempt in the studio, like lifting the most bricks; one in the field, where pulling jumbo jets on runways was a recurring favorite; and an in-depth profile of a colorful record breaker. Jez Edwards, the show's final host, found America fertile ground for these profiles. "I went to the U.S. a lot. You've got some interesting blokes there. I was always dumbfounded by the hobbies that became passions that then took over people's lives. Like this guy we interviewed, he was a sales guy from California, he started the International Banana Club. He holds the record, and I don't think anyone else is vying for this one, for having the largest collection of banana-related materials. He dresses in a banana suit, and people send him banana stuff all the time from all around the world, and then he gives them banana merit points." Fittingly, current *Guinness World Records* editor Craig Glenday is a proud member of the International Banana Club.

Despite the preponderance of nonhuman records in the book, and those held permanently (first to the moon) or by the deceased (first in flight), the show was entirely about current human record breakers, many of them first-time aspirants, many attempting made-for-TV Guinnessport feats. In fueling this fire, *Record Breakers* was not alone, as the book spawned countless other television shows and still does today. *The Guinness Book of Records* got its first American airtime in April 1970, in the form of a one-hour special sponsored by AT&T and hosted by comedian Flip Wilson. Following this success and the book's continued best-selling status in the United States, 20th Century Fox would sign respected British television host Sir David Frost to produce six prime-time, record-breaking specials based on the book, as well as the *Guinness Game Show*, which ran on NBC for forty-eight weeks from 1979 to 1980. Back in the U.K., Sir Frost, who still hosts *The Week That Was* (and whose interview with Richard Nixon remains the highest-rated television interview of all time), hosted another prime-time Guinness show, this one aimed at a more adult audience. *David Frost Presents the International Guinness Book of World Records* ran from 1981 to 1986, followed by *The Guinness Book of Records Hall of Fame* from 1986 to 1988. From 1987 to 1988 he would host several television specials, all called *The Spectacular World of Guinness Records.* In the United States, FOX brought the book back to the airwaves in 1998 with *Guinness World Records: Primetime,* which ran two seasons, and in 1999 it was replicated in Britain,

Germany, and Scandinavia. According to Stuart Claxton, FOX is preparing yet another series. In 2005 even the Food Network got into the act, with the *Food Network Challenge*, which initially included a few episodes featuring record-breaking cooking events, leading to the show's *Guinness World Record Breakers Week* the following season. More recently, Australian television aired a thirteen-episode series, *Australia's Guinness World Records*. Both France and Germany have ongoing Guinness World Records television series, and as of 2006 *Ultimate Guinness World Records*, produced by Guinness World Records Ltd. itself, was on the airwaves in some thirty-five different countries around the globe. Asia in particular has world-record fever, with several shows on the air in China, Singapore, and other Pacific Rim nations. There seems to be no end in sight: as recently as January 2008, NBC aired a two-hour special, *Guinness World Records: Top 100*. *Smithsonian* magazine reported that by 2005 Guinness-related shows were on the air in at least eighty-five different countries, while the company's revamped website was getting 14 million hits a month—more than 150 million annually. There are also Guinness museums, which began opening in the 1970s in high-profile locations such as New York City's Empire State Building and London's Trocadero, eventually popping up in tourist locations around the world, from Las Vegas to Missouri, Myrtle Beach to Niagara Falls, as well as far-flung locales like Tokyo, Singapore, and India.

By 2005, fully half the records in the book were held by humans, up from just a tiny sliver in the first edition fifty years earlier. Any lingering doubts that Guinnessport and the notion of highly specialized, made-up-to-get-into Guinness feats have become the norm rather than exception can be dispelled with a quick glance at the latest edition. In 2008, coming up with wacky ideas for records seems a more impressive challenge than the feats themselves. Who would have thought that any record-sanctioning body would have gone for such categories as Fastest Time to Place Six Eggs in Eggcups Using the Feet, Fastest Time to Paint a 10-Square Meter Wall, Most Snails on Face, Most Sheets of Glass Pierced with Needles in One Minute, or Heaviest Vehicle Pulled By Rice Bowl Suction on the Stomach? These records beg the question: just what does it take to *not* get accepted by Guinness? Well, they passed on my proposal to hold the croquet game with the most people playing simultaneously, which apparently is more nonsensical than the rice bowl suction thing. At least I hadn't just gone ahead and done it without approval, a fate that has befallen many would-be record holders, like a ten-year-old Guinnessport aspirant from Texas who contacted the book for inclusion after accomplishing the feat of writing the letter *A* 17,841 times. He was turned down. To explain which records were simply too inane for recognition, Stuart Claxton told *Smithsonian* magazine: "We get claims from people who have worn a pair of socks for the longest, or have had a glass of milk in their fridge for seven years." The book apparently prefers more creative made-up events, like the Fastest Time to Walk 50 Meters on Can and String Stilts, a new record listed in the most recent book—separate from the can and string stilt mile—both records held, of course, by Ashrita Furman. He sprinted 164 feet on stilts made entirely from cans and string at the famed ruins of Tikal, in Guatemala, embracing his passion for mystical places and doing his part to keep the Guinnessport alive and well.

A cynic like Jason Daley, the record-keeping magazine editor and columnist, might call such stunts contrived at best, absurd at worst. When Daley left his post as the dispatches editor for *Outside* magazine, he bade farewell with an opinionated editorial titled "Broken Records." Here he finally vented his frustration at all the glory seekers whose "triumphs" had found their way, usually by e-mail, to his editorial desk over his years of covering outdoor, exploration, and athletic records. Daley stated that "an American who logged first ascents on sixty-three Tibetan peaks that were too small for anyone else to have bothered with, then compared himself to Neil Armstrong. . . . So what is actually worth covering? When it comes to records . . . they should carry no more than two qualifiers. First woman to sail around the world? Good. First bi-curious woman to sail around the world with a glass eye? I'll pass. . . . I can't stop the freak frenzy. But I can stop feeding into it. I will no longer pimp contrived, unworthy feats. No more profiles of human slingshots. Sayanora to extreme unicycling. Adios to blindfolded through-hikers and round-the-world pogo stickers."

Chris Sheedy, a former vice president of Guinness World Records, who managed the records research department in London and is now the company's representative in Australia, would probably disagree. "Everyone thinks Guinness World Records gets sillier as they get older, but actually they are losing their imagination," he told a reporter while arguing that the colorful records are no sillier than "real" sports such as butterfly swimming or dressage. "As a child everything you read in the book is deadly serious, from the most pegs attached to someone's face to the fastest climb up Everest." Guinnessport has become such a major piece of the book that while other media outlets and writers like Daley might eschew such efforts, one thing is perfectly clear: practitioners of arcane, implausible, and often disgusting feats, whether done forward, backward, upside down, or underwater, will always have a place in the *Guinness World Records*. Even the late Norris McWhirter himself rose to the defense of Guinnessport, arguing that the most respected sports landmarks—like his friend Roger Bannister's—are simply contrived events. "What made the four-minute mile special is the appeal of round numbers. To say that somebody ran 5,280 feet in less than 1,240 seconds doesn't sound quite the same. . . . Americans have such a high level of achievement. The underachievers are driven into zanier outlets. Life isn't all frivolous, I know that. But it's not all serious either. It's the same with records. There's room for all kinds."

5

---

15 Minutes of Fame

His object was not suicide but money and imperishable fame.

—Schott's Sporting Gaming & Idling Miscellany

It's not my job, but I work at it like it's a job, because let me be frank with you: I like the attention and I don't make any bones about it. I like people recognizing me, noticing me, asking for my autograph, that kind of thing. I have attempted to attain fame throughout my lifetime and this has been my best vehicle. I've been in some movies and acted in some TV shows and I've done a lot of different things, but that Guinness tag has been my most popular thing.

—Jackie "the Texas Snakeman" Bibby

In his moving prologue to the original edition, Rupert Guinness mentions swimming the English Channel as one of the book's highlights. In 1875, when Matthew Webb became the first person to successfully swim the English Channel without a life jacket, he was the Neil Armstrong of his time, and became a model for thousands of adventurers and glory seekers who would follow him.

But why? Webb was a mold for the hybrid adventurer/athlete whose achievements are often lumped in with those of true explorers, but whose actual accomplishments are unnecessary, other than for the fact that no one else has done them before. He neither discovered the Channel, nor was the first to cross it, nor the fastest to do so. At least with Mount Everest, there was no way to the summit except by foot, but thousands had traversed the Channel before Webb did it. The life jacket qualification suggests he was not even the first to swim the Channel but simply the first to swim it unaided. Nonetheless, it was widely acclaimed, and in true record fashion, spawned an industry of derivative Channel "firsts," niches that have since been carved out include first by a woman, by using various swimming strokes, by doing it in the opposite direction, and by swimming the Channel round trip. One swimmer even seized the mantle of first Channel crossing by a Chilean.

The Channel is not the longest body of water to have been swum, nor the most difficult, yet Webb became a world-famous celebrity. The fire of his fame burned so brightly that the risk of its dimming set him on a swimming course of escalating drama that would end badly. His effort to stay in the spotlight eventually brought him to the United States and an insurmountable challenge: attempting to swim the whirlpools and rapids below the thunderous Niagara Falls. He failed in his swim but succeeded in getting into the newspapers, albeit the obituary section, when he drowned. "Of Webb's attempt, one writer opined 'his object was not suicide but money and imperishable fame.'" He would not be the last person driven to questionable actions by these powerful forces.

Pop artist Andy Warhol famously said, "In the future everyone will be world famous for fifteen minutes," and ever since then, this time-based term has defined our society's obsession with a moment in the spotlight, no matter how fleeting. The media panders to this desire: everything from shock-talk shows to so-called reality television with its invented competitions to social networking sites such as FaceBook and MySpace are fueled by the seemingly limitless number of people who crave their fifteen minutes—and are willing to suffer or debase themselves to get it. But long before anyone thought of appearing on national television in exchange for admitting they were their son's uncle or addicted to Internet pornography, long before anyone locked a bunch of twenty-somethings in a house under the watchful eyes of 24/7 cameras or shipped eager volunteers to a deserted island to starve and burn while playing summer camp–style color war games, there was the Guinness book. Even before television played a role, but especially afterward, for the vast majority of those attempting it, making the book was about getting that moment in the sun, about being, or at least feeling, important. With the advent of televised specials in the United States and the prime-time show *Record Breakers* on England's BBC, this temptation was only magnified, because the potential fifteen minutes suddenly meant not only print recognition but also the siren call of being on television. "Now there are a lot of reality shows, but it's the original reality television," explained longtime *Record Breakers* producer Greg Childs. "You have to show the attempt, win or lose. It's either a record or it's not." The show would give hundreds of would-be record breakers their shot at stardom, something the book's readers increasingly craved. Even Ashrita Furman, whose litany of amazing feats is not only inspired by but literally made possible by his deep religious beliefs, admits to the satisfaction his "celebrity" brings, glowing as he recalled his first photo appearance in the book, next to Olympic star Nadia Comaneci.

Ask almost anyone why people want to get into Guinness, and the answer is . . . some sort of fame. Stuart Claxton, a figure often trotted out to monitor celebrity or televised record breakings, answered, "It's an interesting question. I think it is the fifteen minutes of fame element." He also told me that "It is the most frequently asked question. After any record is broken that I have ever attended, the immediate question is 'when am I going to be in the book?' It's all about being in the book. It's like getting into the Hall of Fame, because once the book is printed in any year, it is permanent and you can hold it in your hands forever." Accordingly, on the book's website, one of its FAQs is "Why is my record not in the book?"

The book's current editor, Craig Glenday, told the *Washington Times*, "People tell us it's a dream they've had since childhood," but added the blunt caveat that "On a shallow level it's just about seeing their name in the book." In the same vein, he told another reporter, "For most of these people, the motivation is all about getting their name in the book." Stewart Newport, Guinness World Records' Keeper of the Records, described applicants as "people seeking their fifteen minutes of fame," adding that "they want adulation for being the best in the world at whatever they do." Even GWR creator Norris McWhirter saw the appeal of notoriety early on, remarking of record breakers, "They are desperate to be *the* person who did something, not just *a* person."

It is not just the Guinness World Records staffers who feel this way; many record holders openly state fame as the main or even sole motivation for their attempts. Recognition-crazed Jackie "the Texas Snakeman" Bibby is far from alone in his candid admission. Bibby, whose two main areas of record-breaking expertise are lying in bathtubs filled with hundreds of poisonous snakes and holding live rattlesnakes, as many as ten at a time (and all, according to rules, at least 2.5' long), in his mouth, dangling like a bouquet from his lips—for more than ten seconds. The photo of Bibby with his head bent over a hanging clump of wriggling snakes instantly became an iconic and frequently reproduced Guinness photo, like those of Wadlow or the McCrary twins. As a result, Bibby was honored in 2005 at the book's fiftieth anniversary gala in New York City, when he was named number six of the top ten most popular Guinness World Records of the first fifty years, an award he described to me as "about as prestigious as anything I've ever done."

Joining Bibby as one of the most revered and iconic characters in the book's history is Sridhar Chillal, who let his oft-photographed and freakishly curling fingernails grow unfettered for half a century, the entire existence of the book itself. His five remarkable nails (Chillal grew one hand only, permitting him to pursue a career as a professional photographer) have graced the pages of the book regularly since about 1980, with the longest being his thumb-nail at nearly 5' (57"), while each of the other nails exceed a yard. While Chillal's lifelong dedication to a task begun at age fourteen has ensconced the senior citizen in the highest tier of Guinness lore, this "fame" has come at a high price and with little reward. He told England's *Guardian* newspaper that the anguish of keep-ing his record nails intact has greatly affected his life, as he lives in constant fear of cars, children, and even gusts of wind ("I have so much tension as a result of the worry that my nails are going to break, that with every heartbeat I'm tense"). The physical an-guish is even worse, from problems sleeping ("I can't move, can't turn sides, can't pull over the covers") to pain and injuries from the weight of his nails, which have not only ruined his left hand, now permanently disfigured, but also cause chronic pain in his wrist, elbow, and shoulder. The appendages have even destroyed nerves, leaving him deaf in one ear. This may seem an extreme price to pay for carnival sideshow fingernails, even ones that hold a long-time world record, but not to Chillal, who in 2000 dismissed his injuries with the simple explanation, "What does man not do for fame? He jumps from boats, dives from planes and does stunts on motorcycles. This is also done for fame. Were I to have another life I would do it again."

While Chillal accepts his injuries as part of the price for fame, upon reaching his sixties, the physical ramifications of his nails became harder to bear. In 2000, when Chillal realized he could not go on forever, he did what any self-respecting owner of valu-able objects would do: he put them up for sale on the Internet, offering to cut off and sell all five nails, with an asking price of nearly a quarter of a million dollars. To date, there appears to have been no takers. Interestingly, if Chillal succeeds, he may move into uncharted Guinness territory. Even a modest six-figure payday probably does not compensate for a lifetime of discomfort and irre-versible damage, but if it works, at least he will get some substantial reward besides intangible "glory." Wealth is perhaps the one great feat that consistently evades Guinness World Record holders.

While there are certainly exceptions, the typical Guinness record breaker or setter is not pursuing the limits of human achievement but is in search of the perceived celebrity a verified record brings. The irony of this motivation is that the "fame," the "celebrity," the "immortality," record holders discuss is virtually nonexistent. No one, not even Jackie Bibby, Sridhar Chillal, or Ashrita Furman, the most famous record holders, has ever been able to parlay Guinness records, into riches or even a career. A one-hit wonder pop band that is quickly forgotten may still experience, at least for a little while, the rewards of exotic sports cars, luxury hotels, and eager groupies, but the vast majority of record holders take away nothing more than a certificate and bragging rights. Only a tiny fraction of all official records get printed in the annual book. You can break half a dozen records and still never be able to point to your name on a library shelf. The lucky ones that make the cut can add to their haul a half-inch entry among thousands of others in what is basically a children's book—a children's book with a one-year shelf life. In the rarest cases, record holders also take home a video clip of a television appearance. Yet the title of world record holder is more than enough motivation for most. Again, I ask why?

Jake Halpern is the author of *Fame Junkies*, a comprehensive look at the importance of fame in our society. The book attempts to answer the questions of why so many people seem to worship celebrity, and why are people so attracted to the limelight and the possibility of obtaining fame for themselves? To Halpern, the *Guinness World Records* is a near-perfect vehicle for the fame obsessed and fame challenged, because it is so democratic and its records are more attainable than other kinds of fame. "I think the idea of setting records is one of the oldest forms of pursuing fame. Think about the earliest Greek Olympics where they kept detailed records, the first person to sail around the world, whatever it was. I guess that's all history really is, in some ways, is the setting of these records.

There's a real neurological rush that comes from getting
attention from other people, a high like any other high, not
unlike hitting a jackpot when you gamble or eating chocolate or watching pornography. All these things activate
something in the reward/aversion system. Getting attention has probably always had this affect of making people
feel good, but in a society like the United States, where
there is such a premium put on individual accomplishment,
and the rugged individual and laying claim to everything
you possibly can, whether you are a robber baron or movie
star, I think the idea of getting that recognition and attention is especially attractive. But the reality is that most
people reach some point in their life when they say "I'm not
attractive or talented enough to be a movie star and I'm not
wealthy enough or have enough business savvy to become
Andrew Carnegie, but I could stand on someone's front
porch and bounce a Ping-Pong ball 5,000 times. It may not
be winning an Oscar but it's something and it will immor-
talize me. I will get some momentary recognition and that
will feel good. I'll probably be written up in the local paper,
I might even get on TV, and people who don't pay attention
to me at work will take notice of me for a day, the pretty
secretary who never looks twice at me might ask me how I
did it."

Joachim Suresh, the closest thing there is to a rival of Ashrita
Furman and the holder of about thirty records (many of them quite
impressive physically), was drawn to the book directly as a vehicle
for the kind of Hollywood fame Halpern describes. Born in war-
torn Sri Lanka, Suresh emigrated to Canada in 2003 and began a
charity to raise awareness about the plight of suffering children,
something that had been a goal of his for more than a decade. Back
in Sri Lanka, his original plan was to go into show business and use
his ensuing fame to promote his cause. As he recalled, "I started
thinking I could be Michael Jackson, a singer, a Hollywood star."

But after someone gave him a copy of *Guinness World Records*, he went for Plan B. "I turned all the pages. I see all the stars are there. This is my goal. I have to be number one in the world."

"Everybody in their humdrum ordinary lives aspires to a little bit of immortality. A tiny moment of greatness in all of our routine, everyday lives of working three jobs and scrambling for health insurance. The opportunity the book of records affords each person, even in the most obscure and esoteric ways, is to have their names included with all the other people in the world who have done the greatest, the most, the best," said Ben Sherwood, former executive producer of *Good Morning America* and author of the novel *The Man Who Ate the 747.*

> I've met enough record holders to understand this, and not to get too existential about it, but in a world where most people are living lives of quiet desperation, it's something fun to talk about it, and it's often something fun to do. As you drive across America, as I have done several times in my work as a journalist, you pass through little towns where you will see a sign in the street that says "Home of so and so, Minnesota Twins right fielder 1972." I think that across this great country and across the world people like to put up little signs in their towns or on their streets or on their lawns that say "Home of" and then I'd ask you to fill in the blank, maybe someone who is the fastest yo-yoer in the world. It's a corollary to the little bit of immortality that you can be a local celebrity. All the celebrities don't have to be in Hollywood. You can be at your local bar and they can say, "Oh yeah, we've got the guy who did X," and you can have your picture over the Pabst Blue Ribbon tap and you can be that guy.

In my case, Sherwood is right. It was cool to be a Top 10 Play of the Day on ESPN's *SportsCenter*, cool to be featured in my local paper, and even though I am no longer in current circulation, relegated to the 90 percent of records found only in the book's private database, it is still cool to be a record holder and to have twice been in "The Book." But why? No one except people I tell about it remembers. No financial reward, lasting recognition, sponsorship, or career advancement came of it. I didn't even get a free DVD of the show. The fact that I was on *SportsCenter* and other television shows and in print should not matter, but it does, for the same reason why my first Guinness World Records certificate is ensconced in an ornate gold-colored custom frame, behind matting and conservation glass, packaged with the same care and expense as my college diplomas. Perhaps Guinness records matter for the same reason why so many other framed diplomas hang on walls around the world. Finishing college is an accomplishment that most people are proud of, but in and of itself means little. Even in the cases of the most impressive graduates, the diploma itself does not convey its value. Why then do we ostentatiously put them on our walls for ourselves and others to see? Does being proud of holding a world record in something, anything, differ that much from holding a degree in economics, mathematics, or sociology from an Ivy League school?

In fact, even Ivy League colleges are not immune to the allure recognition by the book brings. In Hanover, New Hampshire, at Dartmouth College's Rauner Library, home to its special collections and most valuable historical objects, visitors can view a pair of socks that once belonged to esteemed alumnus Daniel Webster, a collection of historic college canes, and an empty plastic bag. A plastic bag? Dartmouth cannot part with it, because it once held a handful of snow from the world's largest snowman, constructed by students to a height of 47'6" and recognized by *The Guinness Book of World Records* in 1988. The snow has since melted, along with the record, and the vial inside the plastic bag that once contained the historic water eventually leaked. All that remains of the college's prized relic is the lingering fame of a broken record that lives on, at least in the bag's label. This may be a case of taking what *Newsweek* dubbed "Guinnessitis" a bit too far. The pessimist sees the glass as half empty, while the optimist sees it as half full, but anybody can see that Dartmouth is cataloguing and storing a plastic bag that is fully empty, and tied only tenuously to a record that does not even stand.

In *Sports Illustrated*'s landmark 1979 magazine feature article on the book, in which the term "Guinnessport" was coined, one record holder interviewed was Arron Marshall. A fisherman from Western Australia, Marshall stood under a shower in a shopping mall for 224 hours to claim the longest showering record. As *Sports Illustrated* described, "Marshall's feet ballooned and his body became as wrinkled as a prune, but he said, 'I'll be yahooing around the countryside when I see my name in the record book.'" Even more direct was Salt Lake City gymnastics instructor Rick Murphy, who briefly held the record for covering fifty yards walking in a handstand position, getting into just one volume, the 1975 edition, before his record was eclipsed. That one year was apparently enough, since Murphy stated, "deep down, I was proud to make that book. It's the best thing I've ever done." He is not alone. Numerous record breakers, even those whose tenure was so short they never got into the book itself but hang on to their certificates, describe the feats as the greatest moment of their lives.

"Why do people break Guinness World Records? There's something about being a Guinness World Record holder which will separate you from the rest of your friends, or the population," claimed company spokesman Stuart Claxton in a promotion for an episode of a *Guinness World Records*–based television show. Without their accomplishments, no matter how bizarre, record holders would be just like everyone else, since despite the popularity of the book and the broadening of the way in which records can be achieved, the vast majority of people will still never set or break one, never know how it feels to be a real live Guinness World Record holder. The *Times* of London even coined a term for this pitiful state of affairs most of us live in: "Guinless."

"For the last decade I have been heavily involved in covering outdoor sports news, and record breaking is a huge part of that.

Over the past seven to eight years I have probably averaged an hour a day online reading about all these attempts," said columnist Jason Daley. "If you're not first you're last, there's that perception that life is all about high achievement and if people can do something like that, even if it's as seemingly pointless as pogo sticking for forty-eight hours, we as a society are fascinated with that. But it's not like they're superheroes. They often just have compulsions we can't understand."

Take Lucky Diamond Rich. The most tattooed person alive, Rich chose a hard way to get into the book, spending more than 1,000 hours under the needle, just for his first coat, tattooing his entire body jet black, including eyelids, gums, and genitals. The most painful part of the inking process was the inside of his ears. Then, after all the scabs healed, he started over, covering his body with intricate white lines and designs in assorted colors. It was this attention to detail that let Rich slip into the book past rival Tom "Leopard Man" Leppard, who even filed his teeth into fangs to match his orange body covered with black spots, but only managed to ink 99 percent of his skin. His reward? Rich now has a gimmick none of his fellow street performers in London's Covent Garden can claim. "For me it was a dream come true. I remember being a little kid and thinking that all I want to do is be in the *Guinness World Records* book for something," Rich said in a newspaper interview. "*Guinness World Records* is a celebration of, in a sense, a form of mental illness. It is obsessive-compulsive behavior, it is addiction. People have to have a certain personality or a certain type of mental trait to be in that book and it celebrates that."

Jez Edwards, an acclaimed host of children's television and radio programs in Britain, was the last presenter on *Record Breakers*, hosting the program for its final four years on BBC, 1997–2001. Dealing with record breakers and would-be record breakers day in and day out, he garnered an enormous respect for the practice and effort they put into even the zaniest feats, but he also saw the appeal of simply being in the book—or in his own case, for being associated with the book. "You can have a world record in anything. My advice if you want to get in the book is to look through it and try something no one's done, like hanging upside down. Then you will have something that people all around the world will recognize," and as if to clarify this point, Edwards adds the obvious: "There aren't many people who haven't heard of the book. The show is still on my bio, and the one thing people look at and say 'Oh, you did *Record Breakers*? Brilliant.'"

For self-proclaimed fame seekers like Jackie Bibby, television is the brass ring of world-record setting. Bibby told me that one of the highlights of his entire life was getting recognized by a visiting English tourist on the observation deck of the Empire State Building in New York the day after he was a guest on a talk show there. It did not matter that the tourist was an anonymous stranger; what mattered was the recognition of himself and his achievements. "I like the attention," says Bibby. "I'm an egomaniac with an inferiority complex. I love being noticed and recognized. People know me as the Texas Snakeman, that's my handle. I'm pretty well known and I got a little notoriety from the Guinness thing. You get recognized. I mean I got recognized on top of the Empire State Building by a guy from England last time I was in New York. It's from being on TV. I've been on TV almost sixty times. I get calls from broadcasters and writers and people like you several times a week, year round. I've done two or three radio interviews this week and got probably two or three e-mails about interviews. This goes on all the time. I love it and enjoy talking about it."

It has been this way for Bibby since he won his first rattlesnake roundup, one sponsored by the Brownwood Texas Jaycees, fresh out of high school four decades ago. "I won two trophies and thirty dollars and got my name in the paper. Thirty-nine years later I hold several world records and have been all around the world and was featured in magazines like *Playboy, Newsweek, Time, Parade,* and *Texas* magazine, so I guess it's been pretty good for an old country boy."

Bibby loves to travel and uses his fame to leverage free trips around the world; he will go on virtually any television show or participate in any live performance that will pay his way. He has been flown all around the United States, most frequently to New York and Los Angeles, and has traveled (at the expense of others) to Europe nine times to set snake handling records or do demonstrations. When I spoke to him he was in the midst of heated negotiations to perform a snake stunt in Hong Kong. "The money is never much, I don't make anything. If I break even and get the trips, that's the main thing. That and the prestige and the press." It seems that if anyone could cash in on Guinness World Record fame it would be Bibby, a tireless self-promoter, who, to his credit, undertakes astonishing—and dangerous—stunts with poisonous snakes. Yet he makes it clear that he is still financially dependent on his full-time day job, and is supplemented by nonrecord-related snake wrangling and sales. Ironically, he has worked in the field of chemical dependency for eighteen years and runs the Dublin Outreach Center in Dublin, Texas, a boardinghouse for recovering addicts. But Bibby clearly would rather talk about records than rehabilitation, quickly reminding me that in addition to all his other accolades and appearances, "I'm a Trivial Pursuit question in the twentieth-century edition of Trivial Pursuit." According to *Fame Junkies* author Jake Halpern's hypothesis, serial record setters like Bibby, Furman, and others could perhaps use some professional help with addictive disorders themselves.

> It doesn't surprise me that you would have a situation where someone would break one record, enjoy the satisfaction that brought them, and then quickly kind of say as the attention waned and the rush passed, "well one was not bad but what about two." I would imagine that it would be slightly less satisfying the second time, so they would be inspired to break a more visible record, a record that is more extraordinary or to break it in a more smashing way. You would kind of have to keep one upping yourself so it doesn't become this humdrum experience of "well, I just broke my thirty-seventh record." Because how many times

really are you going to be able to go back to the office or
your church group or whatever and say "I set a Guinness
World Record again." They'll say "Oh, that's great. You've
already been in it thirty times." So you have to say, "Well
this time I walked a thousand miles on one leg while balancing an egg on my head," and they say "Oh, wow, now
that is interesting." You could see how it would have this
hyperbolic effect where you had to keep breaking records
and keep on breaking them in a more sensational way in
order to get the recognition you want.

I tell Halpern, who is not an aficionado of the book, about
Ashrita Furman and Jackie Bibby, and he nods knowingly.

It doesn't surprise me that there are serial record breakers.
People are greedy for attention in the same way they are
greedy for money. How many people make a million dollars in business and say "well, that's enough"? They might
say at the outset "when I make a million I'll quit," or at
the blackjack table "when I'm up $50,000 I'm out of here,"
but the minute they get to $50,000 they say "geez, if I got
this far imagine if I got to $100,000. That's twice as much
money and I could get twice as much stuff and have twice
as much security." You could see how someone would start
off saying "I just want to get in the Guinness book and
then I'll be satisfied." Then they get in and say "well that
was great, but I wouldn't mind a bit more recognition."
Anything that makes you feel good, like money, sex or
winning at gambling, has a potentially compulsive or addictive quality to it and you'd want more and more.

Almost as soon as I set my first Guinness World Record and
basked in the brief limelight, friends started asking me "what's
next?" with alarming regularity. Apparently it is not just record
setters themselves who are affected in the way Halpern describes.

There seemed to be an expectation, almost an obligation, that once I had joined this world-famous club, I'd continue with other feats—one was not enough, even for my limited audience. This sensation was soon fueled by the loss of my record to an anonymous rival. In turn, not only did I begin to ponder more records I could topple, but as Halpern later suggested, I looked at them less for their viability and more for their dramatic appeal—and difficulty for others to break. This was quite a departure from my original logic of seeking out the path of least resistance to get into Guinness. I even began to feel slightly embarrassed by my first record, since it was more a feat of logistics than one of stamina or physical achievement. Anybody who put the same research and creativity in what I did could have broken the golf record, and indeed, my record was quickly eclipsed, in part, as Ashrita describes, because all the media attention I got, along with inclusion in the book, made it a particularly easy target. Next time, I vowed, I would set a difficult record that most people could not pull off, one that I wouldn't be embarrassed by, and one that had a chance of lasting. Despite my second record having also been published in the book and knowing of people making serious plans to topple it, as of this writing it still stands. I don't know why, but that makes me happy.

Maureen Orth, a respected journalist who wrote the book *The Importance of Being Famous,* with a similar slant to Halpern's *Fame Junkies,* wrote "The scorch of fame can be brutal, but the chill of the aftermath is an even stranger, more bitter sensation. . . . To keep the party going, new stories have to be at the ready. So if you want to extend your notoriety . . . you'd better have variations in the pipeline to keep the cameras satisfied." Like Halpern, Orth cites the explosion of media outlets and the increased popularity of reality television, along with the subculture of celebrity- and entertainment-oriented magazines and "news" programs, as part of the shift to a fame-obsessed culture, one that provides the perfect breeding ground for the *Guinness World Records.* "Since I started reporting on the worlds of entertainment and politics, we've moved from a society that admired entertainers with talent, and politicians with intelligence, to a culture in which the goal is just to achieve fame. Being famous now, increasingly, has less to do with talent or with doing anything real, thoughtful or subtle."

Record holders like Jackie Bibby and fingernail grower extraordinaire Sridhar Chillal talk about the fame Guinness brings, but does being in the book really make you famous? "It does in a fashion I guess," admits Halpern.

> Recognition, attention, and validation is the reward. My quick take on the Guinness book's appeal would be that because of the breadth of things it covers, it would make people feel like setting a record that will be written down for posterity as a world record is an attainable goal. I think that would be especially attractive in a time and place where there is a great premium on fame, which there obviously is today. One of the things I look at in my book is the sense today that fame is more attainable than ever, particularly because back in the '70s there were just five TV stations: now there are 500. There's reality TV. In the '60s and '70s the Guinness book would be especially attractive as a venue for being famous, since the thought of getting on TV was a lot more farfetched back then. The other aspect of fame is that in some ways it immortalizes you. You might die, but in some way you will live on in this book. "What does my life amount to? What am I leaving behind?" To be in a book that lists all the world records, that's something.

Carey Low, the book's spokesperson for Canada, a hotbed of record-breaking activity, apparently agrees and told the *Toronto Sun*, "It's human nature to want to go out and be the best. If you can do something that puts you into the Guinness database or book, you're doing something amazing." Increasingly since the early sixties there has been a democratization of records, and the focus has shifted from doing something amazing, to doing something, anything, that will get you in the book—or at least the database. Low's point seems to be today that the amazing part is simply getting in, rather than the feat itself, which would explain a lot of the records of the washing-machine-throwing variety.

Halpern's concept of immortality through accomplishments is not a new idea: it predates the *Guinness World Records* by at least three thousand years. In the *Epic of Gilgamesh*, dating from around the seventh century BCE or earlier, and widely considered the first, or at least the oldest, surviving work of literature, the title character, a mythical hero king of Sumerian legend, spends the entire second half the poem pondering the meaning of immortality after his best friend and fellow stellar warrior, Enkido, is killed. After several opportunities to physically become immortal present themselves but are not availed of, Gilgamesh returns home and considers the strong walls of the powerful city-state he has built and ruled, with the heroic stories of his life carved in stone, and reaches the conclusion that one form of immortality is to be remembered by others for your deeds. No known Western literature predates *Gilgamesh*, and in a very real sense, our history of reading and writing begins with the notion of achieving immortality through deeds and public recognition, a literary tradition that continues through the latest edition of the *Guinness World Records*. This concept of "virtual immortality" resonates throughout history and is so important to the Homeric epics, *The Odyssey* and *The Iliad*, that it becomes the crux for several crucial plot developments. According to Professor Elizabeth Vandiver, a classics professor at Whitman College in Washington State and a winner of the American Philological Association's Excellence in Teaching Award, honor and fame are the chief motivations to the Homeric warrior. She wrote, "The Homeric warrior fights for honor (*time'*) and glory or fame (*kleos*). *Kleos*, usually translated to 'glory' or 'fame,' means what is spoken aloud about one." *Kleos* and *time'* resonate throughout the rest of the tale, and when Achilles, the greatest of the Greek warriors, feels his fame or glory has been diminished, he refuses to fight any longer. Vandiver defines the concept of *kleos aphthiton* as "imperishable glory . . . the only kind of meaningful immortality available to Homeric warriors." Since the Greek view of the afterlife was not one offering much in the way of comfort, she concludes that "only *kleos* provides any significant kind of immortality; the Homeric warrior lives on in what others say about him after he is dead."

If this immortality logic seems overly dramatic for the Guinness World Records–induced fame seeker, consider the case of Philip Rabinowitz, an exceptionally fast senior citizen. Already a Guinness World Record holder as the oldest competitive walker, Rabinowitz, a one-hundred-year-old South African fitness fanatic nicknamed "Rabinoblitz" by friends, was a guest on the radio talk show *All Things Considered*, where he discussed his upcoming attempt to break the world record for the fastest 100-meter-run by a centenarian. When asked why these things were so important to him, Rabinowitz laughingly replied, "When my time goes to go up, I want to tell them there also that I've broken records, they must recognize it there as well."

Michael Roberts, executive editor of *Outside* magazine, agrees. "If you're going for a record, it's all about recognition, not just the achievement itself. If you care about the record, you are claiming something, just like planting your flag. You become immortal in a sense."

The notions of fame and celebrity are so central to the *Guinness World Records* that they go far beyond the journeyman record holders and into the very fabric of the book's editorial. Recent editions have given vastly increased coverage to celebrity subjects, most of whom presumably made no effort to get into the book, but rather seem to be sought out by the book's staffers simply to lend an air of celebrity credibility. If everyday record breakers like Jackie Bibby are "basking in the reflected glory" of the famous Guinness World Records brand by virtue of just being in the book, then the book itself is basking in the reflected glory of Tom Hanks, Tom Cruise, Jennifer Aniston, and Angelina Jolie, all of whom have large photographs spanning the two-page "Movie Stars" chapter of the 2008 edition, a category that didn't even exist as recently as 2005. It is hard to imagine that Tom Cruise went online to the record website and filled out an application requesting that he be named earth's "Most Powerful Actor," or that the notoriously press-shy Jodie Foster sought attention for having received the highest annual earnings among all actresses. It is far more likely that editors actively searched for ways to include more celebrities in the book, since celebrities sell product, and part of the entire Guinness World Records mystique is that by setting records, the person next door can share the pages with movie stars, recording artists, and athletes. There have always been a huge number of records, including those set by humans, that got in as a result of staffers rather than applicants, but these typically have come in the form of sports records or important firsts. Tom Hanks's record for most consecutive best actor Academy Awards is public knowledge and quantifiable in a sense no different than a sports record, but Tom Cruise's record, which the star may never have even heard of, reeks of editorial Guinnessport: there is no similar record for most powerful lawyer or chef.

Interestingly, the book's current love affair with Hanks carried over from the 2007 edition, when he and the rest of the crew and cast of *The Da Vinci Code*, including director Ron Howard, were honored by the book for undertaking the longest nonstop international train journey, a record that seems dubious at best. Apparently the group enjoyed a first-of-its-kind excursion from London to Cannes, in southern France, on the high-speed Eurostar. The actual length of the trip pales in comparison with other point-to-point train routes, such as Ulan Bator to Beijing, but besides coming down to semantics about how one defines a nonstop international journey, this kind of record appears to be a grasp by the book for celebrity recognition, a grasp rewarded by a photo of its trademark certificate in Ron Howard's hands. The same 2007 edition welcomes a laundry list of "celebrity record holders new to Guinness World Records including Johnny Depp, Jennifer Lopez, Drew Barrymore, and Reese Witherspoon." Likewise, on the first page of the 2006 edition is a list titled simply "Record Breaking

Americans," which would suggest a sampling from among the thousands of U.S. record holders; yet with the sole exception of Mr. Versatility himself, Ashrita Furman, the list includes nothing but entertainment and sports celebrities, from Lance Armstrong and Will Smith to David Copperfield and Jessica Simpson. A year-to-year comparison of the editions shows a clear fervor building toward celebrity records and coverage, wanted by the stars or not, peaking in 2007 with a three-page foldout spread or centerfold on "Celebrity Secrets," described as "The Hottest Celebrity Gossip from Guinness World Records." These include some listings that may or may not be, even by Guinness World Records standards, such as the opaque entry that Paris Hilton was voted most over-exposed celebrity of 2005 by "an online research firm." Norris McWhirter would likely turn over in his grave at such nonrecord inclusions. This is joined by a multiple-choice quiz asking which of four actors, Russell Crowe, Robert Downey Jr., Courtney Love, or Errol Flynn holds the Guinness World Record as the most jailed actor, complete with photos of each. The book gives the correct answer as Flynn for his four arrests, though depending on how you define actor, it seems implausible that there has not been a thespian jailed more than four times. On the other hand, it doesn't really matter much, as the purpose of the spread seems to be to jam in as many frivolous, nonrecord celebrity photos as possible, and in this case Flynn serves as an excuse to publish otherwise unwarranted photos of more contemporary movie stars alongside his.

Halpern, the author of *Fame Junkies*, is far from surprised at this turn of editorial events.

> It's all part of the same function that you see now with the mainstream media, everyone is scrambling to do celebrity stories because it moves books, magazines, increases viewers. No one is immune to it and it doesn't surprise me in the least that the Guinness book would do whatever it could to in some fashion or another include celebrities, because if they didn't they would be just about the only publication

on the face of the earth that missed the boat. Even the *New York Times,* which doesn't usually jump into it, covers celebrities. When Rosie O'Donnell and Donald Trump had this big fight it was on the front page of the Arts section. I think that there's this sense now that if you don't cover celebrities you'll either be culturally irrelevant or your sales will plummet or both.

As Stephen Moss wrote in the *Guardian*, in a salute to Norris McWhirter's life and work:

McWhirter bowed out from the GBR in 2001, when the title was sold to a new publisher. He even put his name to a potential rival—*Norris McWhirter's Book of Millennium Records*. There appears to have been some unpleasantness. He may have resented the unrelenting popularization of his great work—the attempt to make a mountain of largely re-dundant facts hip, happening, relevant. That's not the point of the book at all. Take the introduction to the 2004 edi-tion, illustrated by gratuitous pictures of Eminem ("most successful rap artist ever") and Pierce Brosnan ("star of the 20th Bond movie"—what sort of record is that?). "Dive in and be inspired by the greatest the world has to offer," the editor instructs us. Bare-faced hucksterism. Paula Radc-liffe's marathon world record is "incredible, awe-inspiring." Spare us the hyperbole; just give us the facts.

In fact, at age seventy-five Norris McWhirter did indeed object to the wholesale changes to the book he had launched decades ear-lier. In a call for a highbrow British publisher to "rescue" it and restore its reputation as a reference work, McWhirter described the *Guinness Book of Records* as "virtually unrecognizable now, it's gone so downmarket. It's like a stick of multi-coloured liquorice—it doesn't contain many of the basic records." The lifelong sports junkie attacked the emphasis on pop music and football, noting that under his reign the book contained records for eighty-four different sports. His last record work, *Norris McWhirter's Book of Millennium Records,* was written for Virgin Publishing and looks remarkably like the *Guinness World Records,* down to almost identical chapter headings, except for ones such as "Movie Stars," which is notably absent. McWhirter barely acknowledges celebrities in the tome, mentioning them only in the course of their historical impact on such categories as cinema in the twentieth century.

But on the other hand, *Millennium Records* did not become a household name that 65,000 people a year are clamoring to get into, nor one that 3.5 million readers buy annually. The changes to the Guinness book have worked. There was that long period in the seventies and eighties when sales slumped, but they have since rebounded with the wholesale changes, even though not all fans appreciate them. Producer Ben Sherwood, a devoted fan since childhood who has gone behind the scenes at the company and interviewed countless record holders, said recently:

> This business is not motivated by a love of world records or the fascination with human nature. It's not a lofty enterprise the way one wishes it was. It's a book put together by people who are marketing people. It was very difficult for me to come to terms with my childhood imagination of what it was and the facts, that how records get in there and how they choose them is very marketing driven. The entire reconfiguration of the book, with pictures and all that, is aimed at teenage boys, and they've come up with a much spiffier website. It's not a sweet or quaint attachment to the idea of settling barroom disputes. It's about competing with video games and Mutant Ninja Turtles. It's all been done just to compete in the marketplace, whereas what I loved about it was the sort of fuddy-duddiness of it, sort of old fashioned. Old fashioned like an almanac. Now it's like a cross between *Us Magazine* and the *National Enquirer.*

While the pursuit by record breakers of their fifteen minutes of fame and the pandering to celebrities may have cheapened the content of the book, it is also what keeps the franchise going, both in the sheer numbers of people trying to set records and achieve their slice of immortality, and in the colorful characters who have long made the book popular reading. Without the promise of fame, would John Evans ever have balanced more than two tons of bricks on his head, let alone a Mini Cooper automobile? Evans, having set eleven records for balancing things, usually very heavy and bulky things, on top of his head, recalled feeling that he was talentless after leaving school, a self-esteem issue redeemed through Guinnessport. "Now I am one of the world's most talented people. I have been in *Hello!* magazine. I could have been a normal builder, but the records gave me a sniff of being famous. It's not anybody who gets in the book. I've got dedication." As if proving his self-worth, Evans noted that his feat could be read on "Page 46 of the 2000 book. I got five mentions on page 15 of the 2001 edition and I'm on page 35 of the 2005 one."

Evans is far from alone. Christopher Darwin was born with a famous name, but since it was his great-great-grandfather who came up with the theory of evolution, he had to make his own mark. This may be what led twenty-eight-year-old Christopher and his friends in 1989 to carry a complete replica Louis XIV dining room set, much of the furniture strapped to their backs, to the top of Peru's Mount Huascaranin, a staggering 22,205 feet. Their bid to stage the world's highest formal luncheon also included custom thermal tuxedoes and ball gowns, a four-course gourmet meal, and a butler. "The only thing I'm really any good at is eating," Mr. Darwin told the *Wall Street Journal*. "I wanted to be in the *Guinness Book of World Records,* but you can imagine the number of baked beans that I'd have to eat. I decided to do something much simpler." To this end, Darwin formed a group called the Social Climbers, whose eclectic members for the expedition included a stock broker, travel agent, ex-commando, stunt woman, and professional triathlete. Like so many other offbeat Guinness World

Records attempts, this one was being undertaken for charity, to raise $100,000 for Australia's National Heart Foundation. "Of course, I'd like to sound altruistic," Darwin said, "but it's really the excitement, the ego, the chance to make a record."

Whether it is balancing a Mini Cooper on your head or mountain climbing in black tie, Norris McWhirter discussed the phenomenon of exploiting a unique talent in the introduction to a spin-off volume from the main record book, *Guinness: The Stories Behind the Records*, published in 1981 by David Boehm's Sterling Publishing. "The motivations for mastering certain fields of endeavor are also very different." In the case of William Hollingsworth, Norris noted that Hollingsworth had "dedicated months to learning the fine art of balancing a full milk bottle on his head specifically for a listing in Guinness." As a result of seeing such devoted practitioners, McWhirter concluded that "record fever continues to rage as strongly as ever." In the same edition, Boehm himself interviewed world record stilt walker John Russell, who once strode on a pair of thirty-three-foot-high aluminum stilts, a pair taller than any ever built. When Boehm asked him if he knew that his feat had gotten him into the book, Russell replied, as so many others have before and since, "Of course. It's my proudest achievement."

Many Guinness World Record holders have not intentionally set out to get in the book, from Jesse Owens to Neil Armstrong to Tom Cruise. But among all those others, including the 65,000 who log onto the book's website and fill out applications each year, and then spend their days practicing and perfecting odd pursuits, the goal is purely and simply "getting into Guinness." In turn, a large portion of this audience is motivated by the promise of glory and immortality. Anyone who doubts this, who discounts the lure of the promise of fame, no matter how slight or fleeting, need look no farther than one of the most unique record holders of all time. By way of comparison to the Australian marathon shower taker Arron Marshall, whose goal was to go "yahooing around the country" once he saw his name in the book, consider the case of a nameless coed in East Lansing, Michigan. In 1971 this intrepid student broke the women's record for marathon showering, remaining under the running water for ninety-seven hours and one minute, more than four full days. She chose not to have her name printed and became, according to a note in the 1971 record book, what is believed to be the ONLY anonymous record holder in Guinness history, a record-worthy feat in and of itself.

6

Seventy-Two Hours in Hell: Getting Back into Guinness

If it was easy, everyone would do it. Right now there are probably people at the pub down the road making wild plans. But they'll never do them.
— CHRISTOPHER DARWIN, *THE SOCIAL CLIMBERS*

There are but two roads that lead to an important goal and to the doing of great things: strength and perseverance. Strength is the lot of but a few privileged men: but the austere perseverance, harsh and continuous, may be employed by the smallest of us and rarely fails of its purpose, for its silent power grows irresistibly greater with time.
— JOHANN VON GOETHE

"Don't do it."

Shortly before I left to set my poker record at Foxwoods Casino, I spoke on the phone with one of my closest friends, Jim Martel. Jim is an unbelievable trivia whiz—on par with the likes of Ken Jennings—who remembers everything he reads or hears and who used to clean me out betting on *Jeopardy!* in college.

I proudly told him about my upcoming record attempt. His advice was simple: "Don't do it."

"Why not?"

"I read about this guy who did one of those radio DJ marathons, where they stay on the air for like 99 or 102 or 106 hours. He did it and suffered permanent brain damage. He couldn't concentrate, had lasting insomnia, lost his wife, his job, and his house." Jim may be a good friend and great pub trivia player, but he'd make a lousy coach. His comment was not quite in the same league as "win one for the Gipper" as inspirational speeches go. I tried to forget what he said.

Back in 2004, if you had asked me why I was doing it, I couldn't have given a good answer. Unlike my golf record, no magazine was paying me to suffer. It was not until years later, when I spoke to Jake Halpern, the author of *Fame Junkies*, that I could clearly analyze my bizarre motives. Halpern explained to me in vivid detail the process by which something as satisfying as breaking a Guinness World Record, especially one attendant with high-profile publicity, could have an addictive quality. Furthermore, he hypothesized that in addition to wanting to do it again, many people would want to do it on a bigger stage, and in a more dramatic fashion. "It doesn't surprise me that you would have a situation where someone would break one record, enjoy the satisfaction that brought them, and then quickly kind of say as the attention waned and the rush passed, 'well one was not bad but what about two.' I would imagine that it would be slightly less satisfying the second time, so they would be inspired to break a more visible record, a record that is more extraordinary or to break it in a more smashing way."

Halpern didn't know about my two experiences with record breaking and record setting when he provided what he thought was a hypothetical analysis, but he described my situation perfectly, as well as that of thousands of other record holders who have been driven by oddly powerful forces. Whether it is Matthew Webb's swims, Branson's flights, or something as seemingly silly as my very long day playing golf, there are several common aspects of these kinds of experiences that make them addictive. They comprise an alluring cocktail of the pleasing adrenaline rush during the attempt, the satisfaction afterward at having set or broken the record, and the resulting "fame" in the form of inclusion in the book, coverage in print and broadcast media, and perhaps most important, recognition from friends, neighbors, and peers. The *Guinness World Records* book does not have an exclusive on such motivations, but it packages them together in an especially attractive and accessible way. Equivalent venues for the kind of feelings the book offers many of its record breakers would be professional sports or success in movies, television, or as a recording star. For most of us, getting into Guinness is easier.

Still, not every Guinness World Record holder becomes an addict, and the true serial record holders are the exceptions, not the norms. Many of the people simply achieve their singular goal of nabbing a record and then happily move on with their lives, never revisiting the urge. My friend and fellow journalist (and novelist) Steve Eubanks told me about setting a Guinness record very similar to my poker feat, by playing pinball for seventy-two hours straight while in college at the University of Georgia in the 1970s. Steve fondly recalls his record but does not care in the least that it has been shattered and reshattered since. His reason for standing in a bar with his hands duct-taped to the flipper buttons was the simplest of all: "When you are in college, the girls don't care what your world record is for, as long as you have one." After breaking my first record, I was content and would not have picked up the mantle again and succumbed to the urge *Newsweek* described as "Guinnessitis" were it not for the intervention of two other powerful forces: pride, and peer pressure. My friends and associates were impressed by and supportive of my record, and never ceased to stroke my ego, telling anyone who would listen about my status as a world record holder. This made me feel good. But in telling and retelling the story, I became aware of the obvious—while it was a fun and funny thing to do, it was not exactly an epic challenge. The short version is I played golf, then drank whisky and

Ashrita Furman pushes an orange with his nose for one mile as part of an effort to break the record for "Orange Nose Push" in New York City on August 12, 2004. Furman beat the world record with a time of 24 minutes and 36 seconds. (© **SHANNON STAPLETON/Reuters/Corbis**)

Ashrita Furman attempts to set another world record for hula hooping with the world's largest hula hoop in New York's Flushing Meadows Park on July 15, 2005. Furman successfully broke the record of 3 rotations with this hula hoop, which measured 14 feet 7 ¾ inches in diameter. (© **SHANNON STAPLETON/ Reuters/Corbis**)

Portrait of Sir Hugh Eyre Campbell Beaver, the father of the Guinness World Records empire, by Walter Stoneman, bromide print, 1947. (**National Portrait Gallery, London**)

British Olympic sprinters, twins Norris (1925–2004) and Ross (1925–1975) McWhirter, circa 1953, who founded the *Guinness Book of Records* in 1954. (**Getty Images**)

Famed miler Roger Bannister (back) following top pacer Chris Chataway, on the way to a new record of 3 minutes 59.4 seconds at Oxford, on May 6, 1954. Norris McWhirter, a college teammate of both, was hired to provide the track commentary through the public announcement system. Chataway later became a Guinness Brewery employee and was the one responsible for introducing the McWhirters to Guinness execs, leading to their long editorial oversight of the record book. (**Getty Images**)

Norris McWhirter holds the 100 millionth copy of the *Guinness Book* during its launch at the Tate Modern art gallery in London on November 11, 2003. (© **LEE BESFORD/ Reuters/Corbis**)

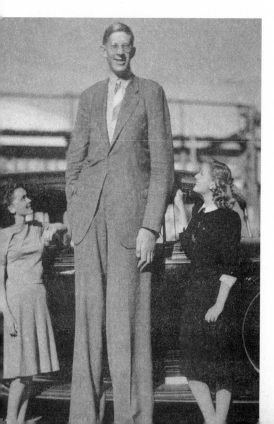

Robert Wadlow, who still holds the record for world's tallest man, in Hollywood in 1938, with actresses Maureen O'Sullivan and Ann Morris. Wadlow, who at his death was 8 feet 11 inches tall, was 8 feet 8 ½ inches tall when this photo was taken. (© **Bettmann/Corbis**)

"The World's Largest Twins," Billy and Benny McCrary, who weigh a combined 1,300 pounds, in Hendersonville, North Carolina, November 25, 1969. (© **Bettmann/Corbis**)

Jackie "the Texas Snakeman" Bibby holds in his mouth ten 2-foot-6-inch-long western diamondback rattlesnakes for 12.5 seconds without any assistance at the CW11 morning show on November 9, 2006, to set a new World Record for Most Live Rattlesnakes Held In Mouth. The event was part of the Guinness World Records Day, where people from all over the globe joined together to attempt amazing records. (**TIMOTHY A. CLARY/ AFP/Getty Images**)

Mountaineer Sir Edmund Hillary sits at base camp, preparing for his successful attempt to be the first to reach the summit of Mount Everest, Nepal, May 1953. (**Express Newspapers/Getty Images**)

Madame Jeanne Calment, of Arles in France, at age 120 in the mid-1990s. She ultimately lived to be 122 years and 164 days old, and she became the longest living confirmed person of all time. When explaining her amazing span, she said, "I've been forgotten by God." (**© Eric Fougére/ Kipa/Corbis**)

Virgin entrepreneur Sir Richard Branson pilots his Gibbs Aquada amphibious "Aquaticar" during a record-breaking crossing of the English Channel, June 14, 2004. (**Carl De Souza/ Getty Images**)

The recipe and pot for the world's largest fondue, created by Chef Terrance Brennan. The finished product weighed a ton, and required a pot 3 feet deep and 8 feet in diameter, weighing 4,000 pounds empty. A Guinness World Records adjudicator was on hand to approve the record-setting fondue. **(Virginia Sherwood/ABC News Wire)**

New York chef Terrance Brennan, owner of restaurants Picholine and Artisanal Bistro, is a frequent guest on NBC's *The Today Show*. While setting the record for the world's largest fondue outside the show's studio in Rockefeller Center, he also taught viewers how to make a more traditionally sized fondue. **(Virginia Sherwood/ABC News Wire)**

Michel Lotito, nicknamed Monsieur Mangetout, or "Mister Eat All," testing his teeth on the bicycle he is going to eat before the public at the 11th Fantastic Record Festival at Every, Paris, 1977. (**Keystone/Getty Images**)

The author completes his Guinness World Record–setting poker marathon at Foxwoods Casino in Ledyard, Connecticut, on June 13th, 2004, while a supportive crowd, including his friends and helpers Joe Kresse (slapping author on back) and Matt Rosenthal (standing with gold Rolex), looks on. (**Foxwoods Resort Casino/Gary Thibeault**)

Foxwoods Poker Room Manager Kathy Raymond lifts the hand of the tired and disoriented author upon completion of his record-setting 72-hour-and-2-minute poker marathon. (**Foxwoods Resort Casino/Gary Thibeault**)

The author at his home with the first "green" edition (1955) of the record book, the 50th anniversary edition (containing his golf record), and several dozen other volumes from his personal collection of record-related paraphernalia. (**Allison Olmsted**)

napped, then played golf. It took some skill in arranging, and as Christopher Darwin noted about pub patrons making wild plans, having actually done it rather than having just talked about it was something . . . but not enough. The record was more a technicality than a human triumph, and the weight of its unimpressiveness began to wear on my shoulders. At the same time, almost since the day I returned from Australia in February 2004, these same friends had been incessantly asking me what was next, when was I going to do it again? This implication that I had not *done enough* seemed like a direct challenge. They were vicariously living the record-breaking experience through me; they wanted me to suffer for them once again. Naturally, I was inclined to oblige.

It was my turn for a little Guinnessport. Having been forced by my editor at *Golf Magazine* to break an existing record, I was still intrigued by the idea of creating a new one and carving out my own bit of immortality. But while some records are made up as an easy way to get in, I wanted mine to be worthy, something truly difficult, an achievement few others could manage, a record that might resist assault and endure but it could only succeed if it was something I could actually accomplish myself. This, of course, ruled out just about every conventional sport. For example, I could not expect to run or bike or ski faster or farther or longer than professional athletes already had. To find a suitable feat, I did a quick inventory of my personal skills. Writing was a strength but one that did not seem relevant to Guinness. That left me with stamina, in the form of a high pain threshold, an evolved level of stubbornness, and a generally tireless nature. I had that going for me, and whatever I was to do, doing it long term would give me an edge over doing it quickly. What else was I really good at, better than just about anyone I knew? The answer was, unfortunately, not very much. There was one thing, but it did not immediately come to mind. It would take the accidental intervention of a magazine assignment to make me realize my destiny and standout skill: playing poker.

I love poker. I always have. My mother taught me to play gin rummy and 500 rummy at a very young age, and just as Ken Jennings reminisced about reading the Guinness book to his parents on long car trips as a child, I played rummy with my mother and brother on lengthy car trips. This soon grew into a fascination for all card games, but by the time I was in high school, I was playing poker almost exclusively. Poker remained one of my many hobbies through college and long after, but it didn't become a true passion until my eye-opening first trip to Las Vegas in 1988, at the tender age of twenty-two.

This was before poker on TV, before poker on the Internet (or even the Internet itself). I had never played with strangers, and something about the idea struck me as seedy, a back-room affair full of cheats and con men. That's why Vegas was such a welcome surprise. The idea of well-run casino card rooms—where you could play for any stakes that suited your budget, low or high, without worrying about cheats, where only the dealer handled the cards, where you played just one game and no one could make up weird rules or add umpteen wild cards—all this struck me as about the greatest thing since sliced bread. It was *real* poker, played in its purest form. I returned often over the years to Vegas for work, and regularly played all night long in between days of conferences or research, even once playing for about forty hours in a single stint before a bachelor party weekend. These sessions left me more invigorated than exhausted, "evidence," at least to me, that I had a gift for marathon poker playing.

As a result of my Vegas discovery, I spent several years pitching magazine editors on poker stories. Long before it became a fad, I took it as a personal mission to educate the public. I wrote stories preaching the fun of the game, why it is the best bet in a casino, and how to get started playing. I sold a few poker shorts to *Playboy*, and then a feature on playing in a tournament to the now defunct *P.O.V.* I've written for the in-house magazines of several casino operators like Harrah's, and even an unlikely poker story for *New York Magazine*, eventually building up a bit of a poker-writing portfolio. Then the *World Poker Tour* was launched, a series of big money tournaments, organized like a professional sports league, that brought the game to TV and changed it forever. Poker suddenly became hot, something to watch in prime time, and interest in the game swept the country like wildfire. The more people watched it, the more people actually went out and played it, not unlike the effect *Record Breakers* had on setting Guinness World Records three decades earlier. It's hard to believe but, prior to the *World Poker Tour* launch in 2002, most casinos, even in Vegas, did not have poker rooms, since the demand was not there, and existing poker rooms were closing at an alarming rate. That turned around quickly, and just as every network suddenly needed its own poker show, every casino needed a poker room. At the same time the *World Poker Tour* became the highest-rated series in the history of cable's Travel Channel, I was writing a lot of CEO and company profiles for *Inc.* magazine, so I pitched a feature on Steve Lipscomb, the colorful attorney, entrepreneur, and filmmaker who had founded the tour and its television show. The magazine agreed, and several months later when the story was done, my editors liked it so much that *Inc.* made it the cover feature.

During my research I interviewed Lipscomb several times, but to see him in action I needed to attend one of his multimillion dollar tournaments. I chose Foxwoods, in Ledyard, Connecticut, and stayed at the vast casino resort for a couple of nights, spending much of my time in the control room with Lipscomb as he directed the production of an episode at a major multiday live tournament. I got to know the casino staff, the Foxwoods public relations department, and the poker room manager, Kathy Raymond, one of the most important executives in the game (now working in Las Vegas). Like everyone who watched the show, my interest in poker expanded daily. I kept in touch with Lipscomb and the others, and subsequently played in a *World Poker Tour* event myself, finishing a very respectable sixteenth. (My cockiness lasted only a few months, until I played in a tournament on the *World Poker Tour*'s short-lived spin-off circuit, the *Professional Poker Tour*, where I got bounced out by the savvy pros almost immediately.) My passion for poker was now running at an all-time high, and like the golf industry, I had an insider's perspective. Poker was a red hot fad; the original series spawned numerous other shows, to the point that poker seemed to always be on television on some channel. Several different new poker magazines and websites were launched, and poker books flooded store shelves. This was all happening at the moment when I was pondering a next record attempt, and finally I made the connection. I consulted Guinness to see if there were any poker records, at least any printed in the book. There were not, but I found an entry for a marathon card game, when eight Italian men and women played "Jass," whatever that is, in a restaurant in Switzerland for twenty-eight consecutive hours over St. Patrick's Day—a truly multicultural event. Twenty-eight hours is not very long in the rarefied world of Guinness records, and I had already played poker for longer than this on several occasions, so I immediately considered getting a group of friends together and playing poker for a longer session in one of our homes. The problem with group events, however, is the weak-link effect: if one person gets tired and succumbs to exhaustion, the record attempt is moot. On the other hand, the beauty of casino poker is that, unlike any other card game, at a busy casino like Foxwoods the games are infinite and essentially go on forever. Most games have no start or end, they simply exist, and when one player leaves another takes his or her place, 24/7. While it wasn't possible to sit down to a prolonged game of Jass, or bridge or rummy or anything else without having cohorts, casino poker gave me the setting for an unlimited individual marathon without having to supply my own posse of players. Given its newfound popularity, I also realized poker should be an easy category in which to get approval for a new record. The Book craves publicity, and would instantly recognize the value of jumping on the poker fad bandwagon while the sport was hot. The limited knowledge of Guinness World Records I had amassed during my golf experience also told me that The Book liked sports where it could defer to established rules and oversight by another authority, whether it was the International Association of Athletic Federations, which governs all track-and-field records, or the casino management at Foxwoods.

I soon refined my idea into an individual record for marathon poker playing, and chose the benchmark of 100 hours. Why? I blithely figured four days seemed like a very impressive length, much manlier than three days, and by extension, if I was going for ninety-six hours anyway, how could I not go for an even hundred? I imagine many new Guinness marathon feats are set with similarly imprecise logic. When Timothy Weber of Germany set a new record in 2003, for "Movie Watching," his mark of 70 hours and 1 minute (thirty-two films), like mine of 72:02, suggests reaching a set goal and then quitting as soon as possible. On the other hand, this begs the question of how Louisa Almedovar and Rich Langley could have not made out for thirty-three more seconds after setting the record for the "Longest Kiss," at 30 hours 59 minutes and 27 seconds, to make it an even thirty-one hours? Maybe they had bad watches. In their defense, they did remain standing the whole time.

New categories for records are always tricky business, for a couple of reasons. First, even though it has not been done before, you have to explain your intent when you apply, and it has to be impressive enough to woo the researchers. One hundred hours I was sure they would go for; ten hours I was sure they would pass on. But where was the unwritten dividing line between humble and heroic? This confusion does not stop once the new record attempt is approved. If Guinness gives the go-ahead for a new category, any attempt could theoretically be argued as a new benchmark. If I quit after five minutes, I could claim that I had set the world record for longest poker playing session at five minutes, having been the only person ever to have done this feat under the Guinness World Records rules for it, which I had essentially just invented. This claim would be ridiculous, so the Keeper of the Records reserves the right to approve or deny attempts that fall short of the stated goal. In theory, if I said I planned to do 100 hours and fell short, after eighty-two, they still might honor it and grant the record if they deemed the attempt worthy. This waffling leaves the record setter in something of a gray area, and provides sufficient motivation for picking a goal that is lofty enough to command the book's respect and approval, but realistic enough to actually do. I knew that people in casinos routinely play poker for twenty-four-hour stints, so asking Guinness to approve anything near this threshold seemed ludicrous. It had to be 100 hours.

My wife had different ideas. Although she is used to this kind of behavior from me, she immediately expressed serious concerns, and I have learned, after more than a decade of marriage in which I have been proven wrong again and again, that on the rare occasions when she draws a line in the sand and takes a strong position against one of my ideas, she is usually right. Going solely on gut instinct—or maybe women's intuition—she pointed out that 100 hours without sleep was, in her words, "a really long time." My argument for the plan was simple: "I played for almost forty-eight hours in Vegas, after flying, while drinking cocktails, without even trying. Now I have a clear goal and should be able to double my earlier effort." Her argument, based on what I had told her about Weber's movie watching and other marathon records in the book, was even simpler: "Why bother, if seventy-two hours would get you the record?"

Good point, and well taken. I reset my official record-breaking sights and filed an online application with Guinness World Records, explaining my intent to play for at least seventy-two hours, and detailing the circumstances: I would do it at a large U.S. casino, in a public game under the standard casino rules open to any casino guests, all monitored by casino management. As I expected, the folks at Guinness World Records gave me the green light.

When the research staff then approved my shot at a new category, they did what they do for every presanctioned attempt: they provided me with a laundry list, three typed pages' worth of rules, stipulations, and details of the required documentation. The key points for my poker stunt were these:

A fifteen-minute break must be taken after every eight completed hours of the record-breaking activity. This is a standard
medical safety rule Guinness has incorporated into most of
its marathon record attempts. However, as Ashrita Furman
found to his chagrin, when he thought he had already broken
the pogo stick jumping record for the first time, these fifteen
minutes cannot be accumulated. You cannot skip one and then
take a half-hour nap after sixteen hours.

I was to maintain a "logbook" recording the start and
finish of play, times of all rest breaks, and changes of casino
personnel.

Officials of the game's governing body had to be present
at all times, and had to ensure that the rules of the game were
followed. No such official could be used to satsify this moni-
toring requirement for more than four hours per session. Each
official had to sign in and sign out of the logbook.

In addition, I needed to have two independent witnesses on
hand at all times. Like casino officials, they had to rotate and
never work more than a four-hour shift, and had to sign the
logbook duly. The witnesses couldn't be relatives of mine nor
be under age eighteen.

Finally, the zinger: I needed a licensed and practicing
member of the medical profession overseeing the record attempt in its entirety. Once again, the doctors or nurses had to
rotate in four-hour shifts, and sign the book. They also could
pull the plug: if it was their professional opinion that I should
quit, I was to stop immediately.

The first two points were easy; the next two were trickier. The
last was borderline impossible. These marathon rules presumably
also apply to the game of Jass in the bar, walking for thirty hours
with a milk bottle on your head, or extended pole-squatting sessions. There have been marathon games of Monopoly, separate
movie- and television-watching marathons, and of course, the oft-

challenged radio DJ record, one of the most popular attempts in the book. It is hard to believe they were all organized under these types of onerous rules. Not many people have enough friends who are doctors or nurses to rotate through voluntary four-hour shifts for three days and nights, and the cost of such round-the-clock oversight would be exorbitant. In addition, some of these marathons go on much longer, spanning four or five days or more. Likewise, having enough unrelated witnesses and rules officials to cover all these shifts would be extremely problematic in any kind of home game setting, or even for the average casino patron. But I had an ace up my sleeve. I chose Foxwoods for my marathon for two reasons. First, because it is the largest casino in the world, a superlative that made it seem especially fitting. More important, from my *World Poker Tour* article, I knew the executives in its public relations department, and I knew the media attention the record could bring to the casino (they would later use my picture in advertisements in the *New York Daily News*). All large casinos have medical staff on hand at all times for emergencies, and the poker room is always manned by a hierarchy of managers, submanagers, and dealers. So when I broached the idea, they not only agreed to help me take care of all the paperwork, filling all the managers in on the details, and to provide nurses and EMTs to monitor the attempt and sign my logbook, they also extended the courtesy of free food and beverage throughout the attempt, served tableside, and a hotel room for the inevitable aftermath, no matter how it went. The logistics of this record were far more daunting than my golf one, and by the end, my logbook had amassed many pages of certificates, signatures, witness statements, and other documentation. Of course, the casino's largesse came at a price: I had wanted to begin my assault on the record book at 9 AM, since I am an early riser and didn't want to "waste" any waking hours, but the casino wanted the morning TV appearance, adding six hours to my sleep deprivation. The casino also arranged a series of radio and newspaper interviews for immediately after the event, when I planned to go to sleep. But these obstacles were minor roadblocks on the path into Guinness.

When I left for Foxwoods there was one secret I was keeping from wife: I still wanted 100 hours and set out with the belief that if I felt great after seventy-two, I would just keep going. As she might have predicted, that was not in the cards, so to speak. Had I insisted on my original four-day goal, things would certainly have ended differently. I can imagine only two possible outcomes: the best case was failure, the worst case death or lasting brain damage. Because as much as I prepared logistically for the attempt, I had done precious little research into the concept of sleep deprivation itself. Instead, I focused on practical matters such as changing my shirt and brushing my teeth, and to that end, I had a duffel bag packed with disposable toothbrushes and mouthwashes, deodorant, baby wipes, six clean shirts, extra socks, underwear, and pants, energy bars, aspirin, and anything else I could think of that might be useful over three or four long days. And nights. The Guinness guidelines stipulated that I take a fifteen-minute "safety break" after every eight hours of play. I'm still not sure why standing on one leg in the bathroom trying to change your pants and brush your teeth at the same time was any safer than sitting in a chair playing cards, but it definitely encouraged better hygiene, and I figured I'd try to get as much as possible done in those fifteen minutes. I thought I had everything figured out, but I had already forgotten the cardinal rule: THERE ARE NO EASY WORLD RECORDS. My ignorance stemmed from the simple fact that I had never stayed up for anywhere near my target time.

My lack of research into the effects of not sleeping was not an oversight. I simply didn't want to know. When I go for long bike rides on unfamiliar terrain, I prefer to not know anything about the route, because that way, you take everything as it comes, rather than worrying about the upcoming big hill you heard about. It is an ignorance-is-bliss approach, and I took the same tactic, intentionally, regarding the sleep issue. That was why I tried to quickly forget my friend Jim's comment about permanent insomnia. I was also in denial. I did not want to confront any evidence that would dissuade me from my attempt, cause me to lose face, and keep me from acquiring another handsome Guinness World Records certificate. I had already told my friends, co-opted the staff at Foxwoods, rounded up a support crew, and based on my previous experience, expected an outpouring of media interest. I couldn't back out. I wouldn't back out. Had I done the obvious online research, I would have learned quite a bit about sleep deprivation, but I did not. I planned to go into the attempt as carefree as possible.

My purposeful ignorance turned out not to matter. The research I should have done in advance, and did do afterward, simply predicted what I corroborated firsthand. I later found out that the military is understandably very concerned with the effects of sleep deprivation, because the reality of war is that sometimes there is no chance for soldiers to sleep during prolonged combat. For this reason, hundreds of studies have been done to determine exactly what happens to mental and physical functions after various periods of time without sleep. Coincidentally, seventy-two hours is a magic number for the military. Numerous subjects, hopefully volunteers, have been poked and prodded and tested after being kept awake for that particular length of time, and the data on this particular duration of exhaustion is ample—and accurate.

One of the many military-sponsored medical studies I read summed up the results of sleep deprivation in a handy little table at the end of a wordy and virtually incomprehensible article jammed with medical jargon, and it read like a perfect description of me right around the time I was trying to get back from my ill-fated trip to the bathroom. The list included:

Body swaying while standing (that's me)
Vacant stares (check)
Slurred speech (got it covered)
Less energetic, cheerful, and alert (leave it to the military to
  fund a study to figure this out)
Loss of interest in surroundings (absolutely)
More irritable ("more" being a gross understatement)
Forgetfulness (I'm pretty sure I had this symptom)

Difficulty speaking clearly (hard to separate this from slurred
  speech, but yes)
Unable to carry on conversation (ditto)
Short-term memory loss (again, I think I had this)

The study's conclusion was that after seventy-two hours without sleep, the ability to perform most tasks was diminished by at
least 50 percent. Another military study more closely focused on
performance found the drop closer to 80 percent. Recent experiments by the University of California at San Diego concluded that
brain activity is actually altered during such extended periods of
wakefulness, and that "the frontal lobe does not function when the
subject is severely sleep deprived." This is important, because as
the authors point out, the frontal lobe is "the thinking part of the
brain, responsible for activities such as speech, temporal memory,
and problem solving." Apparently this includes solving problems
such as how to get back from the bathroom.

Not only did I experience every single symptom described on the
military's checklist, but I had many of them in combination, a sort
of insanity cocktail. According to three of my friends, Joe Kresse,
Matt Rosenthal, and Nalm "JP" Peress, I became increasingly irritable, snapping at other players and the dealers. I also became forgetful
and slow to respond, constantly having to be reminded that it was
my turn to ante, bet, or fold. But the real problem was just beginning
to show up. Other than possible hallucinations, none of the articles
mentioned anything about visual acuity. I suddenly found myself, at
about three in the morning on the last night, with ten hours still to
go, unable to read the cards. I could still see, and I could make out
the faces of the players and the chips and the cards themselves, but
the cards all looked blank, rectangles of white as pure as the driven
snow. I tried holding them closer or farther away, squinting, but it
made no difference. The red and black print, the hearts and spades,
kings and queens, they were all gone. Even if you know nothing
about poker, it is obviously not a game you want to be playing for
money when you don't know what any of the cards are.

I remember the frustration of the blank cards clearly. I remember thinking that I could not go on like that for another ten hours. I remember thinking I might have to pull the plug on the attempt and let the chips fall where they may as far as Guinness granting the record. But I remember little else, because this kicked off a two-hour stretch of complete blackout, where according to witnesses, I was conscious and vaguely lucid, and continued to play, but I cannot remember one single second of that time, except as sort of a waking dream. In my dream, I saw the white gazebo surrounding the elevated table, and I became concerned that I was in the wrong place. I kept trying to make sure that I was still at Foxwoods, still making my bid for the record. Although Foxwoods has the largest poker room of any casino in the nation, with more than eighty tables, each accommodating eight to ten players, in my waking dream I was suddenly playing at a small solitary table, set in a distant corner of the casino, surrounded not by other poker tables but by clanging slot machines. I begged and pleaded with the dealer to help me get back to the official table but they ignored my pleas. I felt lost and hopeless and alone. These conversations never took place. It really was a dream.

In anticipation of my record attempt, the casino had mounted a large, red, digital clock over the table, which was also surrounded by posters trumpeting my GWR attempt. Spectators watched constantly, except in the wee hours. The clock counted the minutes and hours from zero to twenty-four, and after a full day it reset to zero, something that had already happened twice. In fact, it was when the clock reset after forty-eight hours that I completely abandoned all pretensions of making 100 hours and focused on simply surviving the last day. Even at that point, just two days into it, the end could not come soon enough. At nearly six in the morning on Sunday, with just over seven hours to go in my bid, the clock read in the neighborhood of seventeen hours, the time elapsed in the third day. It was these glowing red numbers that suddenly came into focus, like the display on a bedside clock radio, as I "awoke" from whatever dream state I had been in. My blurry eyes focused, the red digits got sharper and sharper until I could read them, and suddenly I was there, at the table, with cards in my hand, cards I could once again read, and I was fully focused. I began to play at close to my normal level, and much to the apparent surprise of my tablemates, began to win again. It was only later, after I had set the record, that my friends would fill in the missing hours for me. Here is what happened:

Shortly after I realized that I could no longer read the cards, JP whispered in my ear that I needed to start folding every hand. He had to remind me several times, but apparently I got the message, and began to fold automatically, like clockwork, after every deal. After all, I had no idea which cards I had. The game I was playing required a fifty-cent ante; they deal roughly thirty-five hands an hour, so I stood to lose about $17 an hour sitting there with this strategy, which seemed preferable to how much I might lose betting on cards I couldn't read. My strategy of playing aggressively at the outset, when I was lucid, had worked, and I was up a considerable amount of money from my many hours of play when I could still see, so the antes didn't matter. What is interesting, especially to JP, is that despite his instructions, two or three times each hour I would deviate from the folding strategy and suddenly play a hand. I cannot remember this, and it happened while I could still not read the cards; yet on each of these rare occasions I did in fact hold excellent cards and win, like some sort of idiot savant on autopilot, recognizing the great hands subconsciously, despite not being able to perceive the cards.

I also became increasingly irritable, distracted, and slow to respond, prompting the night-shift manager of the poker room, a woman who had been very supportive on the previous two nights and wished me nothing but success, to become somewhat concerned. At one point she came over and asked to speak to me. Again, I know this because she later told me, and Joe, Matt, and JP confirmed it, but I have no recollection. Nonetheless, I trust all these witnesses, who helped me reconstruct the ensuing conversation.

"HOW ARE YOU DOING?"

"OKAYIGUESS."

"DO YOU KNOW WHERE YOU ARE?"

"NO."

"WHAT IS YOUR NAME?"

"IDON'TKNOW."

My responses did little to curb her growing discomfort with my condition, and she threatened to pull the plug at the next designated "safety break," laying down a "shape up or ship out" ultimatum to my friends, who themselves were nearly at wit's end. It was James, the dealer, who came to the rescue. James, of whom I also have no recollection whatsoever, had emigrated from Haiti, where he had been an amateur boxer. He explained to my friends that my eyelids had swollen from staying open too long, and it was the swelling that was severely affecting my vision. He suggested a curative treatment of Visine, very strong iced coffee laced with as many sugars as could be dissolved in it, a good dunking of my head in ice water, cold compresses laid across my eyes, a cold wet towel wrapped around my neck, and more Visine.

At this point Joe and JP, both of whom happen to be attorneys, decided to consult my logbook, the notebook diary I was required to keep for Guinness purposes, detailing my hourly activities and safety breaks. The entries for this period are written in an increasingly maniacal and jagged hand that becomes almost indecipherable by four AM on day three, but amazingly, none of the seventy-two required hourly entries was missed. With just over eight hours remaining, I was due another fifteen-minute break very soon. Joe and JP and Matt organized a military-style operation that involved one running to the sundry shop for Visine, one to the hotel room for an ice bucket and towels, and along the way, someone acquired the ginormous iced coffee from the casino's Dunkin' Donuts. Once these items were assembled, they marched me out the nearest fire exit and into the predawn darkness, my first fresh breath of air in days. In went the eye drops, and then I undertook a

forced march back and forth in the parking lot, moving while guzzling the coffee. Then I sat down on a brick curb while they poured
ice water over my head, followed by the compresses over my eyes.
As the clock ticked down on my break, they wrapped the icy, wet
towel around the back of my neck, tucking the front ends into
my soaking, cold shirt collar, and marched me, like a blindfolded
prisoner, back to my seat at the poker table, where they removed
the compresses and applied the second dose of Visine. The results
of this makeshift triage were nothing short of amazing. The red
numerals on the clock came into focus, and just like that, I was
back in the game. The reason the other players had put up with my
boorish behavior was because poker players love playing with an
easy mark, or a drunk, and while they knew about the record attempt, they perceived me in this way, so their tolerance was driven
by selfishness rather than charity. They seemed less than enthusiastic when I returned in a wide-eyed state, and with the finish
line in sight and the circadian rhythms of daybreak helping me, I
proceeded to go on a winning tear through the remaining hours.
At this point, my biggest problem became hypothermia: the air-
conditioning in the casino was combining with my soaking wet
shirt to induce shivering. The suddenly ecstatic poker room manager retreated to her office and produced a fresh T-shirt for me, a
leftover yellow model printed with the logo of the previous year's
New England Poker Finals, now one of my favorite and most sto-
ried garments. The remaining hours raced by; finally, egged on by
public address announcements from the poker room managers and
the sudden entrance of photographers and videographers from various news outlets, a crowd gathered around the table for the record
countdown, watching in awe as I won the last three hands, closing
out in style with three tens to sweep in the final pot, seventy-two
hours and two minutes after I had begun. Approximately 2,300
hands after I had sat down, I had gotten into Guinness.

I still have the video of *ESPN SportsCenter* saved on my TiVo.
It was the second time my record breaking got me onto the sports
news show's Top 10 Plays of the Day, and I did even better than

with my golf record, finishing at number two, behind only the winner of the 2004 NBA Championship and ahead of Sir Richard Branson's own Guinness World Record set that same day—his crossing of the English Channel in the Aquaticar. The clip ESPN used was shot immediately after the event, after that last hand, when I stood from my chair and Kathy Raymond raised my hand. In the video, I am clearly not lucid, and look like a punch-drunk fighter who needs the referee to raise his glove in a salute to victory. Immediately after this, she led me to her office, where for forty-five increasingly disoriented minutes, I fielded questions from one broadcaster and reporter after another, while my friend Matt tried to get them to let me go to sleep. By the time I finished the interviews, I had suddenly become very hungry, and realized my last meal had been dinner about sixteen hours earlier. I insisted Matt join me for lunch before I went to bed, and against his better judgment he did. As soon as I ordered I passed out with my head on the restaurant table. He woke me and got me to my room, where I fulfilled a promise to call my wife and let her know I was done and okay. She was out walking the dog when I called, so I left a reassuring message and then instantly fell asleep, without even bothering to undress or pull back the covers. When I got home the next day, she laughingly insisted I listen to the message, which she had saved on the machine. It is stream of incoherent mumbling, with not one word discernible. "Blah, blah, blah." That must have been comforting. Fortunately, Matt had called her as well.

Once again, the media ate the story up, and the coverage made my golf record seem paltry in comparison. I was on network news affiliates across the country, in Associated Press stories picked up by hundreds of newspapers, and for a day I even did my part to displace the war in Iraq from the front page of the my local paper, the *Valley News*. I was in *Sports Illustrated*, though my Guinness World Record–holding colleague Lance Armstrong did edge me out for the cover with his sixth consecutive Tour de France victory. I was offered a spot in the next year's *World Poker Tour* Celebrity Invitational in Los Angeles. The Texas Snakeman would be proud of me.

After all the usual inquiries about the Guinness book and its records, the question I was asked most often by media and friends alike was "how did you do?" Despite the newfound popularity of Texas Hold 'em, the game that put the *World Poker Tour* on the map and made my attempt possible, and one I play well, I am even better at Seven Card Stud. It is also a much slower version of poker, and since I had to play with my own money, Hold 'em, with its rapid-fire hands, seemed like a bad idea. To further conserve cash, I chose the lowest stakes, $1–$5, less than I usually play for, because as a general rule, the lower the stakes, the lower the caliber of player, reducing my level of competition. My ample casino experience was that I could routinely beat the players in a low-stakes stud game. So my game plan, or best-case scenario, was to win enough in the first thirty hours so that I could coast on my winnings through the "dark times" I imagined would follow, when concentration would be difficult. I set a personal limit of losing no more than a thousand bucks—even a Guinness World Record has its price limit, especially when you already have one. Still, I made sure to bring my ATM card in case I changed my mind.

When I sat down at the table, I bought in for one hundred dollars in chips to start, keeping the rest of my bankroll, nine hundred more dollars—and my ATM card—in my wallet. I didn't need either. I won the third hand, about four minutes into my 72 hours, and was in the black from there on in. Despite the fact that for two hours I could not see the cards, and for many more hours I was faced with a situation summed up by military researcher C. DiGiovanni, M.D. in his comment "The more sleep-deprived that [the] brain is, the more likely any decision it makes will be bad, perhaps disastrously bad." All in all, I won fairly consistently throughout the whole endeavor. I walked away from the table with $373 in chips, a profit of $273, but that was just the tip of the iceberg. In casino tradition, I tipped the dealer after every winning hand, usually one to two dollars each time, all out of my winning chips, and I won about 400 hands, to the tune of $600 in tips. I also tipped the cocktail waitresses generously, since they were my lifeline to all my meals, promptly served and eaten at the table, along with the more than forty cups of coffee, sixty bottles of water, several iced teas, orange juices, and assorted other beverages I consumed. I estimated another $400 in such tips, bringing the winning total to well over a thousand bucks, which the stunned poker managers thought was remarkable for the meager stakes I was playing, with one-dollar bets, even for someone who had not gone crazy.

The most definitive statistic of my endeavor is seventeen hours, which was the length of time I slept, and slept like the dead, after retreating to my room at Foxwoods. I awoke the next morning feeling fine, as if it had never happened, then drove home and immediately went back to work. The lingering effects were less than those of jet lag from a long flight, and the following day I rode my bike sixty miles, getting reacquainted with the great outdoors. The hardest statistic for me to conjure up was the number of different people I played with, since they came and went from the table, staying for radically different lengths of time; my best guess is around seventy-five. These people, reflecting true diversity, are worthy of a book in themselves, with many characters (in the sense my mom uses the word to mean someone who is odd, and not in a good way). I silently nicknamed these playing partners with such suitably colorful titles as TiVo, Bad Ass Willie, and Mr. Clean. The latter was a menacingly huge bald-headed man doing a reasonable impersonation of the Terminator, complete with black motorcycle jacket, boots, and wraparound mirrored sunglasses. If Mr. Clean was one end of the spectrum, the fellow who explained the cookbook he is writing to me in excruciating detail was the other. Poker, just like *Guinness World Records*, takes all kinds.

When I broke the record for greatest distance traveled between two rounds of golf played in the same day, I figured out a whole new methodology, improving on the previous effort by inventing the notion of crossing the international dateline. I thought it an innovative solution to an existing problem, one worthy of Guinness recordom. But the Australian who usurped my record simply lucked into the launch of a longer flight on the same route from

Sydney to North America after I had done all the legwork and research for him, and his raising of the bar struck me as exceptionally uncreative. In any case, that experience led me to try to set a record that might stand, and stand it has. There was some press more than a year ago about a professional poker player going for the record in Vegas, but that never happened. As of this writing, I checked the Guinness World Records website and my record, though no longer in the book, still stands, three years later. The explanation is simple, despite the fact that it got far more media attention than the vast majority of records get: not everyone can play poker for seventy-two hours straight. In fact, very few people can, and I suspect the record may be mine for quite awhile. If someone does break it, unlike with golf, they will earn my respect. I certainly wouldn't try. I feel lucky to have survived it unscathed. I might have another go at long-distance golf down the road, but when people ask me about poker, I always instantly reply "never again." And this time I mean it.

THE CLAIM FORM I FILED WITH GUINNESS AFTER MY POKER ATTEMPT

Guinness Record Attempt:
Longest Casino Poker Session

CLAIM ID: 64041
Gentlemen/Ladies:

   This note is intended to clarify my record attempt and the supporting materials herein.
   On Thursday, June 10th, 2004 at 1:20 PM Eastern Standard Time, I began playing poker in the Foxwoods Resort & Casino in Ledyard, Connecticut. I continued playing continuously, at the same table, until 1:22 PM on Sunday, June 13th, 72 hours and 2 minutes later. I did this under the guidelines presented

by Guinness, with just my 15-minute break every eight hours, and under the rules and guidelines for the Foxwoods casino poker room as stipulated in my proposal.

Enclosed is my personal log, including the prior note from physician and witness thereof.

Also enclosed are witness forms I drew up to cover the various points required in the marathon guidelines. A poker room supervisor who was present during his or her shift filled one of these out every four hours as required, testifying that I was present and playing continuously, as well as verifying the presence of required medical personnel. Each is also signed by two additional witnesses. The on-duty nurses and Emergency Medical Technicians (EMTs) employed by the casino also signed an additional log verifying their presence.

The best additional contact for any other questions or verification would be Kathy Raymond, poker room manager for Foxwoods, who was present at the beginning, end and much of the middle, and directly supervised the other shift managers present. Her information is:

Kathy Raymond
Director of Poker Operations
Foxwoods Resort Casino

Very truly yours,
Larry Olmsted

7

The Cheese Does Not Stand Alone: Giant Food and Guinness

[T]he whale would by all hands be considered a noble dish, were there not so much of him; but when you come to sit down before a meat-pie nearly one hundred feet long, it takes away your appetite.

—HERMAN MELVILLE, *MOBY DICK*

I just thought a ton was a nice round number, so I said, "okay let's do a ton of fondue." It was a new record and they said yes.

—CHEF TERRANCE BRENNAN

Food and drink records have been a mainstay of the Guinness book since the very first edition in 1955, when such accomplished consumers as American Philip Yazdik and Spaniard Dionsio Sanchez entered its pages, for eating seventy-seven hamburgers in one sitting and drinking forty pints of wine in under an hour, respectively. Fittingly, these are catalogued under the section titled "Human Achievements; Endurance and Endeavor," alongside Sir Edmund Hillary's conquest of the highest peak on earth and Commodore Peary's historic journey to the North Pole. Gastronomic records have remained in the book ever since, eventually growing in scope to encompass the eating of everything from mince pies to bicycles and airplanes. But another entire category of food records is a recent and even more significant part of *Guinness World Records* history. Operating under its long-standing premise that bigger is better and biggest is best, the book has eagerly embraced "big food" records of every imaginable sort. Just as the athletic set came to realize that getting into Guinness can be most easily accomplished by finding new items to throw, the culinary minded have turned to finding new foodstuffs to grow.

Giant food records began to appear in the book fairly early on, but have become a competitive and very broad niche for record holders only in the past twenty years. The first two decades of the book saw a handful of enormous cuisine entries for the English and American staples, such as biggest pizza, ice cream sundae, hamburger, and meat pie. Today there are dozens and dozens of increasingly specialized, international, and esoteric giant food records. By 1984 big food had come into its own as a bona fide *GWR* craze: that edition includes a whole camel as the largest standard dish served at a meal, along with the largest banana split, BBQ, cake, Easter egg, haggis, bread, omelet, pastry, mashed potatoes, lollipop, salami, Yorkshire pudding, and curiously, bowl of strawberries, the sole uncooked or unprocessed entry. The most significant change was in the realm of pies, which soon became giant food's equivalent of throwing things; limited only by the imagination, the erstwhile apple pie was joined by cherry pie, meat pie, quince pie, and even pizza pie.

While many seemingly implausible records are listed in the book with no explanation or details at all, giant food records tend to have abridged recipes, listing enormous quantities of the key ingredients, though rarely the complete list. *Guinness Time,* the in-house company newsletter of Guinness PLC (the same edition that carried the obituary of book founder Sir Hugh Beaver in 1967), contained one of the more impressive early giant food records. At the 1962 Seattle Worlds Fair, a six-sided birthday cake was baked, which weighed 25,000 pounds, stood 23 inches high and measured some 60 feet around. The recipe called for 18,000 eggs; 10,500 pounds of flour; 4,000 pounds of sugar; 7,000 pounds of raisins; 2,200 pounds of pecans, and 100 pounds of salt (see vol. 20, no. 2, Spring 1967). While twelve-ton cakes were still unusual in 1962, by the special millennium edition of 2000, with its futuristic, shiny, silver cover, big food had become such an accepted part of the *Guinness World Records* that for the first time an entire chapter appeared titled just that, "Big Food." Whether your taste runs to a one-ton gyro or a single, continuous sausage more than twenty-eight miles long, you can find it there. Notable entries in the new chapter include the biggest curry (2.65 tons), longest sushi roll (three-quarters of a mile), biggest onion bhaji (over six pounds), and tallest chocolate model, appropriately one of a life-size dinosaur.

In a sense, giant food records are perfect for Guinness. Hard to even imagine, that twenty-eight-mile-long sausage is the gastronomic equivalent of Robert Pershing Wadlow, the tallest human being. Enormous foodstuffs also neatly fit—and manage to improve upon—Ben Sherwood's four-point analysis of what makes records so attractive to the media. Certainly giant foods qualify as -ests, and as Sherwood noted, no pun intended, the "media feasts on superlatives." They are also highly visual, perfect for television, and easily captured in a single photo for a magazine or newspaper. Consider the fact that television's *Food Network Challenge* found so much ongoing fodder in the form of record-setting foods that they devoted a special miniseries to it, *Guinness World Record Breakers Week*. Sherwood further posits that superlatives are enhanced when they are in categories that are entertaining, curious, or of freak value, which cakes the size of playing fields certainly are. Giant food record attempts are often undertaken in the name of charity, another leg of Sherwood's chair. There are notable exceptions, however, such as Mama Lena's Pizza House outside of Pittsburgh, which according to the Associated Press took a decidedly more pragmatic, for-profit approach to *Guinness World Records* big-food history when it created "the largest pizza for sale in the world." The Big One is a menu fixture, and for $99 Mama Lena's will make one for any customer. It measures 4.5' x 3', weighs over fifty pounds, and is cut into 150 slices for serving.

Sherwood concludes that much of the appeal of Guinness Record holders is the fact that they can be "folks like you and me." In this case it is the food itself that is "folks": who in America does not see apple pie as the wholesome, ordinary, classless foodstuff that deserves to be elevated to gigantic status? What Scottish heart would not glow at the record-breaking attempt by his good friend the haggis? There is a reason these are called "comfort foods," and in giant food endeavors, they take the place of the quirky guy on your block pogo sticking or spinning a yo-yo on his front porch.

Giant food goes beyond Sherwood's criteria and has two more important dynamics that set it apart and help make it an increasingly popular sector among both readers and record setters. In many cases these records become matters of national or cultural pride, making them more emotionally important than their humanistic counterparts. For instance, sausage records are fought over by various cultures with sausage-making histories, while new entries often include national dishes, such as a unique form of pastry widely consumed in a sole South American country. While an Australian wresting an individual record in plate spinning or juggling away from an Italian might not raise many eyebrows, it is hard to imagine Italians not becoming irritated when the Aussies stole the world's biggest risotto title away from the dish's homeland in 2004, and did so in convincingly emphatic fashion.

More than in any other category, giant food has taken on a corporate component. Who but mammoth chocolate conglomerate Hershey Foods is in the best position to manufacture the world's largest Hershey's Kiss? One could logically assume that even if a competitor tried to use its own chocolate factory, trademarks alone would prevent anyone but Hershey from setting this record, which they did—more than once. Likewise, companies like Coca-

Cola and Snapple have gotten into the *Guinness World Records* big food game, always for promotional value, bringing deep pockets and enormous production capabilities to the table, as it were. In fact, giant food records today are rarely set by individuals (as most other types of human records are) and instead are almost always held by a food company, restaurant, hotel, charity, or country with something to prove and something to sell. The first thing one realizes when pondering some of these records is that the cakes, pizzas, or bowls of strawberries exceed the scope of any oven, pan, or bowl any regular person might have in the kitchen. It is easy to see why someone contemplating the world's largest ice cream cake might look into the existing record and switch gears, deciding that the record of thirty hours of brick carrying is, in fact, more vulnerable. Fittingly, the world's largest ice cream cake was made in the world's largest country, when chefs in Beijing rolled out an eight-ton monstrosity the size of a small swimming pool, standing more than 3' high and measuring 15'8" x 9'10" containing nearly 500 cubic feet of frozen desert. Whose freezer is that going in? Giant food records more often than not require the custom fabrication of everything from pots to burners, not to mention enormous quantities of ingredients, the costs of which can easily run into the thousands, or tens of thousands, of dollars.

Where, for instance, is the average Scottish home cook who decides to assault the haggis record going to lay her hands on more than eighty ox stomachs? To date, the largest haggis on record was assembled by a team of chefs at the Glasgow Hilton Hotel on May 24, 1993. According to the *Glasgow Herald*, it required those eighty such stomachs and weighed in at 667 pounds. When the book calls these records "Big Food," they really mean it. In taking on Italy's largest risotto record, which stood at 440 kilograms (just under 1,000 lbs.), the Australians left no room for doubt. More than 3,000 pounds of Arborio rice went into the pot, along with 660 pounds of cheese, nearly a ton of peas, over 1,100 gallons of vegetable stock, 20-plus gallons of olive oil, almost 50 pounds of crushed garlic, 1,000 pounds of diced onion and celery, and more than 700 pounds of butter (unsalted). The final touch was about 3 pounds of saffron, notable in its own right in the 1972 *Guinness World Records* as the most expensive spice. The result, which stood above not only Italy's risotto but every other rice-based dish on earth, a double record setter, clocked in at a massive 16,522 pounds—more than sixteen times the previous record—and more than three 2008 Chevrolet Suburban SUVs stacked together. The record-setting attempt, done on Sydney's harborfront Circular Quay on November 26, 2004, was organized by the Australian Rice Industry to raise money to combat world hunger. About 4,000 spectators sampled the dish—not even putting a dent in it—in exchange for a donation to Care Australia. The ingredients were donated by food manufacturers and suppliers, and the attempt required a custom-made pan with a seventy-foot circumference.

"At first, it sounds like a simple exercise: make a bowl of soup to beat the current record—a 5,045-litre [1,332-gallon] goulash from Romania. But contemplating just the cooking vessel is a task in itself—where does one find a cooking pot and stove sufficiently large to house enough soup to fill around seventy bath tubs? Let alone the problem of finding the ingredients for the chosen recipe, a chili-beef soup called caldillo," wrote current *Guinness World Records* editor Craig Glenday in his July 2007 online blog about traveling to witness record events, in which he visited the city of Durango, Mexico, to witness soup history in the making.

> The project pulled together the resources of the entire region. A month was spent planning and building the bowl—a UFO-like steel contraption that served as both container and gas cooker; local farmers provided the produce; restaurants put aside their competitive grudges and offered up their chefs; countless volunteers acted as security, servers and cleaners; and local schools put on a day-long variety show. In the end, everyone pulled it off and created one enormous caldillo measuring 5,350 litres [1,413 gallons]. The municipal president Jorge Herrera Del-

gado joined me in taking the first sip—after the thumbs-up from the local health authority advisor on hand to oversee proceedings, of course—and received the official Guinness World Records certificate in front of a queue of thousands desperate to sample the world-beating dish.

While the book has shown a remarkable cultural diversity in its giant foods, from the huge bowl of caldillo to the Indian onion bhaji, the English meat pie, and all-American dishes like apple pie and hot dogs, one giant food that gets little respect is the burrito. That's what the staff of a Taco Bell restaurant in Tennessee found after making a 444-foot-long version that David Boehm (then publisher of the American edition, which included some homegrown records separate from the English version of the book) turned down. Boehm's motive was apparently the lack of universal appeal, something pizza has but burritos don't, at least they didn't in 1988. "We get a call every week for another burrito record," Mr. Boehm said from his New York office. "People in California think burritos are sold everywhere. In New York people haven't heard about burritos." Colossal culinary constructors take note: the book is as fickle and unpredictable about Big Food as any of its other record categories.

One thing that makes these records extra difficult is the rule that the big food products actually be edible. *Guinness World Records* officials sometimes even require record breakers to be certified as such by health inspectors. Of course, they don't have to be edible by humans, at least not if the giant food in question is aimed at dogs. That was the case in 2007 when the Lions Club in Lunenburg, Massachusetts, made the world's largest dog biscuit, at 379 pounds. It was baked using a propane grave thawer on loan from the local cemetery, and removed from the makeshift oven with a forklift (interestingly, the previous dog biscuit record, at just 159 pounds, while small by giant food standards, was held by a true giant, Microsoft Corporation). The biscuit still had to be canine edible under Guinness rules, and participants in the charity event fed pieces to their dogs. Because of such rules, even accomplished chefs can be surprised by the work that goes into a world-record dish. Chef Terrance Brennan is the owner of two highly regarded New York City restaurants, Picholine, and Artisanal Bistro and Wine Bar, both of which have an emphasis on fine cheeses. "At my restaurant Artisanal, we're known for fondue, and about two years ago I thought, 'wouldn't it be great to make the world's largest fondue?' Last year I was too busy with other stuff, so this year (2006) I said 'this is the year we're going to do it.' When you think of 'world record,' the Guinness word comes to mind. I had read the book as a kid, and subconsciously, when you think of records you think of the book. If you are going to set a record, it's got to be the Guinness World Record."

When Brennan started looking into it, the project immediately became more difficult than he had imagined, despite the fact that there was no existing record for fondue, making it easier, at least on paper. True to form, Brennan imagined his undertaking as a charity fundraiser, but the first obstacle was the city's health laws. "I wanted to do it initially in Central Park and have people come pay $2 a portion or something, but it was hard," due to regulations about selling food. Brennan is a frequent celebrity chef guest on the *Today Show*, and his contacts at the network soon got interested in his plans. "Then NBC got a hold of it and wanted an exclusive, and I thought it was a good partnership. They already had a relationship with the *Guinness Book of World Records*, so as long as I could make it a benefit rather than just about the record, NBC was on board." Brennan continued, "I filled out the paperwork, but NBC had the contacts and had done stuff with Guinness before, and they handled everything. I just thought a ton was a nice round number, so I said, 'okay let's do a ton of fondue.' It was a new record and they said yes."

Brennan started testing adaptations of his fondue recipe for much larger quantities, because melting cheese is a fickle science and he was worried, "because at some point is it going to seize. Will it stay smooth? So we figured out how much water we needed

and how to make a slurry to melt the cheese so it stayed smooth."
But the biggest challenge was neither the recipe nor the ingredients,
all of which were donated, but rather a fondue pot big enough for
a recipe exceeding 2,000 pounds. "I called a good friend who has
a food company outside of New Orleans who could help and he
thought this was great. He found me a 200-year-old cast iron vessel
for making sugar, from an old sugarcane plantation. First he had to
sandblast it and clean it up, but then it turned out to have a crack
in it, so he had to find another one like it and start over. Then he
had his team build a metal frame around it that would hold it over
six propane burners, which we had to fabricate. We filled it with
water to measure it and the vessel held 500 gallons. It was eight feet
across and nearly a yard deep and it weighed 4,000 pounds, empty.
We just did our fondue three-quarters of the way up, so if anyone
breaks the record we can come back and top it."

People who witness Ashrita Furman walking loops around the
high school track he trains on near his house, sometimes through
the night, balancing things on his head or carrying a brick or doing
forward rolls, think he is crazy. But what about scouring the South
for two huge antique pots that need to be sandblasted and required a
custom stove, all for a Guinness-sized fondue? Getting the pot finished was only half the challenge. It still needed to be delivered and
set up outside the studio of the *Today Show* at Rockefeller Center.
The two-ton pot, and all its associated burners, framework, and
gas had to be loaded onto a truck and driven from New Orleans to
New York; to make matters even more complicated, the cargo was
classified as hazardous because of its flammable potential. "With
all the security now, since 9/11, they were driving up from Louisiana with these six huge propane tanks. We had told them that they
had to take it over the top level of the George Washington Bridge,
because we had done all the research and found that was the only
way to legally get it into Manhattan, but apparently that commu-
nication never got to the truck driver. So they get to the Holland
Tunnel and the police were really pissed off and they almost got
arrested. They told them 'if you can turn around without backing

up we won't arrest you,' and turned them away. Then they tried the Midtown Tunnel, and they were nicer but still got turned away. They ended up getting through the Lincoln Tunnel."

The fondue attempt also required a special permit from the New York City Fire Department, which had to have a fire truck on hand. With everything apparently in order for the attempt, Brennan was stunned when the *Today Show* called him the day before his attempt to cancel, because a producer was out sick.

We had a regular fondue segment with some recipes planned as well as the record, so they probably just didn't get the gist of it, that we were going for this Guinness record, that we had driven this big vessel up for two days from Louisiana, that someone from Guinness was going to be there, that City Harvest was there to distribute the food to homeless shelters, that the fire department was all lined up, and that we had gotten a permit and they had to have a fire truck there. I said "this has just got to work out, we can't cancel, we had three months of planning." So I called the executive producer I knew and then it was on again. Then it got cancelled again because the fire permit had already been cancelled and they said we couldn't get another one in time. We called everyone we knew who was connected and ended up getting the fire department on board again at the eleventh hour. We got there at 5 AM, got it cranked up, and the actual cooking time was probably about three hours. We gave away all the cheese to City Harvest. We pumped it back out of the kettle into five-gallon white plastic tubs and their chefs took them around to shelters in all five boroughs and used it to make macaroni and cheese, soups, pasta dishes, various things. Our donated fondue fed 5,000 people.

Guinness World Records sent a spokeswoman to the event, and as *Today Show* talent sampled the fondue, which Brennan stirred with three-foot-long French baguettes, she confirmed the new record for the cameras and handed over a preprinted certificate, another perk of being as well-connected as the *Today Show* (typical record breakers have to wait weeks or months for formal approval and their copy by snail mail). Speaking to the television audience, she said with flair, "On behalf of Guinness World Records we'd like to present this record," and handed the chef his certificate. While Brennan was very happy with the effort and its outcome, he quickly conceded that he has no additional giant food records in sight. As with the majority of Guinness undertakings, food or no food, the reality proves much more difficult than the illusion. For the record, his fondue recipe was:

1,900 pounds Gruyère cheese
105 gallons white wine
2 ½ gallons lemon juice
5 gallons garlic juice
21 pounds kosher salt
44 ½ pounds corn starch
½ pound nutmeg
¾ pound black pepper

Even with donated cheese, chefs like Brennan have to dig deep, and often into their own pockets, to fund giant food records, which may explain the recent spate of attempts by some of the largest and wealthiest companies in the food and drink industry, which are much better positioned to pull off these promotional records. This trend began a decade ago when Coca-Cola set the Guinness World Record for the largest ice cream float, and to no one's surprise, decided to forego the traditional root beer for one of the company's own cola products. To mark the relaunch of its Vanilla Coke last year, Coca-Cola went back to the well, breaking its own record, even as Guinness spokesman Derek Musso told the Associated Press that he was not aware of any attempts by anyone else to top the former float record in the intervening nine-plus years.

Musso confirmed that the new 3,000-gallon float, made of Vanilla Coke and ice cream, weighing ten tons, had set the new world record. Once again proving that most giant food records are like stuntman-aided car commercials and bear the caveat "don't try this at home," Coca-Cola dispatched a tanker from its syrup plant, and then pumped the flat syrup into a custom-made fifteen-foot-high soda glass, complete with a device that produced carbon dioxide and carbonated the beverage in the glass. Workers then dropped in buckets full of ice cream by hand. Instead of serving the several hundred witnesses, the ten-ton drink was tossed in the garbage while Coca-Cola gave out smaller ice cream float samples from a kiosk, presumably for health code reasons.

Just as Jackie "the Texas Snakeman" Bibby keeps his record-breaking attempts for holding live rattlesnakes in his mouth well clear of his maximum human potential so that he can easily continue to rebreak his own record as needed, companies like Coca-Cola and Hershey have found that they can carve out their own niches by repeatedly making increasingly bigger versions of the same things. Just four years after Hershey Foods Corp. fashioned the world's "Largest Chocolate Candy," they quintupled the size of their effort. The 2003 record breaker was a Hershey's Rich Dark Kiss standing just over six feet tall and weighing 6,759 pounds. Aided by pastry chefs from the French Culinary Institute, Hershey scientists and engineers built a pyramid of ten-pound chocolate blocks, stuck together with liquefied molten chocolate, and after cooling, this mass was sculpted into the traditional shape of a Hershey's Kiss, albeit almost 700,000 times its normal size. The Kiss was put on display at Chocolate World, a popular attraction *cum* museum in Hershey, Pennsylvania. July 7, 2007, was the 100th birthday of the iconic Kiss, and to celebrate, Hershey's team once again broke out the bulk chocolate, and this time crafted a twelve-foot Kiss, tipping the scales at 30,540 pounds, more than fifteen tons, and earning the similar but slightly different *Guinness World Records* title of "World's Largest Piece of Chocolate." The life-size chocolate dinosaur couldn't have been happy about having his record driven to extinction.

Not all candy records are as static as the giant Kiss, which can be kept in a museum virtually indefinitely. Mentos mints, famous for their characteristic of setting off bubbling geysers when dropped into bottles of soda, orchestrated a brief but creative bit of performance art when Eepybird Perfetti Van Melle, USA, the mints' Kentucky-based manufacturer, enlisted fans in Cincinnati to help set an impressive new record. To celebrate the launch of its new "Mentos Geyser Loading Tube," a tube-shaped candy packaging designed to facilitate such tricks by flawlessly dropping several Mentos into soda bottles simultaneously, the company got 504 people to do just that, all at the same time, resulting in a dancing waters–style fountain show and earning the first-ever *Guinness World Records* title of "Most Mentos and Soda Fountains." As Pete Healy, the company's vice president of marketing told *Candy Industry* magazine, "We're thrilled that millions of people have enjoyed making Mentos Geysers, and posting and watching Mentos Geyser videos online. The new Mentos Geyser loading tube packages are our way of thanking Mentos fans and helping them create even cooler and more elaborate Mentos Geysers." He was not kidding. On the video of the event, which can be viewed on the company's website, along with several other geyser experiments (www.eepybird.com, Guinness World Record Event), the multiple Mentos dropped from the tubes into two-liter bottles of Diet Coke shoot sugary geysers upward of twenty feet into the air. What is notable about the Mentos record is that since it is multiple food and not true giant food, it appears vulnerable to the average person. Predictably, one of the thousands of Guinness fanatics who scour the book looking for records to break quickly seized on mass geysering. Almost immediately some intrepid folks in Texas quickly put together their own Mentos-and-soda team and broke the company's record with 791 fountains. Not to be so easily outdone, Eepybird's Dutch parent company took matters into their own hands, and in Castle Square of Breda, Holland, launched 851 Mentos-and-Diet Coke-powered geysers to retake the world record. Emphasizing how Guinness-mania can take off, the original record setting and the two record-breaking spin-offs all occurred within a period of just five months. By the time you read this, I suspect competitive Mentos geysering will no longer be measured in the three digits.

Guinness World Records Day, an annual festival of record set-ting and breaking organized by the book's marketing folks and now in its third year, is a perfect giant food venue. Once planned, these feats usually can be staged at any time and are done more for publicity than anything else—something the roving media cover-ing the international record-smashing spree can provide. The orig-inal Guinness World Records Day in 2005 kicked off with giant food as one of its very first official deeds as shoppers and staffers at the main Birmingham branch of venerable English supermar-ket, Selfridges, assembled the world's tallest free-standing tower of doughnuts. The tower should not be confused with the record for the biggest single doughnut, sixteen feet in diameter and weighing a ton and a half. The event also took brand promotion a step fur-ther by teaming the well-known retailer up with doughnut manu-facturer Krispy Kreme, who supplied the hardware for the tower in the form of 2,544 doughnuts.

Not every giant food attempt ends as successfully as the dough-nut tower or enormous ice cream float, even when sponsored and concocted by a deep-pocketed international food producer. Such was the case when beverage manufacturer Snapple visited New York City in an attempt to break the record for "World's Largest Ice Pop," and instead became the victim of the world's largest ice pop meltdown. As *PR Week*, a trade publication for the public rela-tions industry, wryly noted, "In retrospect, 'Returning the Favor' might not have been the best tagline for the Snapple PR stunt that turned into a kiwi-strawberry tidal wave in New York City last week. An attempt by the soft-drink company to break the Guin-ness World Record for the 'World's Largest Ice Pop,' turned into a fiasco when the 35,000-pound ice pop melted on a hot summer day, sending bystanders scurrying to escape the world's largest pool of all-natural beverage. . . . The spectacular failure of the ice pop generated hundreds of news stories across America, but most pointed to the ineptitude of the idea's execution rather than the quality of Snapple's new ice pops." To rub salt on Snapple's wounds, the *New York Post* reported that several minor injuries were caused by the juice flood, and attorney Michael Lasky told *PR Week* "that Snapple might have neglected to 'plan protectively' to keep itself from legal liability in the case." In one of the few cases of anyone being shy about *Guinness World Records* publicity, good or bad, representatives from Snapple and its public relations firm did not return the magazine's calls.

The range of recipes suitable for supersizing seems limited only by the imagination, but some themes have caught on more than others. There are foods, there are giant foods, and then there are giant sausages, perhaps the most hotly fought subcategory of enormous edibles in the *Guinness World Records* book. When a single unbroken sausage measuring an unimaginable twenty-eight miles in length—longer than the marathon that has been the basis for so many colorful Guinness World Records over the years—was entered in the debut Big Foods chapter in 2000, who could have dreamed it wouldn't last? Apparently the natives of Melon, a town in Spain's Galicia region, famous for its spicy chorizo sausage, who did not know about the feat when they cooked a giant chorizo measuring 360 feet long and tried to enter it in the book. While a sausage longer than a football field sounds impressive at first glance, it is strictly minor league by *Guinness World Records* standards, especially given that the 2000 standard was shattered in the same year the book came out, when one J. J. Tranfield of Sheffield, England, broke the record, originally set in Canada, with his thirty-six-mile-long sausage. Upon finding out that Melon had fallen more than thirty-five miles short of world record status, its mayor, Alberto Pardellas, got on the phone with the Guinness researchers in London and may have talked his way into the book. The *Times* reported that "The local mayor thinks he's persuaded Guinness to create a specialist chorizo category, thus allowing his town's comparatively puny product its chance of glory. He explained that the attempt was 'to publicize our town's main industry, which is sausage-making.'" While such an attempt to snatch victory from the jaws of defeat sounds a bit contrived, Mayor Pardellas was simply relying on precedent, as the 2000 edition did list lengths and weights for several sausage subcategories, and his town's chorizo would fall squarely between the world's largest salami (68') and longest bratwurst (over a mile). Amazingly, another sausage subcategory, a brand new record for Longest Hot Dog, appears in the 2008 edition immediately adjacent to an explanatory graphic box titled "Claims We Don't Want to See," which in addition to the understandable "Fastest Surgery" and "Fattest Cat" lists "Longest French Fry" and "Largest Potato Chip"—with the explanation that "there's no merit in these claims so thanks but NO!" This bewildering logic is a clear case of *Guinness World Records* sending mixed messages, leaving the reader to ponder why bratwurst, hot dogs, salami—or for that matter onion bhaji—is inherently more worthwhile than various forms of fried potatoes. It does show that there is still nothing quite as appealing to the editors as sausage, yet while the book has proven extremely flexible in its larger-than-life sausage records, don't expect to see the largest sausage house or sausage dam or other architectural sausage undertakings anytime soon. "We also disappointed the Hungarian village with the tradition of making a wall from sausages," *Guinness World Records* editor Craig Glenday, the same official who anointed the world's largest soup in Mexico, told the *London Telegraph*. "It is possibly the biggest wall made of sausages in the world, but we have to draw the line somewhere."

8

Records Go Global

Like I was in Malaysia last year, and they are totally into records, it's just incredible. I was a celebrity in Malaysia and I didn't even know until I got there.

—ASHRITA FURMAN, HOLDER OF THE MOST GUINNESS WORLD RECORDS

Is there a record for the nation with too much free time? Canadians rocked the book this year, shattering more than 100 world records.

—*TIME* MAGAZINE, 2006

No country takes the setting and breaking of world records more seriously than tiny Singapore—at least by some accounts. No less of an authority than Ashrita Furman himself describes the place as a hotbed of all things record breaking. In addition, Singapore has its own record book and record-setting club to augment Guinness. But then, so does India, where record attempts are regularly front page news. India has also proven very fertile ground for new Guinness World Records museums, and its residents overwhelm the book's London office with record-related correspondence. The arguments for India as record central are strong, but so are those for Australia, though statistics Down Under may be skewed by a handful of especially obsessed serial record setters. China is bursting onto the scene at what may be a *record* record pace, and in Malaysia Ashrita is a pop star. It seems that Guinness record mania is more prevalent in the Pacific Rim, unless you count Canada, which has an exceptionally high per capita record tally and buys more copies of the book per person than anyplace else. The United States still dominates record setting, and England and Germany are in the top five. Despite the natural competitiveness the book has inspired, it may be impossible to pick a national winner: Guinnessitis has gone global, and about the only thing everyone can agree on is that the leader of the craze is *not* record-deprived Chile.

It took the first edition of the *Guinness Book of Records* just a few months to hit the best-seller list and less than two years to emigrate to the United States, now its largest market. Within a decade there were editions being published in French, German, Norwegian, Spanish, Japanese, Finnish, Danish, Swedish, Czech, and Dutch. The book's universal appeal has never ebbed, and since its inception more than half a century ago, it has been translated into thirty-seven languages and spawned television shows, museums, and a legacy of global record breaking that transcends all cultural barriers. All of this success with so many radically different readers proves that the book's allure is not due primarily to pub culture or English traditions but to its very human appeal. The world's tallest man is still a man, whether it's Robert Wadlow or the various living record holders of that title, be they Mongolian or Ukrainian, as the last two have been. The human element shines through to all people—and so do the fifteen minutes of fame and Guinnessport fascination of the book. These just seem to appeal to people in some places more than in others.

Early on, the McWhirters saw a markedly more passionate response to the getting-into-Guinness phenomenon in the United States than on their home turf. They attributed this to America's fascination with exploring and taming frontiers. But while the book still sells more copies and generates more records in the United States, it is more beloved, and in some cases worshiped, in other countries and cultures. In pure world record bulk, the United States is followed by Britain, Australia, and Germany, but devotion to the book seems to be greatest in the Pacific Rim and Canada. The privately held company is as guarded about its finances as its record database, and depending whom you listen to, claims for the highest numbers of record holders per capita cite various nations including Canada and Singapore, while many record pundits believe India is the hottest of all Guinness hotbeds. These nations are certainly extreme examples of Guinnessitis by any measures, and they are not alone.

"In my research I came across articles about India's cult-like obsession with records," recalls Ben Sherwood, who did exhaustive research for his novel *The Man Who Ate the 747.* "I think they have the greatest number of record holders, even if it's not per capita, and the people who hold the records are revered in cult-like status. They sell a tremendous number of books there." Actually, India is only tenth on the list of most records by a nation, but its followers make up for this with fervent dedication. In the 1990s, record mania in India grew so much that one out of five pieces of mail received at the company's London headquarters came from there. Ashrita Furman recalled reading "in India about how Guinness World Records there are like Olympic medals," and recounted the story of the Indian who sought to obtain widespread respect by breaking his orange-pushing record. Certainly India has produced some of the most bizarre attempts at Guinness immortality, even by the book's lofty standards of bizarre, pushing the limits so often as to constantly have records declined. Examples include the doctor's teenage son who tried to get into the book as the youngest surgeon, a four-year-old boy who tried to run a forty-three-mile marathon (he was stopped by doctors and his coach was jailed), and a seventeen-month-old toddler who ate fifty Bhut Jolokia peppers, which are recognized by Guinness and the rest of the world as the hottest on earth, in under four hours.

These attempts are less safe, but hardly less unusual, than many
Indian efforts that did make the book. "India is a land obsessed
with superlatives, especially the kind that get you into the *Guinness World Records* book," writes the Associated Press's regional
reporter Sam Dolnick. "Here, a Guinness record is the stuff of
national headlines." Dolnick cites successful examples of Indians
achieving record status including Radhakant Bajpai, who grew
ear hair more than five inches long; Vadivelu Karunakaren, who
quite literally followed in Ashrita Furman's footsteps by skipping
ten miles in under an hour; and Arvind Morarbhai Pandya, who
took the timeless Guinness tradition of going backward to new
heights by running 940 miles backward in just over twenty-six
days. Dolnick points out that records aren't just personal in India
but matters of civic pride, and as a result are the frequent subject of
headlines of major newspapers. He reports that a leading paper, the
Hindustan Times, ran more than fifty stories on Guinness World
Records in one year, with bold headlines such as UTTAR PRADESH
BOY CAN WRITE ON MUSTARD SEEDS! and ORISSA MAN CLAIMS A
RECORD FOR CRACKING OPEN 72 COCONUTS BY ELBOW! Not to be
outdone, another important daily, the *Times of India*, which Dol-
nick says covers Guinness bids like political campaigns, bannered,
MAN LOOKS TO SET WORLD RECORD PULLING VEHICLES WITH
MUSTACHE.

Dolnick attributes India's records passion to a gamut of reasons,
ranging from its true national superlatives (largest democracy,
largest youth population) to its sudden wealth and opportunity
against a background of strict cultural hierarchy and history of a
caste system. He even posits that records may be a bid for Western
approval and recognition of the nation's superpower-to-be status.
In this environment, the records give people who are neither part
of the newly minted millionaire generation nor born into upper
classes a chance to achieve social respect. "Persons who have no
money wish to do something in their lives, so the poor people try
to break records by their strength or their will," said Guinness
Rishi, sixty-six years old, whose business card lists nineteen re-

cords (the vast majority not or not yet acknowledged by Guinness) and who hires himself out as a record-setting consultant. Because of his feats, which include drinking a bottle of ketchup in thirty-nine seconds, he believes that "People consider me an extraordinary person, not an ordinary person." The obvious proof of his love of the book is that Rishi changed his first name from Har Parkash to Guinness, shortly after participating as a member of a team that kept a motor scooter in motion for a world record 1,001 hours, his sole official record. Lack of authentic certificates has not stopped his political career: Rishi has served as the president of the Guinness World Record Holder Club of India.

Guinness Rishi, with his dozen-plus unrecognized records, and all the would-be child surgeons, marathoners, and chili eaters, demonstrate the Indian propensity to forge ahead with record attempts without regard for the book's approval, much more so than in other countries. As Guinness World Records spokeswoman Amarilis Espinoza told the Associated Press, due to India's incredible record-setting determination, "they just go ahead and do it," whereas other would-be record setters usually ask first, partially explaining the plethora of seemingly unsafe ideas. This shoot-first, ask-questions-later approach to record breaking has also led India to pioneer an unusual niche in record-breaking lore—that of litigation against the venerable book. "The fascination with records there is unbelievable, and they are really into it, so much so that they are litigious about it. If you don't pay attention and at least give their records consideration, you will hear from the Indian courts. There was this thing a few years ago where an Indian guy broke a record that had been retired and he went to court to reopen the record. Retiring a record is not unusual for Guinness World Records, but getting sued over it is very unusual," said Robert "Bob" Masterson, the president of Ripley's Entertainment. The company's most famous product, the regularly updated *Ripley's Believe It or Not* book, is viewed by Guinness and the publishing industry as one of the record book's largest and most direct competitors, if not its biggest. In an unusual state of affairs, Ripley's Entertainment owns the license to build and operate all the Guinness World Records Museums. This unique relationship came about when the brewing giant Guinness PLC still owned the book but was trying to get out of the record-making-and-breaking business. According to Masterson, Guinness had subcontracted the management of their museums around the world, which were losing money and had to be subsidized annually, when Masterson approached them and offered to take the red ink off the company's hands. Ripley's Entertainment, a subsidiary of one of Canada's largest privately owned companies, now has the rights in perpetuity to museums based on the *Guinness World Records* and related special edition titles, in addition to its own Ripley's-based attractions, wax museums, and water parks.

One of Masterson's first moves was to shutter money-losing museums in less popular locations, including Las Vegas and Gatlinburg, Tennessee, and replace them with new museums in record hotbeds like Tokyo, London (opening in 2008), and India. "We signed a deal in Bangalore, India, to do a Guinness museum, a Ripley's museum, and a wax museum. The first India location should be open by fall of 2008, and we can see opening maybe four Guinness museums there, including Mumbai and Delhi. It [record mania] is so popular in India that the Guinness book was not able to keep up with the number of requests, so they came up with their own book of records, not sanctioned by Guinness World Records, but in India it has become almost as popular."

India is just one country where the fascination with records has led to a homegrown competitor to *Guinness World Records*. Titled the *Limca Record Book*, it was created by Coca-Cola India, and named for the locally popular Limca soft drink. Originally released in 1990, the book has been printed in seventeen annual editions and records the exploits of Indian record breakers. Similarly, Guinness-obsessed Singapore elevates national record pride with the *Singapore Book of Records*, published by an organization called Record Breakers Singapore, or RBS. RBS is the work of Helen and John Taylor, who claim to have amassed seventy-nine world records for fuel economy and speed driving, and boast "over twenty years major World Record Breaking Event Organizing experience between them, from Singapore to Australia, USA, U.K., Europe, South America and the Caribbean." The first edition of RBS was published in 2005, followed by an updated 2007 version. The book's website explains its mission and purpose: "The Singapore public love [sic] Records and trivia, thus the book will be a great success. Annual publication covering fastest, biggest, smallest, richest, oldest, longest, heaviest, shortest, loudest, tallest, lightest, youngest, greatest and so on." Entry into the book seems limited to Singaporeans, thus finally making already-spoken-for "firsts" once again available. Move over Sir Edmund Hillary: Dr. Robert Goh and Edwin Siew now claim the record for the first alpine ascent of an 8,000-meter peak, Mount Xixabangma, in 2002, some forty-nine years after Hillary climbed the even taller Mount Everest. It would take another three years before the Everest record could be claimed by Teo Yen Kai, who in 2005, according to RBS, became the first Singaporean to scale the world's highest peak. The book also gives some credit to the same Edwin Siew of Mount Xixabangma fame, who climbed Everest in 1998 with partner Khoo Swee Chiow, but who apparently got only partial credit as a permanent Singapore resident.

Singaporeans also vie for places in the actual *Guinness World Records* book, and as of 2006 held some forty-five records, considerably fewer than Ashrita Furman alone has. It is not many, especially if you look at the nation's total as one record out of every thousand in the massive Guinness database, or one for every 100,000 residents, but it is more impressive if you look at the tiny country's record possession rate per capita as nearly double that of the rest of the world. Right in line with global statistics, only about 8 percent of the Singaporean records made it into the 2007 book for a grand total of four. But Singapore's pride and the scope of its collection is a microcosm of the rest of the world's, including such high-tech feats as the fastest text message in English, held by a sixteen-year-old boy; the longest chain of people on inline skates; the most people wearing hats made of balloons; and the longest scuba dive, at a whopping 220 hours. While this was done in a controlled environment, and presumably with the Guinness-mandated safety breaks, it is still three times longer than my own marathon poker stint and falls into the realm of the truly astonishing. The scuba record holder, the same Khoo Swee Chiow who climbed Everest, also sounded just like may of his compatriots across the globe when he told reporters, "People have called me stupid, ridiculous, wasting time and other names. But I generally ignore people who talk a lot. I prefer to do rather than talk."

Unlike India and Singapore, Canada does not have its own non-Guinness record book, but it does have an insatiable cultural thirst for records, and is home to one of the greatest world-record landmarks of all, the CN Tower. The broadcasting tower, while not technically a building, does have the Guinness distinction of being the tallest freestanding structure on earth, and this status has in turn made it a magnet to everyone from parachuting BASE jumpers to would-be record holders, including Ashrita Furman, who pogo stick jumped up its 1,899 steps for a memorable record and a segment on the *Record Breakers* television show. He is not alone. Toronto stuntman and past Canadian motocross champion Terry McGauran rode a motorcycle up the tower's stairwells in 1984 to promote his skills to the film industry. "It wasn't really a crazy thing for me, nor a daredevil thing either. I did it to promote my business, so the Toronto industry would know I was around." The always elaborate Guinness World Records rules required that once he started, his feet could never touch the ground, so when his rear tire slipped after eight flights and the bike came crashing down on top of him, the uninjured McGauran showed the kind of moxie world-record setting often requires: he rode down, turned around, and started over again. In 1989 Lloyd Stamm, head of the service department at a Vancouver Suzuki dealership, took a different approach to using the tower for a motor vehicle record. Stamm drove a Suzuki Samurai off-road vehicle to the base of the tower, and with the help of eight mechanics and fifty-four United Way volunteers, he then proceeded to take it apart and carry it to the top in pieces. Determined to not only succeed but to do so quickly, Stamm's team had practiced disassembling and reassembling the car in advance some fifteen times. They assaulted the tower only when they knew they could go from car to pieces and back to drivable condition in under two hours. It took about three more hours for the team to carry the 1,865-pound vehicle to the top, in sixty-one pieces, the largest of which was the engine block (around 100 pounds), which required two people to carry it—all of this for charity, of course. Stamm himself had the stamina for only one trip, carrying up the left front fender, but some of his volunteer army, which included seasoned triathletes, made several trips each. "They were tireless," Stamm recalled. "They were in way too good shape. They looked like they move pianos for a living. Here I was thinking, 'God, I can't move another step.' And these guys blow by with the engine." Of course, Guinness rules required the team to fully assemble the car, now stranded on the observation deck, into working order. The entire feat took just five hours and thirty-eight minutes. Not to be outdone, the CN Tower itself recently earned a new spot in the *Guinness World Records,* its second, when it was recognized in 2006 for having the world's highest wine cellar. Even Ashrita was impressed by the tower, to which he returned and shaved almost half a minute off his record pogo stick jumping time. "Most building staffs are stuffy about what they let people do," he said from experience, having been turned away by the Empire State Building and Eiffel Tower, among others. "But the CN Tower, they're crazy. It's fantastic that they're so open-minded. Maybe it's because they're Canadian."

That could explain a lot of things. Like how Canada broke over 100 records—more than twice Singapore's all-time tally—in 2006 alone. Or why, according to the book's spokesperson for Canada, Carey Low, in that same year Canadians submitted a whopping 1,433 record claims. This tally included seven different Canadians who demanded recognition for having the longest arm hair. While Guinness does not consider this category worthy of a record, it is

notable that no other nation claimed any arm hair records whatsoever, leaving the score in this noncategory Canada 7, Rest of World
0. Low's explanation? "Canadians have long arm hair."

As the *Ottawa Citizen* noted, "For good or ill, Canada has
made its mark as one of the world's most conscientious countries at
trying to break weird and wonderful records." The nation is among
the world's top five in records, and editor Craig Glenday told the
paper that his organization receives more interest per capita from
Canada than from any other country in the world. Sales corrobo-
rate this interest, with the nation of just 33 million snapping up
some 200,000 copies annually out of the total 3.5 million sold. That
means a country with less than half a percent of the world's population buys 6 percent of the books, a rate more than ten times that
of its peers.

At the opposite end of the global spectrum for all-things-
Guinness is Chile, which stands out for its dearth of record-setting
accomplishments. Four times the population of Singapore, Chile
submitted only twenty-seven claims in the decade from 1990 to
1999. Of these, just ten were approved by Guinness World Records.
To look at it another way, in ten years nearly 17 million Chileans
could not equal a third of Ashrita Furman's record output for 2006
alone—or 2007. Ashrita has broken as many world records in a
month as it took Chile the entire nineties to do. Chile may have
South America's strongest economy, but it is poor in Guinness
World Records certificates, averaging just one per year. Ashrita
has claimed two in one minute. Even I got two in 2004. Failed attempts ranged from a thirty-hour singing marathon, well short of
the record but trying for a niche based on entirely Latin American
songs, to the world's largest fry up, which, as the *Financial Times*
put it, "cost some 706 animals dearly." Perhaps the nation's biggest success comes as no surprise, since one of the only things the
book seems to love more than giant food is nationalistic giant food,
which may explain why the record for the world's largest Pisco
Sour, a Chilean cocktail, was approved unusually quickly.

Guinness World Records in now entering the second half of its first century, but its global reach is still growing, and the record-setting tome may have awakened a sleeping dragon in the world's largest country. Only after the relaxation of China's Communist rule was the book first allowed to be published and sold in Mandarin in the late 1990s. Since then, record setting has taken hold as a social phenomenon, though the Chinese, a bit late to the party, do not seem to have figured out the ground rules as well as some of their global competitors. According to Wu Xiaohong, a former college lecturer who became the Guinness adjudicator in China, less than 1 percent of the claims she receives warrant being passed on to her London colleagues—who then reject nine out of every ten. Still, London's *Daily Telegraph* reported in 2005 that a craze of record breaking is sweeping the nation that already had the world's largest population, largest army, and largest wall. In 2004 alone, twenty new records were granted, minuscule for such a large country, but represented a growth rate of 25 percent and finally took China's total over 100, enough to put it in the world's top 10 for the first time. Expect much more from the country that recently gave us Bao Xi Shun, the world's tallest living man until 2007, especially if Miss Wu's theory is correct: "As Chinese people live more comfortable lives, they have more time to do things they like. They have the time to live out their dreams. People phone us from all over China. Everyone wants to be the best. They sense that the book of records has given them a channel. They have found a stage they can show themselves on. Society in China is changing. China is opening up to the world and it wants to catch up with the developed countries."

Even as China roars onto the world record scene, some developed countries are heading in the opposite direction, most notably the very place where the *Guinness Book of Records* was conceived, Ireland. At the outset, Ireland had tons of records, especially since the original *Guinness Book of Records* had extensive entries for things like the largest stone and highest point for each of the various components of the British Isles. But times have changed, and today everyone from the Germans to the Aussies hold more records than the denizens of County Wexford and its surroundings. The passion, interest, and pride in the book still runs high in Ireland, and the decline of Irish record setting has not gone unnoticed. Since the fiftieth anniversary of the book, several articles have recounted this theme, and the *Irish News*, *Irish Independent*, and *Daily Mail* have all done stories analyzing specifically how Ireland fares in the modern book compared with the original. The answer, according to the *Daily Mail*, is not so good. "How has Ireland fared in this edit? Is our stock up or down in the record world of 2007? Alas the news is more bad than good. First off, there's no more space left for Sir Hugh's original County Wexford query about grouse. Neither is there room for the world's oldest cow, Big Bertha, a Fresian, born on St. Patrick's Day in 1945 in County Kerry, who passed on to the great milking shed in the sky in 1993 aged 48. Big Bertha also held the record for lifetime breeding as she produced 39 calves—but both categories have now been dropped from the book."

The Irish do hold quite a few records, but like everyone else, most of them have been discarded from the book to make room for new entrants like washing machine throwing. Interestingly, Ireland seems to have a disproportionate number of very successful entertainers, the basis for many of its records. Previous appearances in the book that have disappeared and may or may not be official record holders today include the likes of U2, Live Aid organizer Bob Geldof, dancing zillionaire Michael Flatley, boy bands Boyzone and Westlife, John Devine (world's fastest tap dancer), dramatist Samuel Beckett, author Bram Stoker, and actress Greer Garson. Most amazing, especially if, like me, you've never heard of him, is Daniel O'Donnell, whom the *Daily Mail* describes as "the most consistent chart artist ever in Britain, with at least one new Top 40 album every year between 1991 and 2006." Go figure.

Despite the loss of *Riverdance* mastermind Flatley and his highest-paid dancer record, Irish Dance remains in the book under Mass Participation, for the 7,764 dancers who strutted their stuff in the streets of Cork. Anyone who has driven the winding country roads of Ireland and shuddered at the inability to see around any bends because the view is always obscured by dense foliage will not be surprised to find that the world's tallest hedge, more than thirty feet high, can be found in County Offaly. But perhaps Ireland's greatest claim to record-setting dominance comes in the sport of hurling, for which the island holds all five records listed in the book, supporting the *Irish Independent*'s (unofficial) assertion that the country is the world's greatest hurling nation.

Admittedly, competition in hurling is not as spirited on the global stage as it is for many other Guinness records. Therefore Ireland's most surprising dominance, especially given stiff competition from its record-mad Anglo counterparts, India, and the equally Guinness-obsessed Pacific Rim, is its status as the Greatest Tea-Drinking Nation on Earth. The Irish consume 1,184 cups of tea per person each year, more than three a day for every man, woman, and child. As the *Independent* notes, "That's a staggering amount of tea. And yet, it's one of the less interesting records. Compared to the wealth of totally useless information on offer throughout the book (Largest Underpants, Oldest Twins, Most Produced WWII Fighter), a statistic on tea consumption shouldn't seem very important. But it was an Irish record. Other records may be bigger or flashier—most cockroaches eaten in a minute, anyone?—but this one is ours." The publishers have not forgotten the civic pride that the book enjoys on the Emerald Isle, and any perceived slight or loss of ground in record setting might be at least partially offset by the fact that the country received a unique nod from Guinness with the 1994 release, *The Guinness Book of Irish Facts & Feats*. Why India, Canada, and many other countries have not received their own self-selected editions rather than just translations of the master book is anybody's guess. It might just be a matter of time.

Whether it is the Irish clinging to their national Guinness pride of bygone decades, the Chinese embracing record setting as an element of growing political and economic freedom, or India emulating Western superpowers, there is little doubt that the appeal of *Guinness World Records* is global—and growing. New museums bring records to life in India and beyond, the addition of the Mandarin edition made the book accessible to virtually every country on earth, and the reach of television is now just as broad. In the last two years alone, new record-related shows produced by Guinness World Records TV have been added in Australia, Italy, the Philippines, Vietnam, Indonesia, Cambodia, and China, where it is broadcast on China Central Television, the largest network in the largest nation on earth. Even more recently, an Arabic language version of the show was produced and immediately snapped up by stations in eighteen different countries: Bahrain, Brunei, Iraq, Jordan, Kuwait, UAE, Lebanon, Oman, Qatar, Saudi Arabia, Syria, Yemen, Algeria, Egypt, Libya, Morocco, Sudan, and Tunisia. These newcomers join the dozens of countries that already had *Guinness World Records*–based shows on the air, including Japan, France, Germany, Spain, Sweden, and Finland, bringing the current total to some eighty-five countries where record breaking has gone prime time. Considering the explosion of bizarre feats that resulted from the BBC's *Record Breakers*, the ramifications of similar broadcasts suddenly expanded to every corner of the globe defies the imagination. Right now, chefs craving their moment in the spotlight might be whipping up the world's largest bowl of kimchi, the heaviest falafel, the grandest adobo, or the biggest doner kebab. Wait . . . that one is already in The Book.

9

The Dark Side: Guinness Records Gone Bad

Between 10,000 to 20,000 claims are rejected because the attempts are too harmful, such as the bid by a 10-year-old boy to push 135 pins into his thumb.

—TORONTO SUN, JULY 15, 2007

A 10-year-old girl in China's Hunan Province swam for three hours in a tributary of Yangtze river Tuesday with hands and feet bound, hoping she would be inscribed into the Guinness book of world records some day. "Next time, she will swim further and I'll follow her in a boat to ensure safety," said the father.

—INDO-ASIAN NEWS SERVICE, OCTOBER 4, 2007

Many would-be record breakers fail in their attempts, but rarely do things go so badly as they did for the late Hans Rezac. The effect of record setting is widely varied among its practitioners, and many people have set a Guinness World Record, enjoyed their moment in the sun, and then gone back to life as usual, putting the book and its feats behind them for good. Others, as

Fame Junkies author Jake Halpern theorized, become addicted to the rush that record setting brings, just as if they were hooked on chocolate, gambling, sex, or drugs, and cannot let go, finding fulfillment only in more, and often more dramatic, feats. Among those disposed toward serial record breaking, camps are divided, with Ashrita Furman and Joachim Suresh at one extreme, accumulating Guinness World Records like teenagers collect baseball cards, but in relatively harmless pursuits, with no signs of constantly ascending drama or difficulty. Ashrita might pull off an astonishing feat of physical endurance for one record, and then break the most finger snaps in a minute record the next, while some of his records are measured in seconds rather than miles or hours. He has come back sore, bruised, bloodied, and disoriented from his attempts, but when he fails and does not do enough crunches or jumping jacks in an hour to break a record, he lives to fight another day. Not so for those who follow in the fatal footsteps of Channel-swimming pioneer Matthew Webb. It appears that in his second and third bids for record book immortality, Hans Rezac found himself closer to Webb's end of the danger spectrum than Furman's.

The Vienna pub owner was a passionate skydiver who had jumped his way into the *Guinness Book of Records* once and was determined to do so again. Opportunity knocked in 1997, when Rezac joined very elite company by successfully stepping out of a plane and landing on the North Pole. This was a rare and impressive feat, but his jump was not groundbreaking, and he was not the first to do it. Parlaying the North Pole jump into his second record would require upping the ante. To get into Guinness, Rezac needed to complete a second jump on the South Pole—in the same year—something no one had ever done.

Parachuting has a long and rich history in the pages of *Guinness World Records*, and it is a category where firsts, especially regarding the North and South poles, are exalted and immortalized, never vanishing long even when they have been equaled or exceeded. The sport has always been given a fair amount of space and attention in the book, often with its own section in the sports chapter, and in many editions, numerous records, charts, and photos as well. The 1986 book has a large picture of parachutist Dr. Jack Wheeler, called the "real Indiana Jones" by the *Wall Street Journal*, standing with his chute at the North Pole, a first described in the caption as "A record that cannot be bettered after setting." With the South Pole conquered much earlier, for the first few decades of *Guinness World Records* history the North Pole remained parachuting's Holy Grail; in 1972 the record for most northerly jump was still at 89°30′ N, on the polar ice cap but tantalizingly shy of the pole itself, which sits at a latitude of 90°00′ N, a mark begging to be broken. Which happened when Dr. Wheeler landed on the pole in 1981. With both the North and South poles claimed individually as parachuting prizes, and jumps at the ends of the earth, while still rare, becoming increasingly commonplace, the only record left up for grabs at the polar extremes was to jump both in the same year, which is exactly what Rezac set out to do.

According to the *Washington Post*, Rezac partnered with three other experienced parachutists to make the trip to Antarctica. Such excursions, like guided mountain climbing expeditions to Everest and other high peaks, are prohibitively expensive for all but the wealthiest to undertake alone. The foursome, who didn't know each other beforehand, found themselves teamed by destiny and a need to defray logistical costs, which clocked in at $22,000 a person (though some members of the trip received discounts based on their reputations and the visibility they could bring the tour operator). Rezac's partners that day included three Americans: Michael Kearns, 39, a computer graphics manager and former Air Force captain with about 750 jumps; Ray Miller, 43, who like Rezac, 49, had skydived over the North Pole; and Steve Mulholland, 36, a specialist in BASE (Building, Antennae, Span, Earth) jumping—a plane-free subspecialty that involves leaping off terrestrial heights such as skyscrapers, mountains, and bridges. Mulholland's claim to fame was for the first authorized jump from Seattle's sixty-story Space Needle. According to the *Post*, Rezac was not alone in his bid for glory, since in addition to his two-poles-in-one-year effort he also planned to join all three of his companions in an attempt to set a record for the first "four-way skydive" over the South Pole. While such maneuvers are common among parachutists who jump and practice together, this was a spur of the moment record decision. The group of strangers had decided on this plan of action once they were in Chile preparing for the final leg of their trip, enticed by a bonus shot at world record glory. But on December 6, 1997, just eighteen seconds after they left the safety of their plane at 8,000 feet, with the air temperature at minus 100 degrees, the group claimed a much different record, one for the worst civilian skydiving accident in thirty years. Two never opened their chutes at all, the other two opened their chutes too late. Of the latter, only Kearns, the most experienced of the jumpers, survived but with multiple injuries. Kearns could not explain what happened to his comrades, but contributing factors may have included altitude-induced hypoxia (a sort of drunkenness brought on by thin air), faster-than-normal free fall in thin air, and a lack of visual reference over the flat, white, ice mass so acute that it is difficult to tell up from down. Tellingly, Kearns was the only one of the four who wore an automatic safety device that would explode a charge and deploy his chute if he failed to do it manually. This happened, and it probably saved his life.

There is nothing new about accidents and death in the world of exploration and adventure. The race to be the first, highest, and fastest has resulted in the losses of hundreds, perhaps thousands of lives. As billionaire adventurer Sir Richard Branson puts it, "I think another *Guinness Book of Records* entry I should be applying for is for having been pulled out of the water six times by helicopter. Most of my adventures have ended up in some kind of catastrophe or another." Even when he succeeded, things rarely went smoothly. "Having crossed the Atlantic, we went and also became the first hot air balloon to cross the Pacific. Even though we were aiming for Los Angeles, we missed it by two and a half thousand miles and crashed in the Arctic. Of course, we had clothes suitable for Los Angeles weather but not minus 60 degrees." Of all his many records, Branson quite bluntly admits he is proudest of his first transatlantic balloon crossing, due to its inherent danger. "Because before we did it, six people had tried and five of them died. It was certainly man against the elements and it was one of my first big adventures, one which we were delighted to have succeeded and survived." Shortly after I spoke with Branson, and just before I was to interview his good friend Steve Fossett for this book, Fossett, a career adventurer and the first to fly a plane solo around the world without refueling, died in a plane crash while scouting yet another world record attempt.

When people attempt to push limits in adventures like exploration, mountaineering, or aviation, some of them are going to die in the effort. In light of this reality, and given some of the activities it awards certificates for, it is amazing that the *Guinness World Records* book does not seem to have directly claimed many lives. With records for motorcycle jumping, sword swallowing, and high altitude tightrope walking, the lack of "death by record setting" surrounding the book is nothing short of serendipitous. As a fatality, Rezac was a rare Guinness-chasing exception, but there have been plenty of close calls, and a number of records and record categories have been quietly dropped or modified over the years because of their implicit danger. It is worth noting that the book includes many records not specifically undertaken in order to "Get into Guinness," and it is important to differentiate between those feats that editors have chosen from the public domain to include in the book, and those undertaken specifically to earn a spot in its pages. Hillary climbed his mountain, Neil Armstrong walked on the moon, and Roger Bannister broke the four-minute mile, all for higher purposes; these types of sometimes dangerous pursuits go on with or without the existence of the book, as those undertaking them are driven by other motivations.

Not so for Jackie "the Texas Snakeman" Bibby, who literally puts his life on the line every time he breaks one of his rattlesnake records, dangerous stunts he clearly admits are undertaken explicitly for *Guinness World Records* recognition. In fact, Bibby has been bitten by his poisonous snakes on nine different occasions, but not yet while formally attempting to set a Guinness World Record (though his practice for such attempts is part of an increasingly gray area). Likewise, Ashrita's most serious injury, a laceration to his hand that severed a nerve and required surgery, came while practicing for, but not yet attempting, the Guinness World Record for glass balancing—something he clearly never would have been doing had it not been for the existence of the book. The book dodged yet another bullet when one of its other snake-related record holders was killed during a public performance rather than an actual record bid. Boonreung Buachan, known as "the Snake Man," was Jackie Bibby's Thai soul mate and the holder of the Guinness World Record for spending the most time penned up with snakes. He got into the book in 1998 after living in a glass box with poisonous snakes for seven days. Buachan died in 2004 after being bitten by one of his cobras.

Over the years the book has periodically tried to create a safer record-breaking atmosphere, sometimes through sensible rules, other times through mere lip service. Medical precautions and observations are now de rigueur in the specific rules for many kinds of record attempts, including almost every marathon event. In fact, London's *Independent* reported that Guinness banned all endurance-based records on the grounds of safety in 1990, and then reintroduced them in 1999 with strict guidelines. But the various editions of the book throughout the 1990s do not bear this out, and indeed include numerous records for extremely lengthy events set during that period, ranging from Ashrita Furman's seventy-one-mile brick carry to a 3,233-mile bed push and a fifty-eight-hour clapping session. Just what endurance events, if any, were banned is unclear. In this same vein, on several occasions the company has announced records or categories that have been banned, or in Guinness-speak "retired," so that the last person to set them holds the record forever. This happened with Ashrita's nausea- and dementia-inspiring somersault record over the route of Paul Revere's ride. But like the alleged endurance ban, there have been many cases where Guinness World Records staffers have stated in interviews that certain records or types of records are no longer sanctioned . . . only to go ahead and welcome them back—or at least welcome variations so close to the banned version as to not be able to justify any sort of safety rationale. Perhaps the book wants to work both sides of the fence, knowing that the lure of danger is what creates its appeal to its core audience, while posturing in a manner that might discourage litigation when things go bad.

No category of records has generated so much confusion on this point as eating-related feats. Printed warnings of possible danger began to appear in the book in the early 1970s, and these admonitions were soon strengthened by specific prohibitions on records involving the consumption of spirits (any amount) or "large quantities" of beer. Competitive eating seems to be endemic these days, having even made it onto the airwaves, at least on ESPN2, publicly anchored by the popular annual July 4 Nathan's Coney Island hot dog eating contest. Competitive eating as sport, if you can call it that, has evolved into an almost Guinnesslike phenomenon with its own official record-keeping body, while the fastest eaters of everything from Spam to cow brains have become celebrities to a niche but fast-growing international fan base. But despite its newfound popularity, speed eating and gluttony records as a genre were banned by Guinness World Records as early as 1989—sort of. In May 1989, the London *Times* reported, "Now that it is officially acknowledged that eating can seriously damage your health, the *Guinness Book of Records* is to abandon all its records for gluttony and fast feeding." The article quotes the book's then-editor Donald McFarlan as saying, "We now regard these records as unhealthy and outmoded in the light of growing concern about health issues." McFarlan added that the only such eating record being retained is that of greatest omnivore, "for its historical and nostalgic value."

The greatest omnivore title is one of the book's most enduring, and has long been the sole province of Frenchman Michel Lotito, better known by his nickname M. Mangetout, French for Mr. Eat Everything. Lotito has achieved membership in the rarefied pantheon of all-time Guinness greats, a fan favorite on par with the Texas Snakeman, Robert Wadlow, and the McCrary twins. Greatest, like oddest (his record has also appeared under Oddest Diet), ugliest, or most artistic, is a vague definition, and this is one of the rare *Guinness World Records* instances of an editorial judgment call outside the realm of measurable comparables. But Lotito's case for the record seems open and shut, as the Grenoble native has consumed an impressive diet of things widely considered inedible, including eighteen bicycles, fifteen shopping carriages, seven television sets, six chandeliers, two beds, a pair of skis, a computer, and an entire airplane. "I believe he was the only man to ever have a coffin inside of him, rather than the other way around, when he died," current *Guinness World Records* editor Craig Glenday said of Mangetout.

Lotito was the inspiration for the title character in Ben Sherwood's novel *The Man Who Ate the 747* (2000). Sherwood got an unusual level of behind-the-scenes access to the company's record operations through his friendship with Mark Young, then the editor of the American edition. He went through company files, read record submissions, and attended record breakings before writing the novel, which displays a high level of realism and expertise. "My interest was in the perspective of fiction. You'll notice it's not called the *Guinness Book of Records* in my book, because that's a copyrighted name and you can't do that, so mine is called the *Book of Records*. Then I fictionalized it to make it what I wanted it to be, a guy running around under pressure to deliver more and bigger and better records." That guy running around is the novel's protagonist, a sort of romantic traveling record detective who has no real-life counterpart, but was an inspired amalgam of the book's Keeper of the Records and Sherwood's childhood view of how the book *should* be run—in the pursuit of the greater glory of superlatives rather than profit. In his novel, the man from the *Book of Records* finds his way to Superior, Nebraska, a town named for superlatives, where a local farmer is systematically grinding up and swallowing an entire jumbo jet, a 747 that had crashed in his cornfields years earlier and lain abandoned ever since. The researcher visits the farm and vividly describes what he sees as the greatest of the many record attempts he has ever witnessed. As the devout chewer nears completion, the London home office of Sherwood's fictional *Book of Records* suddenly pulls the plug on the attempt, deciding it is too dangerous and scoffing at overly litigious American society. In a memorable phone exchange with his superior, the traveling record verifier is told "problem is, we've got copycats. A woman in Ghana is eating an office building. A family in Morocco is eating a bridge. A man in Malaysia is eating an ocean liner. We don't know where it will stop." Through this absurdist exaggeration of implausible ingestion, Sherwood hits the nail on the head vis-à-vis the world of Guinness records, and his novel is a clear case of art imitating the real life of record copycats.

While the attempt to eat a 747 is intentionally preposterous, Lotito did in fact eat his way into *Guinness World Records* by consuming an entire airplane, ground up in similar fashion, albeit it was "only" a four-seat Cessna 104 single-engine plane, a so-called "light aircraft"—at least until you try to eat one. While airplane eating might no longer be endorsed by the book today, speed eating is back with a vengeance as part of the acceptable *Guinness World Records* realm, despite the 1989 ban, and there are time-based records featured prominently in the current book for mass consumption of everything from Tabasco sauce and jalapeño chili peppers to brussels sprouts and doughnuts, this last with separate records for powdered and jelly versions. The spirits ban seems to have remained in force, though, and while it is hard to imagine anyone sanctioning record attempts for vodka guzzling or the like, the almost-as-politically-incorrect beer-chugging records remain (including those for Guinness-style stout). There is even a record for beer chugging while upside down, not widely considered a paragon of safe behavior. Despite the apparent danger of encouraging very fast beer drinking, this category has a rich history going back to the very first edition in 1955, the only one without any made-for-Guinness achievements. The original green book put today's chuggers, who are limited by rules to a couple of liters at most, to shame, with gluttonous speed records for both beer (twenty-four pints in fifty-two minutes) and wine (forty pints in fifty-nine minutes). Even back in 1971, what editor could have possibly thought it a good idea for the book to include a record for the world's Heaviest Drinker? Of course, they didn't call it that. The more eloquent title for this record is "Most Alcoholic Subject." By any name, the London-based hard drinker was impressive, averaging over four bottles of port each day, or nearly a gallon of fortified wine, appreciably higher in alcohol content than other still wines. He kept this frenetic pace up for twenty-three straight years until his not surprising death at 61. Had he lived in the greener modern era he might also have qualified for "Biggest Recycler," as it was estimated that he produced some 35,688 "empties."

The earliest printed warning regarding the potential dangers of record breaking in the book itself I could find was in the 1971 edition. It added a note printed in red type to the otherwise black-and-white section on gastronomic records, suggesting that while no one was known to have succumbed in the course of setting an eating or drinking contest, such attempts are "extremely unadvisable" medically. This was a lesson learned the hard way by Bennet D'Angelo, when he made ice cream history and the pages of *Guinness World Records* by winning a contest in which he shoveled down three and a half pounds of the frozen dessert in just ninety seconds. Afterward, he felt sick, his face was numb for much of the day, and when the feeling finally returned he discovered that the cold had loosened a tooth and his filling had fallen out. He was not alone: all twenty-seven other contestants fell ill as well.

The 1971 warning, in slightly different verbiage, continued to appear annually until 1979, when it was significantly strengthened with the addition of specific prohibitions. "GWR will list no records involving consumption of more than two liters of beer or any involving spirits." The editors were probably less concerned by D'Angelo's ice cream eating antics than by the Welshman who tried to appeal to the book's history by setting a record for drinking its eponymous stout. He devoured sixty-five pints of Guinness in fifty minutes and thirty-seconds, but the editors took exception to his technique, telling the *Times*, "This gentleman regurgitates what he has drunk halfway through. We are powerless to stop him, but we feel that such spectacles are not in the interest of anyone." Despite the rule modifications, the new quantity limit still left plenty of room for the several remaining beer speed-drinking records, including fastest yard of ale and fastest Oxford University sconce, both around two pints worth. Those interested at taking a go at the upside-down beer-drinking record will be glad to know that it was made safe by the switch from the risky "most beer consumed while inverted" to the apparently harmless "fastest time to down (or up?) an Imperial Pint," which remains in the book to this day—at a staggering three seconds. It seems surprising that the 1979 edition would still include this unusual beer record, especially since eight years earlier, while considering the ban on gastronomic records in 1971, a Guinness official told the *Times* that, "Some of the records have got to such extremes that it is dangerous to try to break them. Someone did do himself an injury recently trying to break the record for drinking beer when standing on one's head." The 1979 notice also bars eating records for "potentially dangerous" foodstuffs including—but not limited to—live ants, chewing gum, marshmallows, and raw eggs with shells. To the careful reader, this suggests that presumably dead ants, shelled raw eggs, and hard-boiled eggs still in their shells would be allowed, which makes one wonder whether the egg safety concern was rawness or the shells, neither of which are addressed fully by the prohibition. In a rare direct editorial comment at the end of this warning, apparently aimed at Michel Lotito, the editors called eating a bicycle "the ultimate in stupidity" but included it nonetheless with the rationale that it was not likely to be repeated. Not all banned eating records were discarded in the interest of safety, as when David Boehm, longtime publisher and rule interpreter of the American edition, dropped competitive goldfish consumption from the approved list. His rationale? The goldfish being used were getting progressively smaller, making the record less competitive. "The goldfish got down to the size of caviar," complained Boehm.

It is interesting that Guinness considers eating live ants dangerous, but holding live scorpions (largest, at seven inches, warranting a two-page spread) and poisonous rattlesnakes (most, twelve) in the mouth is encouraged both in print and photos and by rolling out Texas Snakeman, Jackie Bibby, on television and at special events. Then again, Bibby, who has been bitten by rattlesnakes many times with no long-term ill effects, may feel that even his riskier stunt of sitting in a bathtub with over a hundred rattlers is safe. Rattlesnake bites are not usually lethal, and antivenin is widely available at hospitals. This is not the case for many other breeds of poisonous snakes, and one wonders what the book would say if Bibby decided to break Peter Snyman's much older snake record. In 1979, the same year the book banned chewing-gum records as too dangerous, Snyman, who paved the way for folks like Bibby, spent fifty days and seven hours in an 80-square-foot cage, the size of a bathroom, with two dozen highly poisonous snakes, a lethally impressive assortment that included black mambas, cobras, puff adders, and boomslangs. Why? To set the record for "Snake Pit Duration," of course.

Despite regular and changing warnings and prohibitions, and frequent mentions by Guinness World Records spokespeople in interviews touting safety that the book has stopped accepting eating records, they continued to appear in myriad forms. In 1996 Guinness staffer Carole Jones told the *Los Angeles Times* that gluttony as a category had been "Taken out in 1990. Even how many pancakes can be eaten in a minute can be quite dangerous to the individual. Also, with so many people starving in the world, it's not really diplomatic." However, four years later the 2000 millennium edition still included the record for the most watches eaten. Likewise, the ban on "gluttony and speed eating" records apparently does not apply to speed-eating contests if they involve pizza. Guinness World Records not only accepted the attempt of Belgium's Tom Waes as recently as December 2, 2006, but also showcased it on their website. Waes ate a twelve-inch pizza in 19.91 seconds, making him the world's fastest pizza eater, at least at the one-foot-size category. If mere pancake eating is considered dangerous, why does the 2008 edition include recognition for the most sausages swallowed whole in one minute, a much more dangerous-sounding pursuit, or for that matter, speed and quantity records for eating or drinking more than two dozen different items, from Tabasco sauce to meatballs to that old standby, beer? But the safety conscious will be glad to know that marshmallows and live ants aren't among the resurrected categories appearing in print.

Food and endurance records may be just too good to let go, having been staples of the book since its very inception, but they are not the only dangerous record-setting pursuits to be banned and then brought back into the fold. The safety-conscious 1980 edition included a printed claim that no further disc jockey marathons would be listed after Dave Belmondo took the mark to 2,016 hours. Since this number so far exceeds all marathon efforts for other pursuits and any records for anyone ever staying awake, it seems completely implausible. Alternatively, it may have been set under different rules and standards than those governing other marathon records, or even other DJ marathon records; ever since piano smashing in its early days, the book has had a penchant for adjusting its rules on the fly. In any case, despite the admonition, the DJ marathon record is going nowhere—it has remained one of the most attempted and most published of all the book's records. In fact, the Guinness World Records Web site lists it as the answer to the frequently asked question, Which Record Is Broken Most Often?, saying it is attempted every month. The 2008 book lists the record at a mere 125 hours, and states that on average the record is broken three times a year. This suggests that whatever bizarre circumstances led to the Belmondo 2,016-hour record have since been rectified.

Another safety notice once printed in the book but then widely ignored pertained to the bed of nails record, which was officially "retired" in the same 1980 edition. Weights placed on the chests of record setters had by that time passed three quarters of a ton, and the book noted that "no further claims for publication will be entertained or published." The ban was poorly worded and apparently refers not to the "standard" bed of nails record, which is for simply lying on nails, but rather to the so-called iron maiden record where the participant is sandwiched between two beds of nails. In either case, piling weights on makes it more interesting. The iron maiden feat was so popular that on New Year's Day 1977, when Sterling Publishing founder David Boehm held a record-breaking festival to usher in the New Year at New York's Guinness World Records Museum, he featured it. Master Chi, whose real name was Ronald Chamberlain, lay sandwiched between two beds of nails while 1,410 pounds were piled on top of him, setting a new record. Not one to jump into things, Master Chi was cautious and first warmed up by lying on a single bed of nails and having an assistant strike his chest with an ax. Then he had his helper break a cinder block with a blow from a sledgehammer, made more challenging by virtue of the block sitting atop a metal spike placed point down on his chest. It was only after such elaborate preparation that he broke the iron maiden record. At that point Guinness apparently realized that not every record breaker can be trusted to show such caution and professionalism as Master Chi, and they banned the event three years later. This must have been very hard news for Master Chi to hear, since he had previously announced plans to better his mark by being run over by a forty-four-passenger bus while in the iron maiden. Fortunately, Master Chi, who claimed that "pain is only when you accept it," had a back-up plan: to someday jump out of an airplane a mile above the ocean and see what happened (it appears he never tried this). The two variations on bed of nails records had previously been printed together as paired entries, and even though the iron maiden vanished after the 1980 ban, the standard record continued to appear . . . and continued to be broken. Despite the original rationale, both iron maiden and bed of nails weight records were eventually deemed too sexy to pass up: a triple-decker bed of nails record returned in 2000 and the most recent book includes Chad Netherland's record for having hundreds of pounds of concrete blocks broken on his chest with a sledgehammer while lying on a bed of nails. Netherland is a serial record breaker specializing in feats of strength and apparent danger; he is also an employee of rival Ripley's Entertainment, publishers of the *Ripley's Believe It or Not*.

The book's on-again, off-again approach to safety does have some shining moments. In one eerily prescient act of rationality in 1989, the book banned all "youngest records" for pilots, a decision that was unfortunately validated in 1996 when seven-year-old Jessica Dubroff was killed attempting to become the youngest ever to fly across the United States, along with her father Lloyd Dubroff and flight instructor Joe Reid. Like so many copycat records, the stunt was inspired when Jessica's father read about another young girl's cross-country flight. Jessica had been given a flight in a private plane as a present for her sixth birthday, and amazingly was piloting a transcontinental flight just a year later, only to crash the day before she and her father were scheduled to appear on NBC's *Today Show*, according to the *Washington Post*. The paper reported that both the National Aeronautic Association and the *Guinness Book of Records* had stopped recording such feats. Guinness spokesman Mark Young explained that the pilots were getting dangerously young. "First we'd get a request for an eleven-year-old, then a ten-year-old, then a nine-year-old. A parent would call us, or a flying school, but usually the parent." The book's decision to stop recording children's long-distance flights resulted in calls from angry moms and dads, said Young. "Parents tell us that we are stopping kids from fulfilling their ambitions. 'How can you not recognize these kids when you are recognizing ball-juggling, rope-jumping, all those things?'"

In many cases it seems that aviation and the Guinness book do not mix well, whether it is instances of people eating planes, flying them, or jumping out of them. The same goes for helicopters, as Jennifer Murray and Colin Bodill found out. In 2003, Murray, a sixty-three-year-old British grandmother, and her friend Bodill were trying to become the first to fly a helicopter, a Bell 407, around the world via the North and South poles, in an effort dubbed Polar First. They did not succeed and were lucky to walk away, Mrs. Murray with a broken arm and her copilot with chest injuries, after they crashed into Antarctica during a blizzard, a third of the way through the journey. Mrs. Murray was no unprepared novice and had already set the world record as the first woman to circumnavigate the globe in a helicopter in 1997. Not to be outdone, even as she was about to take off for Polar First, her husband, also sixty-three, was in the process of trying to become the oldest man to walk to the South Pole unsupported. They almost managed what could be a record in itself, an unplanned family reunion in Antarctica.

Some of the unfortunate incidents that have befallen record holders had little to do with their attempts to get into the book but were, rather, products of unique abilities. One such memorable occurrence involved Fort Worth, Texas, denizen William Fucqua, an army enlisted man with an unusual talent, one that allowed him to moonlight profitably as a human mannequin. His special gift? The ability to remain completely motionless for long periods of time. Fucqua got into the book in 1971 for a four-and-a-half-hour stint of utter stillness. Neither the record nor his job seemed especially dangerous, so Fucqua was probably as surprised as anyone when he was stabbed while working in a department store by a gawking husband determined to "prove" to his wife that the human statue was merely a realistic dummy. This kind of job risk may help explain why *Guinness World Records* claimed Fucqua earned a whopping $1,300 an hour back in 1971.

While many prohibited records have resurfaced after a short or long absence, some banned categories have actually stayed out of the book and appear to be gone permanently, such as youngest pilot, speed driving records on public roads, and tug-of-war. While the popularity of gastronomic records makes it difficult for Guinness World Records to ignore, the decision to discard tug-of-war may seem ho-hum to readers today, but the competition was a mainstay of the book for years, claiming its own subhead under the sports section. In 1979 alone there were five different tug-of-war records listed. Change was in the wind as early as 1974, when sailors of the Royal Navy attempted to break the tug-of-war record in Gibraltar but broke the rope instead, fracturing the legs of two seamen and cracking the ribs of a third. On each side were 300 members of the Plymouth and Portsmouth Royal Navy commands respectively, but 600 fit sailors eager for a place in the *Guinness Book of Records* proved too much, even for heavy-duty mooring rope. In 1995, a boy was crushed to death in Germany when another mass tug-of-war went awry. In 2006, Eastport, Maryland's John DiPietro learned of the record book's reluctance-firsthand. DiPietro organizes an epic, annual, townwide tug-of-war known locally as the "Slaughter Across the Water," which he submitted to Guinness World Records as the longest tug-of-war over a body of water, using a 1,700-foot rope. But as DiPietro told the *Washington Post*, "We submitted it to the Guinness Book of World Records, but they won't certify tug-of-war because of the inherent danger." While disappointed not to be included in the book, the event's participants were not dissuaded, because, as DiPietro explained, "We laugh in the face of danger."

Despite the book's best intentions, there often seems to be little reason behind deciding which activities are dangerous and which are not. While the misfortune of the brave British Navy sailors should not be minimized, it is hard for the casual observer to see tug-of-war, a record that has apparently been retired (based on DiPietro's experience) as more dangerous than, say, trying to stop two planes attempting to take off in opposite directions by holding them with ropes. This was described in its pre-attempt press release as a case where the would-be record holder "will literally risk having his arms ripped off." The potentially armless candidate was none other than Chad Netherland, the record holder for having concrete blocks smashed on his chest while lying on a bed of nails. The previous plane restraining record, held by Finnish four-time Olympic power-lifting champion Ilkka Nummisto, was fifty-four

seconds. Netherland intended to go a full minute while holding
back two airplanes trying to take off in opposite directions, a
record never before held by an American. "In life, one's greatest
victory comes with the risk of great failure. This is actually much
more dangerous than having 900 pounds of concrete broken off
my chest with a sledgehammer while lying on a bed of nails—I'm
used to that!" Not only did Netherland succeed, earning his tenth
Guinness World Record, but immediately afterward, presumably
having waited to make sure he still had all his limbs, Netherland
successfully proposed to his girlfriend on the tarmac.

As far back as 1981, David Boehm was worried about dangerous records. As he later wrote, "One of the many disagreements I
had with (director) Marv Minoff and David Frost was their propensity for including—nay, featuring—hazardous stunts on Guinness TV shows." This admonition came from the same Boehm who
hosted Master Chi's iron maiden feat, compete with ax blows to his
bare chest. His concerns came at just about the same time that the
1980 book included several printed warnings and prohibitions, and
company representatives would continue to give these values lip
service. "We just don't want to encourage records that are gratuitously dangerous," Peter Matthews, a consulting editor for Guinness, told the *Los Angeles Times* in 1996.

It is hard to think of things more gratuitously dangerous than
records for smashing concrete on top of someone on a bed of nails
with a sledgehammer or risking being drawn and quartered by
planes, so other than tug-of-war, what attempts does Guinness
World Records actually ban? Overweight pets, for one. Notes in
several recent editions, including 2008, remind readers that "heaviest pet" claims are no longer accepted, since some owners were
force-feeding their animals. "That one got rested," said spokesman
Alistair Richards. These days, at least according to the few rules
it releases, "lightest pet" records are also banned for the similar
potential danger of owners starving a pet, yet the book creatively
gets around this by allowing the record for "smallest" dog. Sleep
deprivation is also banned—for the sake of sleep deprivation. Try

to break the record for staying awake and you will suffer the unfortunate consequences that befell Tony Wright of Cornish, England. In a bid to surpass the 264-hour mark set in 1964 by American Randy Gardner, Wright went more than eleven days without as much as a catnap, staying up for 266 hours, only to discover that Guinness World Records had retired the record for health reasons. Rubbing salt in his wounds, Wright discovered too late that not only could the record not be broken, but that Mr. Gardner was not even the record holder. That would be Toimi Soini of Finland who had beaten Gardner the very next year, in 1965, and was in the book with his record 276 hours until 1990 when it was pulled from print. The catch—and with so-called re-tired records there always seems to be a catch—is that the book still recognizes scores of other marathon records, including my own nonstop poker playing record, which are for all purposes de facto sleep deprivation records and could very realistically exceed those of Wright, Gardner, and Soini, just as long as they aren't called sleep deprivation records.

In Wright's case, he relied upon the book itself as the basis for going forward with an attempt that would presumably not have received pre-approval. But with records retired for being dangerous, sometimes no amount of preparation can ensure the company will not become skittish, such as when Ashrita Furman recounted staffers changing their minds about allowing his assault on the forward roll record. This can be especially frustrating when the attempt undertaken in vain is life threatening. Robert Masterson, president of Ripley's Entertainment, described one such case.

> Here's an example to show the frustration of the public with the way Guinness World Records does things. Because we run the museums, people contact us about how to break records and we tell them how to contact Guinness. Well, there has been a record for the most times someone has kissed a cobra. So a guy from Thailand contacts us and wants to break it, so we put him in touch with Guinness

World Records. They spelled out the whole thing, how he had to do it, how high the table had to be, all these rules, and then he went and got the snakes, did everything the way they explicitly told him to, and he did it, risking his life, and then they tell him "sorry, the record has been retired." I think "why not tell him that in the first place?" Now you've got an enemy for life. He did exactly what they told him to do, could have been killed, then went and told all his friends he had set the record, and he ends up with nothing but frustration to show for it. That kind of stuff happens with them all the time.

While several categories of records have been banned, rested, or retired, others are so patently dangerous they have never been approved in the first place. Such was the fate for the man who inquired about setting a record for spending the longest time in a chamber filled with tear gas. "We didn't want it in the book because of all the other deranged people that would try it," explained editor Donald McFarlan. The applicant for the record for falling down flights of stairs got the same response. Likewise, it may not matter to a lot of world record aspirants, but another type of record unlikely to be embraced by the book is one that involves removing large sections of skin from the body. In 2007, Hong Kong civil servant Barry Kwok sent the book's officials a twenty-two-centimeter flap of sunburned skin he claimed he had peeled from his chest back in 1979 and kept for nearly thirty years. Kwok said it took him and his sister some ninety minutes to remove the patch; he believed it was the largest piece of freestanding burned skin in the world, and one that amazingly came off of his body in the shape of a map of China. Guinness World Records refused to award Kwok his certificate, but the jury is still out as to what would be the fate of future peeled skin aficionados. While current editor Craig Glenday sensibly told the *Birmingham Post*, "We didn't want other people to be ripping their skin to bits to try and beat it," other Guinness World

Records officials told the *Times* that they refused Kwok the record simply because he cannot prove the skin is his.

The unofficial record for a bizarre case of record attempt gone bad has to belong to the Murugesan family. Despite the record mania that India is infamous for, it is hard to imagine just what Dr. K. Murugesan and his wife, also a medical doctor, were thinking when they allowed their fifteen-year-old son to perform a Caesarean section on an apparently unknowing patient in an attempt to get him into the *Guinness World Records* book as "youngest surgeon." The couple own a private maternity clinic where their son Dhileepan Raj performed the operation on an anaesthetized twenty-year-old woman in 2007 while his parents supervised. His proud father videotaped the operation, and later showed it to a chapter of the Indian Medical Association, explaining to the audience that he wanted his son to earn the Guinness record as the world's youngest surgeon. To his surprise, his colleagues were more horrified than impressed, so Dr. Murugesan told them it was no mere whim or fluke—he had been training his son for three years and it was not the teen's first operation. As the *Times* reported, "When the chapter members reacted with horror, accusing him of violating medical ethics, Dr. Murugesan denied any wrongdoing and accused them of being jealous of his son's achievements. He argued that if a ten-year-old is allowed to drive a car and a fifteen-year-old can graduate as a doctor in the United States, then his son should be allowed to be a surgeon. 'We were all shocked, but he just didn't listen,' said Venkatesh Prasad, secretary of the Manaparai Medical Association. 'He said that we were jealous and were not recognizing his son's progress. He had no consideration for the ethics of the surgery.'" Officials immediately began a professional and criminal investigation into the matter, while Amarilis Espinoza, a spokeswoman for the Guinness World Records, told the Associated Press that the book did not endorse such feats because they would encourage "bad medicine." Like thousands of would-be record holders before him, Dr. K. Murugesan apparently made the classic error of not running the particulars of his record attempt by the book in advance. The *Times* further noted that the incident "also reflects the enduring fascination of Indians with setting world records, even when they put lives in danger. Last year a four-year-old boy tried to run a 43-mile marathon in an attempt to enter the Indian version of *Guinness World Records.* Doctors stopped the boy when he showed signs of exhaustion after 40 miles and later found him to be malnourished, anemic and under cardiac stress."

Another victim of the book's safety rules is American performer David Blaine, who has somehow made a living and landed television specials by doing exactly the kind of things Guinness World Record holders have done for years without financial reward—but he does them to far less impressive extents. Blaine has buried himself alive, an oft-challenged category since the very first book, and one in which he is not even remotely competitive. Likewise, he has tried pole squatting, and again does not come near the book's mark. His latest stunt was imprisoning himself in a box, an above-ground variation on burial alive. In September 2003, Blaine was sealed in a Plexiglas box suspended from London's Tower Bridge over the Thames River, with the goal of starving himself for forty-four days. While Blaine often calls himself a magician, this was neither a world record nor a magic trick, but rather some weird hybrid of physical feat and performance art. The attempt, titled "Above the Below," was apparently devised entirely to get media attention, the closest he has so far gotten to having something in common with actual Guinness World Record holders. The book's officials said they had been contacted by the performer, asking for his feats to be recognized, but a spokeswoman replied, "We do wish him well, but he has got a long way to go to beat the incredible Guinness record holders." Likewise, the book dismissed his earlier efforts including being buried alive and living in an ice block, because they did not break any records. Blaine's box-above-the-Thames stunt also failed record official's tests on two counts. The seven-foot temporary home was deemed not as small as current record holders for such confinement, and from a safety standpoint, the book refuses to endorse fasting records, despite having previously featured a hunger strike category. Keeper of the Records Stewart Newport told Glasgow's *Evening Times*, "We have never encouraged actively claims for the longest time to voluntarily go without solid food." Much to his credit, Newport rhetorically asked the question dogging too many record breakings gone bad. "If you beat the 'record' and then die is it a successful attempt?"

In silent answer to Newport's question is Hans Rezac, the jumper whose attempt to set a Guinness World Record by parachuting over the South Pole did not earn him a spot in the book but took his life instead. Would Rezac have jumped if not for the record? No one can say, but it hardly matters: his flight was full of other parachutists, some who lived and some who died, record book or no record book, and they will not be the last to try it. Those seeking the rush of adrenaline, the promise of fame, or the conquest of their fears will continue to be injured or killed, perhaps influenced by the glory that comes with getting into Guinness, perhaps not. "People will do dangerous things whether or not we record them," Craig Glenday told the *Financial Times*. That is certainly true, but it also seems reasonable to assume that more people are likely to try to break such records by virtue of them being certified as records rather than just crazy onetime stunts. In the same article the *Financial Times* noted that "He [Glenday] points to a Japanese craze called banzai skydiving where participants throw out their parachutes, then dive after them to hook up with the bag on the way down. That one makes the book." Just don't try it while eating marshmallows.

Epilogue

What a long, strange trip it's been.

Four years ago I first had the idea to do a humorous article for *Golf Magazine* on trying to golf my way into Guinness. Now this book has been written, and in the course of writing it I traveled the world doing research, with countless hours spent interviewing countless characters who "colorful" does not even begin to describe, and poring over articles and original documents in various libraries in various cities. I have seen the identical flash of recognition in the eyes of hundreds of strangers and friends as the topic brought them back to the iconic record holders of their youth, Robert Wadlow, long fingernail guy, and the McCrary twins astride their motorcycles.

If asked four years ago what really got me started on this book, I'd have said that English newspaper clipping and my article for *Golf*. But I would have been wrong. Now I know that my interest began about thirty years earlier, when I was an elementary school student in New York City. I remember a dog-eared copy of the Guinness book on the library shelf of my classroom at PS 92 in

Queens. All the kids, myself included, loved to flip through its pages and marvel at the records and the photos, accounting for the tired condition of the volume, which was probably a few years out of date, though the inspiration it provided never got old. This all came rushing back to me in late 2004, when an elementary school teacher I know asked me to visit her fifth grade class in Lebanon, New Hampshire, to talk about journalism. I had prepared as best I could for a bunch of eight- and nine-year-olds, but it was hard to get them interested in my work until my friend Sarah let it slip that I was in the *Guinness World Records* book. There was no turning back, and it was all the kids wanted to hear about, with questions reaching a fever pitch. Like me, three decades earlier, they had a well-worn, out-of-date copy of The Book on the classroom bookshelf, and despite living in the era of MTV and DVDs, the Internet and cell phones, they were as fascinated with the accounts of people ascending the stairs of skyscrapers on pogo sticks and holding live rattlesnakes in their mouths as I had been at their age. I now suspect that virtually every classroom in America has held an aging but in no way obsolete copy of the book during all those intervening years, and we as a nation are better for it. For children, and the child in each of us, Guinness World Records are the stuff of dreams.

This fascination is not entirely limited to kids, and the enduring popularity of The Book cuts across all demographics and ages. After all, almost every (human) record setter is an adult, and the books are bought by readers of all ages. I recently visited movie star Bruce Willis's vacation home in the Caribbean's Turks & Caicos islands (he was not there), and snuck a peak at his bookshelf. There were just a handful of volumes, including several on the flora and fauna of the region, alongside the *Guinness World Records*. I suspect that with more than 110 million copies sold, in thirty-seven different languages, his is not the only household, celebrity or nobody, family or childless, young or old, that owns a copy. I have nearly fifty different editions myself.

It is impossible to overstate the social significance of the *Guin-*

ness World Records book, especially in these times. It seems that half the programs on television are so-called reality TV, and many younger people today believe this trend started with shows like *Survivor* and the original *Big Brother*. In fact, all reality television, as well as shock or exploitation talk shows have their roots firmly planted in the Guinness book. It was the first public forum, in print and on the airwaves, for ordinary people to do things, sometimes amazing, sometimes humiliating, but always "real," and then get media exposure as a result. In the same vein, Guinness can be considered the genesis for the success of online self-media outlets like YouTube, MySpace, other social networking sites, and the entire concept of blogging. The Guinness book created the notion of a pathway to media visibility and potential recognition for those outside of the Fourth Estate, even if, as with many blogs, no one reads or cares. The idea that a person could convince themselves that they and their opinions or actions were newsworthy or interesting to strangers, that someone else out there might just want to read about them, began with the book, and technology and the media have sought out myriad variations on this theme ever since.

When I started this project, it was a labor of love as I had an unquenchable passion for all things *Guinness World Records*. When I discovered the history of Sir Hugh Beaver's question and the McWhirter twins, as unique and offbeat and oddly gifted as any of the characters they immortalized, it seemed the stuff of a noble fantasy. But along the way I also got to see some of the less pleasing aspects of the book and its history, the way it warps some of its would-be record holders, the way it panders to the crisis of celebrity worship in our society, the way it twists the media, and the way it has changed and rechanged its mission and style and meaning over the decades.

So what do I think now?

There is still a lot of positive energy surrounding the book. It is after all, a children's book, and it still excites and interests children, which is a good thing. I saw this firsthand in the elementary school classroom I visited, I have seen it in the households of my friends with children, and I have had countless peers tell me it is on their kids' Christmas or Hanukkah wish lists. *National Geographic Kids* magazine runs a monthly Guinness Records feature, and the editor assures me that there is an important educational component, and that the records help teachers teach kids about a wide variety of topics, including geography. Just getting kids to read anything today is becoming an increasing challenge, and the book certainly helps out in that regard.

There is also a kind of purity in the book's pages. Despite some irregularities and the habit of playing favorites with the media and celebrities, for the most part *Guinness World Records* has long had an obsession with fairness and maintaining a level playing field; it is one of the few remaining democratic institutions in our lives. The rules surrounding each record attempt, no matter how odd it appears, are lengthy and detailed and mostly standardized, all in the name of keeping apples only to apples (or oranges to oranges) when it comes to records. The thing that surprises record laymen the most is the fastidious red tape involved in the process. Records approved by Guinness (except the "firsts") are meant to be broken, and to that end each one is documented and administered in a way that makes it as fair as possible to all comers—except me, but we'll get to that. With a few exceptions, the world of Guinness is impartial to race, creed, or bankroll, and in its pages one finds true diversity: anyone with enough self-motivation and drive can enter its hallowed pages. For instance, when breaking the distance golf travel record, I was specifically told that only commercial flights, and no private jets, could be used, lest my record become the unassailable province of eccentric billionaires. While the book is home to its fair share of professional athletes, including many of the all-time greats, it is also the last bastion of pure amateurism, celebrating the drives and passions that were once embodied by the Olympic Games. Fifth graders are routinely told that in America anything is possible, that they can grow up to be doctors or lawyers or even the president. Some are already smart enough to know that these promises aren't completely true, but at the same time they recognize that there are many ways for them to excel. Guinness embodies this belief: there is a spot for them in its pages if they put their minds to it.

That's the good news. The bad is that the book and its staff often show little regard for its most hard-core fans, the record breakers themselves. The record application process appears to be intentionally difficult to navigate; it is tedious, and they are slow to respond, having embraced technology in form but not function. Moving their record mechanics online seems to be no improvement over old-fashioned mail, except that the powers that be can now discourage applicants without actually contacting anyone. Making people wait months to do something the book needs them to do to in order for it to continue to exist seems counterproductive, as does changing rules and record parameters retroactively, and consistently employing a pattern of keeping information that has no monetary value hidden from readers and fans.

There seems to be almost an air of paranoia surrounding the book, dating all the way back to the first lunch meeting the McWhirters had with Sir Beaver in 1955, when Norris McWhirter noted his boss's penchant for secrecy. Being obtuse for the sake of being obtuse has become business as usual at Guinness. I understand why every record cannot be in the book, as they simply wouldn't fit. However, when I suggested to Stuart Claxton, head of business development in the United States, that they also publish an unabridged edition and charge a hundred bucks or more for it, or sell it on CD or DVD, he couldn't give me any reason why they should not do this, except for vague rumblings about the proprietary value of their database. This would be the equivalent of Webster's holding back words from the dictionary, but never selling or productively using them. For half a century they have been operating with some sort of black hole philosophy, sucking in records and then hiding the vast majority of them from outside eyes, never acknowledging that the only value these records have is to readers who will pay to see them and those who want to break them. Yet they choose instead to hide them and get no value at all from the collection. This attitude extends to their interaction with the press, and it didn't make me feel any better about the company when they tried to stop me from writing this book. I went to them openly seeking cooperation and explaining that not only did this book not conflict with their sales—no one interested in records is going to buy my book instead of Guinness, and I don't expect a lot of eight-year-olds as customers—but it might rekindle the interest of many readers my age who had not actually bought one in decades. Every single person I have spoken to in the media and publishing industries—who does not work for Guinness World Records—agrees, but they said no. Not only did Guinness World Records say no, but they first led me to believe they were seriously considering it, apparently in an attempt to extract as much detail about my plans as possible before turning their lawyers loose. The Book could be so much better, but it seems bogged down in poor customer service, inattention to detail, and frustratingly bureaucratic management.

My latest record applications were met with such callous disregard and apparent disorganization that I began to seriously wonder whether I had been blacklisted, a practice that apparently has not even been used on employees of their biggest rival, Ripley's Entertainment. Could the notion of me setting records really be that dangerous? I submitted applications for three different records, including an existing one, through the website, and a week or two later was e-mailed the required record agreement forms to fill out and submit by mail or fax (only). I was also given three "claim ID numbers," sort of social security numbers for record attempts, except they didn't tell me which number went with which record, a piece of information without which you *cannot* fill out the forms. I e-mailed them about this oversight and never got a response. A few weeks later I faxed them the same question, and this time I did get a response. I then faxed in all three applications to London in one batch, twenty-four pages in all, watching as they were scanned by my fax machine, eating up many dollars in long-distance phone bills, and got a receipt showing the successful transmission. They later claimed to have received only one of the three, which seems impossible, so I faxed the other two again—having lost over a month. The impossible repeated itself, and they later claimed to have received only one of these two, so I re-faxed the final one for the third time, again having lost more than a month. Nearly five months since I initially applied, using a process that promises to take no more than five weeks, I still had no answers. The one application they admitted receiving was telling me online that I would receive an answer within four weeks—and had been for more than three months. Something seemed wrong.

Was my paranoia justified? Could the notion of me setting records really be that dangerous?

Apparently, yes. After months of waiting, and repeated inquiries, I got a fax from the Director of Records stating that "While Guinness World Records lawyers are investigating serious concerns regarding with the [*sic*] content of your book and its unauthorized association with Guinness World Records, we will not be in a position to consider any Record applications from you."

Since my actual conversations about this book had never gone beyond the company's public relations personnel, which in turn led to letters from their counsel, it appears as if I was internally "flagged" as a forbidden record-setting applicant. I appreciate that Guinness World Records is privately owned, and understand editor Craig Glenday's sentiment when he told the *Wall Street Journal*, "We get seen sometimes as a public service, as if the taxpayers expect it from us." Nonetheless, it strikes me as incongruous to position oneself as the world's preeminent record-keeping authority, and indeed rely on that reputation to validate your very existence, while at the same time picking and choosing who you think is worthy and unworthy of even being allowed to attempt records. As a casual observer of baseball, it seems obvious to me that the authorities at Major League Baseball, also a for-profit business, do not exactly see eye to eye with players like Barry Bonds, but they do not order the umpires to wave off every home run he hits and label it unofficial. Records are records, and when the self-declared arbiter of such deeds goes beyond apple to apple rule setting and begins discriminating between who can and cannot be a record holder based on their own preferences and prejudices, then it seems clear that their "authority" in such matters becomes nonexistent. So the bottom line of record setting becomes more like the quest of the child to become president: you can do it, as long as you are popular, and the folks at Guinness like you.

Amazingly, after all this hassle and disillusionment, I remain a cautious fan. Why? The first reason is that immediately before this book went to press, Guinness World Records was sold yet again, in early 2008, to longtime rival Ripley's Entertainment. Based on my conversations with the company's former president Robert Masterson (now chairman) and the new president, Jim Pattison Jr., I have high hopes for the future. Masterson made clear that he saw the relationship between the record keepers and record setters as flawed, and Pattison noted that unlike previous speculative owners, he intends to actually oversee operations. Hopefully this will mean more recognition of the people who provide the material that is the grist for the Guinnes World Records profit mill.

But my adoration for the book goes deeper than management squabbles, and is born of more than half a century of intriguing history. The records may have gotten wackier, the design sleazier, and the mission less noble, but there is still something compelling on almost every page. The eyebrows still go up, the mind still races to fathom "how could he (or she) do that?" Having gotten in tune with the book, I now see records everywhere, everyday. They are happening all over the world, all the time, all around us. I get countless e-mails from friends and associates with links to news stories of the new oldest woman or the biggest cake. I have not just set records; I have lived them. I have eaten at the world's oldest restaurant, El Botin in Madrid, where the souvenir postcards are a facsimile of the eatery's Guinness World Records certificate. Goya worked as a dishwasher at El Botin while trying to get his painting career started, and Hemingway was such a fan that he set a scene in the closing pages of *The Sun Also Rises* there. I have gone to China to see Mission Hills, the world's largest golf resort, and visited the top of the world's tallest structure, the CN Tower. I even rode in the world's largest organized bike tour, New York's Five Boro Bike Tour. Records are all around us, and a part of us, and the book is the main reason. It has spawned its own language, and "according to Guinness," carries the same weight with superlatives that "according to Webster's" does for spelling.

Now that I have examined the full spectrum of records and record breaking, the history, the evolution, and the future of the Guinness book, I will answer the one question you are chomping at the bit to know the answer to, at least if you have made it this far: Which is faster, the grouse or the golden plover?

According to the British Trust for Ornithology, the top speed of the European golden plover, aka the whistling or hill plover, is now known to be 60 mph, while for the red grouse, the species most commonly hunted in the British Isles, 40 mph is as fast as it gets. Sir Hugh was a true gentleman, and in this spirit, he won his gentleman's bet: he had wagered on the plover, which was indeed faster. But the original argument was based not just on whether the grouse or plover was speedier, but on which of them was the fastest game bird in Europe. The final answer is neither: The spur-wing goose has a recorded air speed of 88 mph, while the absolute winner, according to the McWhirters, was the wood pigeon.

You now know everything you need to know in order to decide whether you want to be a record breaker yourself, to take your first step down that road toward the absolute, of being the best in the word at something. I hope you do, and in that vein, I will say goodbye the same way I said hello, with the words of Ashrita Furman:

> I hope that after reading this you are inspired to attempt some feat of your own. The particular event is unimportant as long as it gives you the opportunity to dance on the edge of your capacity. But be prepared—the benefits could be both illuminating and far reaching.

Appendix 1

THE STORIES OF MY FAVORITE RECORDS

When I first proposed writing this book, I was asked for six examples of especially shocking or entertaining records. That was two years ago, and there was so much to choose from that it was virtually impossible to narrow the field. Now the difficulty of the same task has increased geometrically: in the 2008 book alone, even among just the records designated as brand new, the incomprehensible oddness of many leap off the page. Every time I think I have found the most perverse or bizarre, another catches my eye and outdoes it—just when it seems like records can't get any crazier, they do just that. Recent additions to the litany include feats of mind-boggling eccentricity, ranging from the most people fake-tanned in an hour by one person using chemical spray (67), most panes of (safety) glass run through, most fish snorted in one minute (meaning sucked into the mouth and ejected through the nose: the yoga instructor who managed eight also holds the same record for one hour, at 509 fish snorted) to the heaviest weight pulled (a Volkswagen car) with the eyelids—not to be confused with the heaviest vehicle pulled by hooks stuck through the skin (a van, using two hooks impaled into the small of the back). Some are just weird, others disgusting, and while many are made up Guinnessport, some do make you wonder how one ever discovers they even have a talent for sticking hooks through their flesh or attaching chains to their eyelids and pulling things. Ultimately, the nonstop weirdness of it all threatens to make even the most absurd feats seem mundane. Fortunately, the mix still contains some records that are more entertaining than deranged.

Just as the purpose of the tiny sampling of records chosen by the book's editors is to shock and titillate readers, so was the purpose of my selection of representative records to shock would-be publishers of this work. Now that I have gotten that part out of the way, I have been able to focus more on records that are simply interesting, not because of their gross-out factor, but for other reasons such as the sheer audacity of the achievement or the creativity and good humor behind the record itself. But the *Guinness World Records* provides little insight into the stories behind these remarkable achievements, simply squeezing them into as few words as possible. So given the increasingly hard-to-imagine things humans have done to get into Guinness—and on rare occasions for other reasons—I would like to take a look behind some of more quixotic things that have been deemed certificate worthy, some of the records that have stood out and become my favorites.

Keeping Up with the Norbergs: I have to assume Norberg is a fairly popular Swedish surname, because in 2004 an impressive 583 Norbergs got together in Sweden and set the record for the largest gathering of people with the same last name. This kind of record does not go unnoticed, and the record was soon shattered when more than 1,200 people with the surname—no surprise here—Jones got together to break the record. Interestingly, organizers were able to add a bona fide celebrity element to this momentous occasion, as singer and former James Bond girl Grace Jones, as well as opera singer Dame Gwyneth

Jones, performed for the assembled Joneses. This 2007 gathering raises the obvious question: where are the Smiths in all this? The Smith clan holds a special place in Guinness lore, as the very first edition in 1955 awarded them the title of commonest surname in Great Britain, with over 800,000 Smiths in England and Wales alone. A year later, the first American edition proved that once again the United States was number one, with more than 1.5 million Smiths, also the nation's most popular name. Half a century later, with a little organization, the Smiths could finally live up to their record potential.

Accidental Hero: Some pursue Guinness greatness, while others have it thrust upon them. The latter was the case of Toby Hoffman, an otherwise unknown member of the stage crew for KTLA, the station that broadcast the U.S. version of the *Guinness Records* show hosted by Sir David Frost and created by David Boehm. As Boehm recalled in *The Fascination of Book Publishing* "You never know when a record is going to be set on a TV stage. The plan was to have a man we had brought in from Europe show how he could lift 15 or more bricks from the floor at one time by pressing them all together while they were lined up horizontally. The bricks had arrived the evening before the show, and one of the workers engaged in moving equipment around was Toby Hoffman, whose huge biceps made the girls in the audience gasp. Toby asked me what the bricks were to be used for. I told him. Right away he went over to the bricks, lined them up and lifted them onto a platform. 'Wait a minute,' I gasped. 'How many bricks did you lift?' We counted them—17. The next day the European tried three times and the most he could lift was 15. The TV announcer proclaimed this was a world record, but I and my assistant who had seen Toby too, knew better. Toby went into the book."

A Dark Day in the City of Light: Not all of the many elaborate events planned for the last few Guinness World Records Days have gone as smoothly as organizers would like. When asked to think of a location famous for romance, many would immediately say Paris, and this is what the brains behind the attempt to break the record for most people kissing at once must have thought, too. But despite its passionate reputation, a paltry 1,188 Parisians showed up for the 2006 endeavor, while just a few countries to the east, the true romantics—11,570 of them—could be found smooching in Budapest. With a turnout nearly ten times that of the City of Light, it was the capital of Hungary that went into the record book. On the very same day, Nishio, Japan, a city famous for its green tea, managed to get 14,718 people to sip simultaneously while sitting barefoot on almost a mile of red carpet. This easily eclipsed the participants in the kissing record, perhaps demonstrating the priorities of would-be Guinness World Records holders.

An Oldie but a Goodie: In April 2004, stuntman Eric Scott flew 152 feet above London to break the Guinness World Record for highest rocket-belt powered flight. But what is most interesting about this tidbit, reported in *Popular Science* and evidence that even scientific innovation has its place in the book, is that the purpose of Scott's flight was to break the record. Break, mind you, not set, suggesting that his was not the first success in the pantheon of rocket-belt rides. This record seems especially vulnerable, given that in this case the sky is indeed the limit. Scott did not even come close to the height of Toronto's CN Tower, a rocket-belt flight that would be historically worthy of Guinness recognition.

If Only Cards Were Edible: Architect Bryan Berg is to card houses what every chef in the Big Food chapter of the book is to big food. He simply dominates his niche in a way even Ashrita is unable to do. Since Berg set his first record in 1992, while still in high school, the Cardstacker, as the book describes him (Berg calls himself a "card structure specialist") has never relinquished the title for building the tallest house of cards. His creations are so lofty the only one who can beat them is himself. And to add a bit of theater to the whole thing, he always topples the result himself in a grand gesture of destruction. Just how impressive are Berg's works? The repeat and multiple record holder built a house of cards 25 feet high in 1999, and then seized a second Guinness World Record for the world's largest card structure in 2004 when he built a detailed replica of Cinderella's Castle for Walt Disney World. Berg then put the super in superlative by breaking his new record in 2005, with an homage to New York's famous skyline, complete with playing card scale re-creations of Yankee Stadium, the Empire State Building, Times Square, and several other Big Apple landmarks. This mini-city required 178,000 cards, more than three thousand decks worth. At the 2007 Texas State Fair, he improved on his 1999 tallest record by constructing a replica skyscraper, more than 25'9" tall, and surrounded by several smaller buildings to form a city skyline. The work took him a month to build adding 70–200 decks worth each day, or about 10–125 pounds of cards. His other works have included elaborate cathedrals and domes, and the three-dimensional structures are so complex it seems impossible that they are made entirely from playing cards with no cutting, folding, gluing, or other means of support. The lack of challengers to the record he has held continuously for sixteen years must have gotten boring for Berg, who helped would-be rivals when he published detailed card-construction tips and techniques in his book *Stacking the Deck: Secrets of the World's Master Card Architect*. It is another title he justly deserves.

But Can Your Weird Fingernails Do This? Growing beards, mustaches, fingernails, and even ear hair of immense proportions has long been a classic methodology for entering Guinness's pages. But that was not enough for Antanas Kontrimas, who had been growing his beard for more than twenty-five years as of 2004. Anyone can stop shaving, but in a true case of pick up or shut up, the Lithuanian strongman let his beard do the talking on September 11, 2004, when he lifted a 136-pound woman with his beard. In addition to setting a Guinness World Record, Kontrimas also earned a spot on the "Strength Feats" list of *Joe Weider's Muscle & Fitness* magazine, an annual roundup of the most impressive strongman feats of the year. Apparently Kontrimas used all the time he saved by not shaving to plan and practice beard-lifting feats, hoisting such things as a sack of grain and a keg of beer with his facial hair while training for his first woman. His beard has also towed a Land Rover and a plane. Despite this distinctive repertoire, Kontrimas was not the magazine's only Strength Feat winner to set a Guinness World Record. The same list honors Canadian Kevin Fast, a doctor of theology from Toronto, who specializes in pulling very big things (not with his beard). Upon learning that his 100-foot vehicle pulling record had been unofficially broken, Fast wasted no time wresting it back, leaving nothing to chance: he immediately towed three fire trucks linked together and weighing a combined 102,933 pounds, covering 100 feet in just over two minutes. "Afterward," according to *Muscle & Fitness*, "feeling very sick, Fast announced his retirement."

Man's Record-Setting Best Friend: Dogs are no strangers to the pages of *Guinness World Records*, a tradition dating all the way back to Jacko, the terrier with an insatiable appetite for rats. Since Jacko, dogs have been recognized as biggest (its owner first came to Guinness thinking he had the world's smallest horse—really) and smallest, best at balancing glasses on their heads and skipping rope, and a favorite of mine is the golden retriever who can pick up and hold five tennis balls in his mouth at once. But no canine record is as uniquely Guinnessport as that held by the late Josh the Wonder Dog, who in his lifetime became the "most petted dog in America." Josh was a black and tawny brown stray who in 1984 serendipitously found his way to the Pasadena front lawn of Richard Lynn Stack, an author of children's books. In a fortuitous act of timing, Stack had just finished writing his first book, *The*

Doggonest Christmas, a week earlier. The coincidence continued: Josh bore a striking resemblance to the illustrated book's
main canine character, drawn by Stack's uncle. Stack immediately adopted Josh, but three years later their lives changed
dramatically when an insane person went on a canine shooting spree and shot three dogs in Stack's neighborhood. Only
Josh survived, but he was left unable to wag his tail because of
damage to his spinal cord. After barely surviving, Josh soon
became a spokesdog for overcoming adversity. Stack penned
two fictional children's books inspired by Josh, then helped
the Wonder Dog cowrite his autobiography, which included
inspirational aphorisms like "Josh Says: Go for your dreams!"
In 1989 Stack quit his day job as an attorney and began tour-
ing the country with Josh in an RV, visiting elementary schools
to spread the inspirational message. At each of these sessions,
children would line up to pet Josh, and Stack began keeping a
log of each petting. Josh ended up living to an estimated age of
sixteen, or over 110 in human terms, and he visited more than
2,000 schools. Shortly before he died from cancer, Josh entered
the 1997 record book as most petted dog when his owner presented Guinness with signed affidavits documenting the petting
sessions. By the end, Josh the Wonder Dog had been petted by
more than 408,000 people, a Guinness Record just about any
dog would be truly envious of.

Hungry for Breasts: Where else but in Berkeley, California,
would mothers—a lot of mothers—celebrate World Breastfeeding Week by trying to break the Guinness World Record for
mass breastfeeding? On Thursday, August 3, 2006, organizers
asked babies citywide to latch on at exactly 2 PM. Sucking its
way into Guinness was no mere pipe dream for Berkeley: four
years earlier, the city had first set the breastfeeding record by
satisfying the needs of 1,130 hungry babies. The city mothers
rested on their laurels, until the certificate was shipped off to
the Philippines in 2006 after 3,738 nursing mothers displayed
solidarity in Manila. If such slights are worthy of counterattack

by folks like Ashrita Furman and his rivals, why should nursing mothers be any less driven by pride? The gauntlet had been thrown down and Berkeley women responded like any other displaced Guinness Record holder would, by taking up the challenge and picking up lots of babies.

Pub Trivia—Without the Trivia: The book itself is the result of pubs and pub patrons, so it is only fitting that it contains a pub crawl record for mass bar hopping. It is even more fitting that the record is rekindling the heat of barroom disagreements. In 2005, residents of Maryborough, a small city in Australia, invented the category and set the first record by enlisting 1,198 drinkers to blitz all of the town's seventeen pubs. The next year, the city went after its own record and found 2,237 participants who consumed about 50,000 drinks throughout Maryborough. The numbers are staggering, or maybe just Guinness-worthy, at an average of more than twenty-two drinks per person. Rules stipulate that each participant consume at least half a pint of beverage in each of at least ten different pubs. The drink can be nonalcoholic, but having spent a fair amount of time in Australia, I don't imagine a lot of record setters chose that option. In fact, one of the organizers told a local newspaper that part of the logistical difficulty in the bid is getting the drinkers to fill out and return their "crawl cards," noting that "It's a problem getting them to hand them in at the end of the crawl when they're 'tired and emotional,' shall we say." This problem was demonstrated in 2006 when rivals in London tried to wrest the title away from Maryborough and reportedly got 2,700 patrons to visit ten different pubs, but apparently were unable to sort out the paperwork and get approval from the book. Since Maryborough's record still made the 2008 edition, it seems more than a few of the English pub crawlers also had trouble completing their cards. While this news probably went over well in the rural city that mocked its more famous rival for a poor showing, given London's population of 7 million compared with Maryborough's 25,000, the Aussies will not be sitting back and awaiting the next threat. They have decided to make the record-breaking pub crawl an annual event, to be held on the weekend of the Queen's birthday, and I hope to make it Down Under one of these years and do my best to turn in a card.

There Is No "I" in Team: When EchoStar Communications Corporation, which operates the DISH Network satellite television service, pit eight American football fanatics against each other in a survival-of-the-fittest sleep deprivation contest, the corporate types forgot one thing: football fans love teamwork. After winning contests to represent their favorite teams as "Ultimate Football Fans," the eight contestants were put in front of the TV in an attempt to break the Guinness World Record for TV watching, which was 69 hours and 48 minutes. The last man standing, or in this case sitting, would win a luxury trip to the NFL Pro Bowl in Hawaii. But after one of the eight left early on, the remaining seven did something the organizers had not expected: they came together as a team, helping each other fend off sleep so they could all break the record together. "We decided early on that we could all work together to break the record, so we set aside our personal goals to join in this pact so everyone would turn out a winner," said Chris Chambers, representing the Dallas Cowboys. Sitting next to one another in a single row of reclining chairs and watching nothing but football, the remaining seven banded together, ignoring the rivalries of their preferred teams and encouraging each other. When they had broken the record and made it to a full seventy hours, they followed their agreed-upon plan and all turned their heads and looked away from the screens simultaneously, ending their bids at exactly the same time—in a tie. So moving was the unexpected camaraderie that the DISH Network decided to award all seven contestants the Hawaiian trip, as well as the reclining chairs, large high-definition television sets, and a satellite receiver. Some of the record attempts I pored over made me want to cry in despair, and while this one did not quite move me to tears, if it had, they would have been tears of joy at the feel-good nature of the result. By the standards of the *Guinness World Records*, it qualifies as pretty touching stuff.

The World Walk: This one did move me to tears, and will remain my personal favorite Guinness World Record, in large part because setting the record was of no concern to Steven Newman when he undertook an extremely challenging endeavor that severely tested his will and beliefs, and was almost abandoned several times. From 1983 to 1987, Newman went on a truly amazing journey, which landed him in the pages of the 1988 Guinness—for all the right reasons. As he recalled telling his bewildered parents in his touching memoir *Worldwalk*, "On the first of April, 1983, I will step out the front door to start a journey never before made by anyone. . . . What I am trying to do is walk around the world . . . alone." Newman didn't do this to get into Guinness, which happened later as a by-product of the publicity he received, because the aspiring journalist found a newspaper that wanted him to file a weekly column documenting his four-year, 15,000-mile journey through twenty countries. Newman, who worked for several years at a dangerous and menial job as a uranium miner in Wyoming to save up the money for the trip, had never even been abroad before starting his journey, and the only foreign language he spoke was high school Spanish. His parents understandably found the idea, which he sprung on them after nearly two years of secretive planning, hard to fathom, so he explained his real motivation:

> This walk is something I *must* do if I am ever to get a true sense of what the world and its peoples are like. I want to do this as a learning experience, to find out what all those other people's dreams and hopes and fears are, but

also as a test to see if the world is still a place where love and compassion prevail. And a place where romance and adventure abound as much as they did in the days of Marco Polo and Sir Francis Drake. I want to do it alone, without sponsors, so that I can have total freedom to do anything and go anywhere I want to. Except for a librarian or two who've helped me find the right maps, I've done everything alone on this project. I've done it because I want to show others, particularly the young, that an individual can realize his or her dreams without outside resources. I will have only a backpack to carry my supplies, so that I will have to depend upon the generosity of others to help feed and shelter me. Hopefully that will get me into many homes, so I can see what their everyday life is like. . . . Because if they don't, I'll probably never last. You see, I've set two conditions for myself: never to pay for any accommodations, except if my health is in jeopardy or I am way behind on my writing, and never to eat in any restaurants fancier than a sidewalk café or teahouse.

Newman was also surprised to experience the kind of fleeting celebrity so synonymous with the book. After he completed the first leg of his overland journey, from Ohio to Boston, where he planned to board a plane to Ireland, he instead found himself headed back to the place he had just spent weeks walking from, New York. This time he covered the distance by plane, to appear on the CBS News. As Newman recalled, "So from canned baked beans and peanut butter sandwiches and sleeping on the bare ground in a ragged blanket that rightfully belonged in a back-alley Dumpster, I was whisked away—still grimy and sweaty from the day's walking—in twenty minutes from Boston to New York over the same countryside I had taken a month to cross on foot. . . . When I landed at Kennedy Airport in New York, I had less than five dollars in my pocket. Yet what followed for the next twenty hours was chauffeured limousines, a two-hundred-dollar room at the Parker Meridien Hotel in Manhattan, and room service on spiffy trays—all at CBS's expense. I couldn't eat at the restaurant in the hotel because I had no tie and jacket. It was the closest I had ever been to feeling like a celebrity or millionaire."

If anyone deserves a place in Guinness, it is Newman, who despite challenges and self-doubts, succeeded and did so spectacularly, staying in the homes of dozens of well-meaning strangers, and being wined and dined by American farmers and Australian Aborigines. Even the poorest denizens of Africa and desert Bedouin took him in, fed him, and sheltered him. His is what we would like more Guinness World Records to be: amazing in a way that goes beyond shock value, impossibly difficult in its commitment, and truly one of a kind, with a barrier to betterment that even the most banal Guinness World Records rules cannot begin to hint at. Instead, Newman imposed his own set of rules, ones that undermined his attempt and made it much more difficult—and dangerous—than it had to be, and by doing so he found self-redemption and won admiration from the world's citizens and readers of his fine book recounting the journey. *Worldwalk* is now out of print, but a used copy would be an excellent investment. To cap his touching story, his four-year odyssey even resulted in finding love. He married a schoolteacher he met on a national tour visiting schools and telling students about his walk.

Appendix 2

**THE LONG WAY INTO GUINNESS:
AN ODE TO DRUDGERY**

The main thing that record holders share is their stubbornness.

—Norris McWhirter

After spending 147 days buried in a coffin six feet below the parking lot of a Mansfield, England, pub—eating, breathing, and excreting via a nine-inch-wide plastic tube—GEOFF SMITH emerges triumphant, having broken a buried-alive record set by his mother, Emma, in 1968.

—Outside, June 2004

The title of this book is *Getting into Guinness,* because that is what both the book and our culture have evolved toward, reaching a point where the goal is usually not lofty achievement or exploring the limits of the human condition, but rather of getting one's name into print for a host of often selfish reasons.

But not every record is undertaken to get into the book. Some are the result of higher purposes, some of a mental defect, some of religious passion. What many of the records that are apparently not the result of record seeking have in common is that they are endeavors of the longest kind. This is an –est not seen as frequently as fastest, tallest or strongest, for the very real reason that the longest records take the longest time to set. While reading and contemplating thousands of records and nonrecords for this book, I began to mentally sort them in groups by theme. One theme that especially impressed me were those records based not on danger, or whimsy, or giant food, but on drudgery. These are the ones that are often pursued for some other reason than the book, because frankly, no fifteen minutes of fame or local hero syndrome is enough to make up for years and sometimes a lifetime of toil. While serial record setters like Ashrita Furman might devote decades to breaking dozens or hundreds of different records, this unique personality spends the same vast lengths of time on a single feat. Whether they require not cutting one's nails for half a century or walking around the world—more than once—these records are, by the nature of the scope involved, the most difficult to break. I call these "drudgery records" because their main distinction is in the single-minded devotion they require. So before we close the page on all things Guinness World Records related, I would like to pay a short tribute to some very long achievements.

I have already mentioned Steven Newman's four-year trek by foot around the globe, which the Ohio native undertook as "a learning experience," in order "to get a true sense of what the world and its peoples are like." He did that beautifully, and anyone who reads his memoir *Worldwalk* will come away convinced that the Guinness World Record he received for his effort was perhaps the least important part of the process. In fact, Newman does not even mention The Book in his book, but his record is reserved for the book's jacket as a marketing effort of the publisher. His may be the most moving such tale of drudgery, but it is not the only one. Consider these longests:

A Cross to Bear: When evangelist Arthur Blessitt decided to
carry a twelve-foot-long, forty-pound wooden cross on his
back, he did not think small. Blessitt left California on Christmas Day 1969, with the intent of taking his cross to every
nation on earth. Nearly forty years later he has visited around
200 countries and shouldered his load for almost 40,000 miles.
His pilgrimage is nothing less than the world's longest walk,
according to Guinness. But the mileage was not the only challenge Blessitt faced: he endured standing before a firing squad,
walked through war zones in fifty different countries, and as
of 2002 had been arrested or imprisoned two dozen times. But
there is no quit in Blessitt, who is still out there, somewhere,
walking.

World Run—or Not?: Having already been beaten to the
World Walk by Newman, and the longest walk period by
Blessit, the obvious goal left for Robert Garside was to become
the first person to run around the world. So he left Piccadilly
Circus with just a pack on his back and began running. This
reflects the longtime *Guinness World Records* obsession with
track sports and running in general, which has generated many
different records from the ongoing quest to run the mile faster
to the endless marathoning records (fastest, most, backward,
juggling, pushing a baby carriage, dressed as Elvis, dressed
as chain gang, and so on). But Garside stands atop this distinguished heap, at least according to London's *Daily Mail*,
which described his effort as: "HAVING outrun everyone in the
history of mankind." But had he? Almost immediately after
Guinness granted him a place in its book, huge holes began to
appear in Garside's story, including photos posted on his own
website that conflicted, often by thousands of miles, with his
official diary of the run. A notable lack of witnesses did not
help his cause. Then it was discovered that after being turned
away at the Russian-Kazakh border, he simply flew to India,
skipping 2,000 miles. Not only did he eventually admit having

made up a dramatic story about being robbed in Pakistan, he had never even been to Pakistan. Yet he has shown the same kind of single-minded perseverance drudgery records require to finish in sticking to his claim. He put forth the simple explanation that due to such difficulties he voided the first yearlong leg of his trip, from London to India, and then began again, completing his global run the second time around in an additional two years. And Guinness World Records believes this. Marco Frigatti, the head of records told the *Daily Mail* that his team spent more than three years examining fifteen boxes of credit card receipts and hundreds of time-coded tapes, and making follow-up calls to independent witnesses, adding that Guinness also kept in close contact with Garside during every leg of the twenty-nine-nation journey across six continents. Along the way, his diary describes how he was shot at by Russian Gypsies, ran across battlefields in Afghanistan, was robbed at gunpoint (twice), jailed in China for suspicion of espionage, and survived by scavenging food and drinking water from streams, all done without any support crew.

Still, his run has bred conspiracy theories within the long-distance running community, fueled by evidence of made-up visa troubles to explain suspicious flights, and an amazing seventy-mile-per-day pace from Mexico City to the American border described in his documentation. These smoking guns have inspired many doubters, including former *Runner's World* editor Steven Seaton, who said, "I don't care what Guinness says. To do what Garside claims, to run some of those South American routes at altitude, in the jungle, on broken trails, on his own and with a rucksack—not a chance." It probably didn't help that Garside had previously gotten sponsorship help from the magazine for the infamous Marathon des Sables, a hellacious endurance slog through the Sahara desert, and then never showed up for the race. Whether he did what he claimed or not, there is no doubt that Garside spent the better part of his three years traveling on foot through some exceptionally difficult landscape, and that certainly fits the drudgery category of effort. Interestingly, he also kicked off a bit of a journalistic marathon, as the English papers closely followed the unraveling of his story. The *Daily Mail* called him a "globe-trotting cheat," but Guinness stuck by him, even after he admitted taking days off and cutting out hundreds or thousands of miles with flights, because rules pertaining to such epic journeys allow for rest days and traversing bodies of water by ship or plane. Taking a position that is the polar opposite of what I have seen as business as usual, and after dismissing many other claims for lack of paperwork, Guinness's Stewart Newport explained the controversy away by saying, "There is a certain amount of trust."

Think Small: Eric Peters's tale is the opposite of Garside's declining glory. Instead of being met with a hero's reception that turned into disbelief, he began with disbelief and eventually proved his way into Guinness. Peters was a poor Englishman who spent two years while on the dole converting a fiberglass barrel less than six feet long into a sailboat. Then, armed with only nuts, olive oil, and some water, he spent forty-six days at sea piloting the smallest craft ever to be sailed across the Atlantic Ocean, from the Canary Islands to Guadeloupe. It seems that the doubt surrounding his effort was, in large part, due to his lack of sponsorship, prenotification, or marketing of his effort, and for a while Peters was penalized for simply doing it the old-fashioned way and going about it alone, through grit and determination. But both Guinness and the seafaring community became convinced, with the book's spokesman Colin Smith reporting that "Our experts are satisfied. There is no question at all," which in turn prompted London's *Times* to coin yet another important term in the lexicon spawned by the book when it described Peters as "Guinless no longer."

Eight if by Land, None if by Sea: Combining the spirits of Newman, Peters, and Blessitt was George Meegan, a British merchant seaman who found that his talent on land exceeded that on water when he walked nearly 20,000 miles from the southernmost point in the Western Hemisphere, Tierra del Fuego, to the northernmost, in Alaska. It took him a full seven years and involved a lot of towering mountains, frigid conditions, extremely rough terrain, and often very limited infrastructure, but when he was done he had amassed a whopping eight different Guinness World Records with his one stroll. These included the Longest Walk of All Time (now held by Blessitt) and First Crossing of the Western Hemisphere on Foot.

Interestingly, Meegan fathered two children with his Japanese wife during the walk, giving one the name *Ayumi*, Japanese for "walk," and the other the middle name *Susumu*, which appropriately translates as "keep going." When he finally reached the Beaufort Sea in northern Alaska after 2,426 days on the road, Meegan said, "I thought 'Oh my God it's over. The end of my dreams.' It was a terribly sad experience. It was a bereavement."

Frequent Flier Miles: Few road warriors, even the most harried, can relate to Charles Veley. When Veley stepped onto unoccupied Bouvet Island in the southern Atlantic Ocean in 2003, a journey that had first required him to be lowered from a helicopter onto a research vessel, he made *Guinness World Records* history. It was the 350th different country, enclave, island, federation, or disputed territory Veley had visited in his barnstorming, whirlwind tour that made him the World's Most Traveled Man. No one has visited as many places as he has, and amazingly, he did it all in just three years of nonstop travel, spanning nearly 1 million miles. Veley was already accomplished, a Harvard graduate who flew F15s in the Navy's Top Gun program and then built a multibillion-dollar software company before embarking on his journey. His motive? His parents had not liked to travel, and as a child he never had a vacation. A million miles later—and a million dollars out of his own pocket—Veley got into Guinness.

Bums, but No Bum's Rush: When I first met Ashrita Furman, he reminded me of the many ski bums I know, folks who have managed to build their life around doing the activity that gives them endless pleasure. For ski bums or surf bums, it is the slopes and waves that make life interesting, and for Ashrita it is setting Guinness World Records. For Rainer Hertrich and Dale Webster it is both. While an extremely avid skier might boast of getting in a hundred-plus days in a season, Hertrich skied his way into Guinness by racking up over 1,000 consecutive days of skiing without missing one. British skier and respected journalist Arnie Wilson had previously set the standard by skiing every day for a year, 365 in a row, carefully planning flights and drives across oceans and continents so as to never be too far from the slopes and getting in at least a single run each day. Sometimes that meant climbing the hills at night or in the predawn darkness, when lifts were not operating, in order to get in a run before an early flight. His adventure was as much travel-based as skiing, and it took him to countless resorts around the globe. While Hertrich has kept it up for more than three years, he keeps the logistics a bit simpler by spending the entire North American winter season in Colorado, where he works at a ski resort, the shoulder season in Oregon, where he works on the always frosty slopes of Mount Hood, and then he heads to South America, where stunned locals have dubbed him "Gringo loco de Guinness," keeping his record streak entirely within the Western Hemisphere. It still was not easy: Hertrich has kept the streak alive by skiing with a separated shoulder, bruised ribs, and a wrenched thumb, and venturing out into temperatures of 20 degrees below zero. He also eschews single-run days, working as hard at accumulating hours as years: he has racked up well over 30 million vertical feet, and in the average day skis a height greater than Mount Everest. His single-day best is an unbelievable 115,000 vertical feet. As impressive as Hertrich's streak is, Dale Webster, who was featured prominently in the renowned surfing documentary *Step Into Liquid*, puts his land-based peer to shame. As of mid-2006 he had surfed for more than 11,200 straight days—more than thirty years. He goes through about one wetsuit and one board annually, and has surfed through tropical storms, frigid water and weather, and even with painful kidney stones. Both Hertrich and Webster have made it into Guinness, and neither seems to know when to stop. After breaking the record, Hertrich posted the following message on his online diary: "Great day, snow, and fun!!! I think I'll have to wake up alive one more time and ski tomorrow." And he did. And he still does. Likewise, Webster said, "I could stop and end the damn thing tomorrow, but I know I won't."

Clearly, Webster has the Guinness spirit. There is something inspirational about endeavors that span years or decades rather than hours, and walks or runs more easily measured in continents than miles. But even in the lofty world of drudgery, where most of these accomplishments were not done primarily for the book, there is still the occasional attempt at what might be called ultramarathon Guinnessport. While the book rejected the presumably (especially when considering his attention span) long effort of a ten-year-old who wrote out the letter *A* some 17,841 times, they were moved to include the world record for typing all the numbers from one to one million. It was harder than the *A* thing, because Les Stewart, the Australian who did it, not only spelled out each number in words, rather than numerals, on a manual typewriter, he also did it all with just one finger, a result of being partially paralyzed in the Vietnam War. It took him nearly 20,000 sheets of paper and sixteen years. Similarly, in a fitting nod to itself, the 2008 edition of *Guinness World Records* includes perhaps the most extreme case of Guinnessport ever. The record for

Books Typed Backwards, is held by an Italian who typed fifty-seven books in reverse order—and in their original languages—beginning in 1992 and entering the current edition as a new record, presumably taking about fifteen years for the effort. Titles included such classics as *The Odyssey*, Shakespeare's plays, and of course, the *2002 Guinness World Records*.

Appendix 3

SO YOU WANT TO BE A RECORD BREAKER?

So you want to be a record breaker? Or maybe a record setter? As long as your goal is to get into Guinness, it doesn't matter much, because many of the logistical steps you will need to take are identical. Just remember before embarking on any record quest the two cardinal rules of world recordom:

1. Setting or breaking a world record is always harder than you think. They may seem silly or inane, but most people do not, and never will, have a world record. Even the world's top record holder, Ashrita Furman, failed in his first few attempts.

2. Do all the research in advance. Thousands of records have been rejected because they didn't get advance approval. Some were simply wasted time, because they never would have been approved, but others would have set records, except that they were not conducted under official rules. If you do the most push-ups in an hour but don't have the right number of wit-

nesses, it won't matter. The only thing worse than failing in an attempt to get a Guinness World Record is succeeding and still not getting one.

How should you go about it? There is no easy answer, because why and how some records are accepted and some rejected are subjects of mystery and often, it appears, whim. Some seemingly normal activities, like tug-of-war, will be deemed too dangerous, while seemingly suicidal ones, like jumping out of a plane in the hopes of catching up to a free-falling parachute, or "banzai skydiving," are allowed. Make no assumptions about how Guinness will react to a proposal.

For that reason, it is easier, at least logistically, to break existing records. There are a few exceptions to this rule, such as printed records that have been retired, which is why you always have to remember rule 2 above. You do not want to end up like Englishman Tony Wright, who relied solely on what he had read in a copy of the book when he stayed awake for 266 straight hours to break the record of 264 set more than forty years earlier. Had Wright checked, he would have found the reason for the record's longevity: it was retired and deemed unbreakable for health and safety reasons. He may be named Wright but he took the wrong approach to getting in. Don't make that mistake. It also gives you a greater chance of being in the book if you break a record that is already printed. Let's face it, everyone would rather be in the book than just have the certificate at home on the wall. So for the most part, if you can find a record in the book that you can break, that is the single easiest path to being a world record holder. So let's call that Plan A.

PLAN A

1. Find a record in the book you think you can break. This is not that easy to do, but Ashrita finds ten or more of these a year. The book indicates, usually with red stars, which records are new in the current edition. These are often the easiest to surpass.

2. Go to the book's website, www.guinnessworldrecords.com. The layout changes periodically but you will find a button titled something like "Become a Record Breaker." Follow this link and fill out an e-form stating which record you intend to break, giving them all the information they ask for.

3. Unless the record has been retired, they will send you a form by e-mail (if it has been retired they will just say no at this point) in several weeks. You will need to sign this and return it to London by fax or mail. It is basically a legal agreement, giving them permission to use your image and name, and protecting them from lawsuits. Once you sign and return this, in the neighborhood of four to eight weeks you should receive the rules under which you can undertake your attempt, and the requirements for documenting it, including the number and nature of witnesses, and probably video, photographic, or media evidence as well. In some cases other materials will be required, such as airline boarding passes were for my travel-based record. Follow all these instructions to the letter.

4. Assuming you have gotten advance permission, then break the record and document it properly, and after you mail in all the required information, you should be a world record holder and receive a certificate to that effect in the mail in a few weeks or months. Unless someone else breaks the record around the same time, or unless you get unlucky like the Thai cobra kisser that Ripley's Entertainment president Robert Masterson recalled, the one who got permission and broke an existing record under the required rules only to be told afterward that the record was too dangerous to break. Just remember that those things happen.

What, you might ask, is the downside of Plan A? Well, records in the book attract a lot more attention and if you found one that seemed easy to break, you can bet other people, maybe a lot, maybe even Ashrita, did too. Furman talked about the orange pushing record getting harder and harder to break by the week or month as he trained for it; this can be a major disadvantage and must be weighed against the major advantage of Plan A—that it is most likely to get you into the book. If the record itself is more important than an entry in the book, try Plan B.

PLAN B
Find a record not in the book that you think you can break. Not a day goes by when a record is not set, and almost all of these make the news somewhere. Journalists have access to global media databases of articles such as Lexis-Nexis. If you cannot get access to such a network at the office or through friends, try a public or college library. Many of them, especially at educational institutions, have free access to periodical databases. I regularly visit my local college library and run searches for terms like "Guinness World Records," "Guinness Records," and "World Records," and there are new stories almost every day. Ashrita did this and found out about a new record for throwing the Guinness book itself the farthest, one that never appeared in print. On average these kinds of records are just as easy to break as those in the book, but receive much less competition. You might be the only one to try and break it. If you do break it, there is more chance it will last. The downside is that the editors have already decided this record is not bookworthy and probably will not change their minds, though they do bring records back or publish older ones for the first time, on occasion. If you go with Plan B, after finding a vulnerable record, simply follow steps 2–4 above.

Paradoxically, setting a new record is both easier and more difficult than breaking an existing one. It is difficult because you need pre-approval, to essentially convince Guinness World Records of the worthiness of your proposed feat. If they go for it, however, it is often easier because the threshold is lower, since no one else has done it before, and let's face it, you probably should not be proposing feats you cannot do . . . or you don't deserve to get into Guinness. They probably would accept the first man to fly without mechanical assistance, but you probably won't get off the ground by flapping your arms. So one key is to walk a fine line and make the record sound as impressive as possible while still being within the realm of possibility, or what Norris McWhirter called "at the edge of possibility." Setting a new record will be Plan C, and requires all the same steps as Plan A above, except that in step 1 you have to provide more description and justification of your intended record when you fill out the form online. Think of this as a bit of an essay contest, an opportunity to convince the jury. For example, here is an actual claim proposal for a new record I submitted to Guinness World Records:

ATTEMPT DETAILS

Attempt Title: Most Bicycle Ascents of the Alpe d'Huez in One Day
Attempt Date: Monday, July 25, 2005
Attempt Location: France
Details: The Alpe d'Huez is the most famous bicycle mountain ascent in the world, a normal fixture on the Tour de France, and the site of last year's Tour Centennial individual time trial won by Lance Armstrong. Bicycle enthusiasts come from all over the world to do the climb, which is approximately 14 miles long and has 21 famous switchback turns, ending at a ski area atop the pass in the French Alps. The vast majority of cyclists climb it once and are satisfied they met the challenge, as do the racers in the Tour de France. Some gluttons for climbing punishment make it a point to climb it twice in one day, which is considered a badge of honor. I intend to climb it at least five times in the same calendar day, a feat which I can find no evidence of anyone ever having done. This is the bicycling equivalent of Mount Everest. I intend to do it on my own, or I may do it with a cycling friend, Mr. James Offensend, but in that case we would still both complete all the ascents individually and would be happy to be co-record holders. We would

drive back to the start after each ascent, which any challenger could do, but the entire ascent, following the Tour de France time trial route of 2004 (which is the standard climb of this ride) would be human powered. As a current holder of two Guinness World Records I am very familiar with your policies and standards and would be prepared to provide witnesses and other required information, and I think this certainly is a qualified goal, especially since there are so few bicycling records. In addition, it meets the sporting concept of being eminently breakable and easy for other enthusiasts to challenge. I thank you in advance for your consideration. Lawrence Olmsted

First off, there were several things I attempted to do in this claim. I made the following very clear: that the Alpe d'Huez, a mountain pass in France, is the *most famous* climb in the *most famous* bike race on earth, the Tour de France, and one that puts me on the same plane as a true champion like Lance Armstrong. I also made it clear that avid cyclists from around the world come on pilgrimages to climb it, and made sure to describe it as cycling's equivalent of Everest, a mountain the folks at Guinness know well. I did this to establish the traditional quality of the climb, just as the English Channel is the traditional standard for open water swimming. Then I had to set a threshold, at the very "edge of possibility," one that would seem much more impressive than the twice-in-a-day climbs, and after much deliberation, I chose a minimum of five, having learned from my poker attempt that it is better to shoot just a bit below your maximum potential, which I thought would be six. Knowing it would be an easier ride with company, I left open the option of doing it with or without a regular riding partner of mine. Finally, I felt they would give me more consideration as a two-time record holder, or at least take the idea more seriously.

They said no.

They also said no to my pitch for most people playing croquet simultaneously, although they have many such records, from most people playing Twister to most people wearing Groucho Marx fake glasses and noses at the same time. You just never know what will impress that fickle bunch. Still, there are some generalizations you should keep in mind.

TIPS FOR NEW RECORD APPROVAL:

1. Read recent editions of the book and note the new records. This probably means they were just approved for the first time, so looking at a bunch will give you a feeling for what the editors like.
2. Think of variations on existing records. Throwing, pulling, lifting, or balancing new things has worked many, many times. Bricks, beer kegs, other people, and cars are all popular things to lift or put on your head. So maybe you can try something new but colorful. Alternatively, you can change the method rather than the item: people push cars, pull them, pull them with their eyelids, with their beards, or with hooks attached through their skin, move them all sorts of ways. Variations do not have to be this dramatic; they can be as simple as doing something backward, upside down, or underwater. Even my poker record, while new, was essentially a variation on many other marathons, from card playing to really long games of Monopoly.
3. Try group records. The book gives a lot of latitude to mass participation records, from people drinking tea together to huge group head shavings to chains of bras. Then again, this was my croquet logic.
4. Do it for charity. This is especially true for group records.
5. Do it first. Firsts are a whole special class of records and, among record aficionados, considered the best because they can never be surpassed. However, the book is fickle about its firsts, and on its website gives examples of good and bad firsts. Good ones are "absolute," and have fewer qualifiers. First woman on the moon is still up for grabs and would be ac-

cepted. First woman from Singapore on the moon would not. Likewise, they usually will not split hairs, and while they have categories for various first flights (transatlantic, transpacific, around the world) by various types of aircraft (plane, hot air balloon) they state that they will not accept variations by class or type of plane, for example. In general, they like firsts of lasting historical significance: Mount Everest, yes, Mount In Your Backyard, no.

6. Avoid the no-nos. While they cannot be assumed to be absolutes, there are certain types of records Guinness has stated it does not accept. These include age-based records with a few exceptions. They do maintain youngest and oldest categories for such feats as running marathons and climbing Everest, but not for doing push-ups. Certainly no –ests by a certain age, like fastest mile by a teenager. Likewise, for the most part, they do not accept nationality-based claims, and they absolutely do not like ones defined by race or religion. They do not accept heaviest or lightest pet records, and in the pet record categories that are acceptable, they do not differentiate by breed. They do not accept speed records involving motorized vehicles on public roads, *Cannonball Run*–style. And due to an especially bad experience, they do not accept any chain letter records, whether by mail or e-mail.

So if getting into Guinness is your goal, choose from Plan A, B, or C above, and good luck. Having multiple ideas will better your odds, and you might as well submit them all at once, rather than waiting to hear. Patience is also a virtue as GWR is often very slow to respond. When you get approval and are ready to go, follow Ashrita's advice and fire off a fax (they won't read e-mails) to verify that the record threshold has not changed in the interim. If and when you do make it to the finish line and become a Guinness World Record holder, your first question will likely be, "So, will I be in the book?"

The sad answer is probably not. Only about 8 percent of the officially recognized records get into print, or less than one in ten. This meager selection is based on editorial judgment of entertainment value and variety, and very hard to predict. More outlandish records, especially those with equally outlandish photographs, seem more likely to be published. Records that are already in the book are more likely to be continued once broken. About 20 percent of the content turns over annually, so a record may appear once, as my poker marathon record did in 2006, and then disappear, despite not having been broken. It takes hard work, talent, and dedication to set or break a record. It takes a lot of luck to see it in print. The easiest way to statistically ensure that you will see your name in print is to break or set about ten records.

Appendix 4

A RECORD-BREAKING TIMELINE

1759: Arthur Guinness starts making stout at the St. James Gate brewery in Dublin. He later signs a 9,000-year lease on the property. By the end of the nineteenth century, Arthur Guinness & Sons is the world's largest brewery.

September 1954: Sir Hugh Beaver, KBE, managing director of Arthur Guinness & Sons goes bird hunting in County Wexford, Ireland, leading to an argument over which bird is faster, the grouse or the golden plover. His inability to answer this question leads to the creation of the *Guinness Book of Records*.

May 1955: Sir Beaver hosts twin brothers Norris and Ross McWhirter at a lunch meeting at the company's London headquarters, where he commissions them to start a new company, Superlatives Ltd., and create a record book for the brewery.

August 27, 1955: The first-ever copy of *The Guinness Book of Records* is published by Guinness Superlatives Ltd., Ludgate House, Fleet Street, London.

1956: David Boehm, founder of Sterling Publishing, buys U.S.

rights to the book, which he renames *Guinness Book of World Records*.

1960: Sir Hugh Beaver retires.

1962: Boehm licenses paperback rights to Bantam, which publishes the first paperback edition of *Guinness Book of World Records*, which sells more than 50 million copies.

April 1970: The first U.S. television special based on the book airs. This one-hour show is sponsored by AT&T and hosted by comedian Flip Wilson.

1972: *Record Breakers* television show is launched on the British Broadcasting Corporation (BBC). It will run in prime time for more than thirty years.

1973: Guinness PLC signs updated contracts with Sterling Publishing and Bantam extending their rights through 2016. Sterling partners with host Sir David Frost and 20th Century Fox to produce six prime-time specials, along with twenty-four game show episodes, based on the Guinness book.

1975: Ross McWhirter is assassinated at his home by Irish Republican Army gunmen after organizing an effort to stop terrorist bombings. *Newsweek* claims that after twenty years the *Guinness Book of World Records* "has set a record as the largest selling book—after the Bible: 26.3 million copies."

1979: Ashrita Furman sets his first Guinness World Record by doing 27,000 jumping jacks. He goes on to set and hold more than anyone in history.

1985: Norris McWhirter retires as editor of the book after thirty years.

1989: Boehm and Sterling sell the rights to the U.S. edition back to Guinness for $8 million.

1995: Guinness Publishing lures executive Chris Irwin away from the BBC and names him managing director. After he arrives to find records stored in forty-two filing cabinets with no database, Irwin tells the *Wall Street Journal* that "the book had become ossified," and "The place was a time warp. A lady would come though the office with a tea trolley." From the late 1970s until the mid-

1990s, sales of the book had been falling steadily by about 5 percent a year. Nearly forty employees are eliminated or replaced, a new editorial team brought on board, and the headquarters is relocated from the suburbs to downtown London. Irwin says, "It wasn't the easiest transition. We feel that we have one of the world's great brands, but it had got stuck." Guinness Publishing sells two museums and rights to operate and open seven more future locations to Ripley's Entertainment.

1996: The annual edition features an extensive redesign, with greatly increased emphasis on color photographs. Categories were updated and modernized and more celebrity elements appear.

1997: Guinness PLC and rival Grand Met combine in a $22 billion merger forming Diageo, with a strategy to become a pure wine and spirits company by divesting unrelated businesses. Positioning it for sale, the record book gets a name change. "We're called Guinness World Records now," says Alistair Richards, chief operating officer. "Diageo wanted a name to be one that had the least chance of confusion with their Guinness brand. Therefore they wanted the word 'Guinness' to be as close to the words 'world records' as possible. To the man in the street that probably doesn't make much sense. But to a lot of businesspeople and lawyers at the time it was terribly important."

1995–98: Following the organizational changes and revamp of the book, sales triple. Success is greatest in the United States, where sales had declined from 1.4 million in the mid-1970s to 408,000 in 1995 before climbing to 1.3 million by 1998. Projections in 1999 are for the book to sell 2.4 million copies in English and 1.3 million in other languages all in hardcover, plus another 900,000 in paperback in the United States.

1998: *Guinness World Records: Primetime* debuts on FOX in the United States.

1999: *Guinness World Records: Primetime* is replicated in Britain, Germany, and Scandinavia. A new breed of Guinness World Records museum opens in Orlando, operated under license by Ripley's Entertainment with an emphasis on interactive exhibits.

The official target reader switches from ten- to fifteen-year-olds to seven- to fifteen-year-old boys.

July 1, 1999: Guinness Publishing, a branch of Diageo PLC, officially changes its name to Guinness World Records Ltd. The company decides to move away from publishing numerous ancillary titles such as *The Guinness Book of Military Blunders* and the *Ultimate Joke Encyclopedia.*

2000: Diageo sells Pillsbury to General Mills.

2001: Diageo sells Guinness World Records Ltd. to Gullane Entertainment for £45.5 million. Gullane is a leading English children's entertainment company that owns such valuable brands as Thomas the Tank Engine. The book of records, aimed at young adolescents, seems to fit the company's niche, but some analysts believe Gullane overpaid for the record-related properties.

2002: Following financial struggles subsequent to its acquisition of the book, Gullane is acquired by rival entertainment company HIT Entertainment. HIT's original offer is £225 million, but when Gullane posts lower than expected earnings for 2001–02, the sale price is lowered to £139 million. HIT, which owns Bob the Builder and Barney the Dinosaur, quickly puts the Guinness World Records Ltd. piece of its Gullane purchase up for sale, but after receiving some respectable bids, changes its mind and keeps the company, believing its business has great potential for improvement and forecasting that profits can be doubled in two to three years. In the same year, Diageo continues its strategy by selling fast-food chain Burger King.

2003: Diageo acquires liquor giant Seagrams.

April 19, 2004: Norris McWhirter dies while playing tennis.

November 2004: 100 millionth copy of Guinness book is sold.

2005: HIT is taken private by Sunshine Acquisitions, a private holding company that in turn is part of large U.S. venture capitalist Apax Partners, the de facto owners of the Guinness World Records properties. In London, Diageo closes the Park Royal Brewery, where the book was born, and relocates operations to St.

James Gate in Dublin, still in the infancy of the 9,000-year lease signed by Sir Arthur Guinness in 1759.

November 9, 2005: The first annual Guinness World Records Day is held.

December 2007: London's *Times* reports that Guinness World Records is once again up for sale, at an asking price of £60 million.

January 2008: Guinness World Records Ltd. launches a companion site exclusively for video and computer gaming records, www.gwrgamersedition.com.

February 2008: Guinness World Records Ltd. is purchased by Jim Pattison Group, a privately-held Canadian company that also owns longtime Guinness rival Ripley's Entertainment. Reuter's estimates the reported purchase price at $118 million.

Acknowledgments

There are many people without whom this book would have been impossible to write, and many more without whom it would have been so much more difficult. Like an Academy Award recipient, I don't have time to thank them all before the music starts playing to rush me off the stage, but I will do my best to hurry through without insulting anyone.

First and foremost, my lovely wife, Allison, who for years has been subjected to my repeated absences as my work takes me to all corners of the globe, and who has long been the one who has to fret while I put myself though sometimes dangerous stunts. Also on the home front, a shout out to Armstrong, Stretch, and the puppy Sundance, who spent much of his youth under, next to, or on my office chair while I wrote this book. They may never have mastered holding five tennis balls in their mouths simultaneously, but if Guinness ever adds a record for best-looking golden retriever in history, it would be a three-way tie.

My life has been made much easier—and far more entertaining—by virtue of all the experts and record holders who generously took the time out to discuss their exploits, obsessions, and madness with me, including but not limited to Ashrita Furman, Jackie "the Texas Snakeman" Bibby, Sir Richard Branson, Ben Sherwood, Jake Halpern, Greg Childs, Ken Jennings, Jez Edwards, Terence Brennan, Michael Roberts, Mark Frary, Nobby Orens, and Jason Daley.

Kudos to the great nation of Australia, which not only provided the fodder for so many of the funny stories herein but also hosted my first record bid and continues to prove on a daily basis that life can and should be fun. I'll be back.

My own record setting, health, and sanity would probably not be what it is today without the unparalleled support of a group of friends who quite literally got me through my darkest hours, including Joe Feeney, Tony Matos, Dave McGrath, and anyone else I forgot in my mindless stupor, all led by the unbeatable dream team of Matt Rosenthal, Joe Kresse, and Naim "JP" Peress.

I cannot imagine a writer, no matter how lofty his or her reputation, who wouldn't want to be in my shoes when it comes to representation. When it comes to agents, Jill Kneerim is to the profession what Ashrita Furman is to setting Guinness World Records: if she says it can be done, she does it. And her house is cheaper than an airport hotel.

One last group that I cannot overlook: all the folks, friends and strangers alike, whom I have mentioned this project to over the past two years. The unanimous enthusiasm of your reactions has been the secret ingredient behind my inspiration, a constant reminder that this was a good and worthwhile idea, and that you really do want to hear this story. Major career undertakings, no matter how promising, are always accompanied by some self-doubt. Your passion for this project erased my worries. And if every one of you does what you said and buys a copy, I will be in good shape.

Finally, I cannot forget Sir Hugh Beaver, Norris McWhirter, and Ross McWhirter, the three men who, for the best reasons and with the noblest intentions, brought the *Guinness Book of Records* into the world without the slightest inkling that they were changing publishing history and the course of contemporary human events. Okay, so in doing so they may also have created exploitation talk shows and reality TV, but don't blame them—they didn't mean to. They just wanted what we all want: answers.

Endnotes

vii. Adrian Hilton recited the *Complete Works of Shakespeare*: *Investor's Business Daily*, Mar. 30, 2007.

CHAPTER 1 MEET ASHRITA, RECORD BREAKER FOR GOD

1. *Just for the Record:* www.ashrita.com.
2. second most widely read book: *Oregonian*, Nov. 18, 1990, T6.
3. *"People* magazine called me": *New York Times*, June 12, 2003, 1.
3. "Ashrita is by far": *New York Times*, June 12, 2003, 1.
3. As of Jan. 2008: www.ashrita.com.
3. Russian weight lifter: *New York Times*, June 12, 2003, 1.
4. To match Alekseyev's: www.ashrita.com.
6. "bookwormish": *New York Times*, May 11, 1988, 16.
6. "I had this fascination about the book": *Christian Science Monitor*, Dec. 22, 2000, 12.
7. According to his official biography, Chinmoy . . . : www .srichinmoy.org.

7. Chinmoy had a colorful athletic past of his own (feats): www.srichinmoy.org.

8. World Harmony Run: www.worldharmonyrun.org.

9. At 5'10" and 165 pounds: *Christian Science Monitor*, Dec. 22, 2000, 12.

10. "In pursuit of excellence, sort of": *Globe and Mail*, Jan. 18, 1986, A6.

10. The "King of World Records": *Toronto Star*, June 27, 1990, A6.

10. Guinness's "King Of Strange Feats": *New York Times*, June 12, 2003, 1.

10. "Mr. Versatility": *Christian Science Monitor*, Dec. 22, 2000, 12.

21. James Carville to tell him, "You're not crazy": *Washington Post*, Nov. 3, 1995, F1.

22. Empire State Building, World Trade Center, and Eiffel Tower turning down his request: *Toronto Sun*, June 24, 2001, 22.

24. According to the *New York Times: New York Times,* June 12, 2003, B1

29. His Website refers to him as "Suresh Joachim": www .sureshjoachim.org.

30. Almost very nearly impossible.": Greg Childs, former *Record Breakers* producer for BBC.

CHAPTER 2 THE GREATEST RECORD OF ALL: BIRDS, BEAVER, BEER, AND SIR HUGH'S IMPOSSIBLE QUESTION

32. *"The next best thing":* Dr. Laurence J. Peter, *Peter's Quotations* (New York: Bantam/William Morrow, 1977), xiii.

32. *The original edition has an introduction by the chairman of Arthur Guinness & Co: Independent* (London), Oct. 29, 2004, 37.

33. "all started by a mouse": *The Quotable Walt Disney* (New York: Disney Editions, 2001).

34. "America's crime rate": Ken Jennings, *Brainiac: Adventures*

in the Curious, Competitive, Compulsive World of Trivia Buffs (New York: Villard, 2006), 74.

35. Hugh Beaver moved around: Collection of Personal Records of Sir Hugh Beaver at British Library of Political and Economic Science, London School of Economics.
36. In addition to running the world's largest brewery: Ibid.
37. According to his 1967 obituary: *Guinness Time* (no copyright), vol. 20, no. 2, Spring 1967.
37. But the most accurate account seems to come from Norris McWhirter: Norris McWhirter, *Ross* (London: Churchill Press, 1976).
37. Guinness was on tap in some 84,400 pubs throughout the British Isles: *Herald* (Glasgow), Aug. 18, 1997, 10.
38. It is known that the shoot occurred at Castlebridge House: *Sunday Mail*, Nov. 27, 1988.
38. the first edition was written in just sixteen weeks: *Daily Telegraph*, Apr. 21, 2004, 25.
38. For what it's worth, both the *New York Times*: *New York Times*, Oct. 7, 1992, C1.
38. the *Scotsman* attributed the genesis of Sir Beaver's idea to 1954: *Scotsman*, Nov. 17, 2004, 16.
38. Beaver's meticulously detailed personal appointment diaries: Collection of Personal Records of Sir Hugh Beaver at British Library of Political and Economic Science, London School of Economics.
39. *"My dear Hugh"*: Ibid.
40. Like everything else Sir Beaver undertook, this moment was recorded in precise pencil-written letters. Ibid.
41. born just twenty minutes apart: David Boehm, ed., *The Fascination of Book Publishing* (Salt Lake City: Sterling Publishing, 1994), 9.
41. the twins' grandfather, also William McWhirter: *Daily Telegraph*, Apr. 21, 2004, 25.
41. "From an early age my twin brother, Ross, and I": *Advertiser* (Brisbane), Oct. 27, 1993.

41. their time together at Marlborough prep school: *Irish Times*, Apr. 24, 2004, 14.

41. "They memorized every important date": Boehm, *Fascination*, 9.

41. They were standout athletes who competed at the national and international level in track, and also excelled at rugby: McWhirter, *Ross*, 87.

42. Also on the track team was Chris Chataway: Boehm, *Fascination*, 11.

42. "It would have taken a clairvoyant": McWhirter, *Ross*, 85.

42. "It never occurred to either of us": Ibid., 75.

42. the twins formulated a plan to set up: Ibid., 94.

42. their first book, *Get to your Marks*: Ibid., 94–95.

43. On Mar. 2, 1951 McWhirter Twins Ltd. was formally registered as a business: Ibid., 101.

43. The twins clinched the deal . . . using "superlative objects and people": Ibid., 106.

43. Norris's work with BBC radio also took a major step forward: *Irish Times*, Apr. 24, 2004, 14.

44. "Ladies and Gentleman. Here is the result of event number nine, the one mile.": McWhirter, *Ross*, 134.

44. "The total crowd was estimated at 1,200 and I have met all 10,000 of them since!": Ibid., 131.

45. Norris reported that scalpers: Ibid., 136.

45. Chataway had just given up full-time athletics : Boehm, *Fascination*, 11.

45. one morning, Sir Beaver and Smiley began chatting: McWhirter, *Ross,* 141.

45. "It seemed that Sir Hugh had an instinct for confidentiality": Ibid., 142.

46. As Norris recalled the fateful meeting: Ibid., 142–44.

47. They had only sixteen weeks: *Daily Telegraph*, Apr. 21, 2004, 25.

47. "The work on the book could be summed up as extracting '-ests'": McWhirter, *Ross*, 148.

48. "People who have a total resistance to giving information": Ibid.

48. On August 27, 1955: Ibid.

48. the original book contained some 8,000 records: *Sports Illustrated*, May 3, 2004, vol. 100, no. 18, 227.

49. Sir Beaver promptly wrote back to the twins: McWhirter, *Ross*, 149–50.

50. "The realization dawned on us quite quickly that the book": Ibid., 150.

50. "The earliest roots of trivia": Jennings, *Brainiac*, 55.

50. "It is also historically misleading": *Guardian*, Apr. 22, 2004, 6.

51. "Pub trivia, like 1960s rock and roll": Jennings, *Brainiac*, 215.

52. both McWhirters married women: McWhirter, *Ross*, 112–13.

52. the name changed out of misguided concerns: Boehm, *Fascination*, 15.

53. "In the United States people will not buy anything unless it is advertised": McWhirter, *Ross*, 151.

53. *Le Livre des Extremes*: (Paris: Hachette, 1962).

53. *Rekorde Rekorde Rekorde*: (Vienna: Carl Ueberreuter, 1964).

54. Obituary of Sir Hugh Beaver, K.B.E (1890–1967): *Guinness Time* (no copyright), vol. 20, no. 2, Spring 1967.

**CHAPTER 3 GETTING INTO GUINNESS
GETS PERSONAL**

55. "While some records": Peter Matthews, *Glasgow Herald*, Aug. 18, 1997, 10.

61. "We get seen sometimes as a public service": *Wall Street Journal*, June 10, 2006, 1.

61. "We thought we were in the book for sure.": *Sports Illustrated*, July 30, 1979, 68.

66. historically, about three-quarters of the record categories repeat: Ibid.

CHAPTER 4 GUINNESSPORT: GETTING INTO GUINNESS GOES PRIME TIME

70. *"If you want to settle a pub argument in 2004"*: *Independent* (London), Oct. 29, 2004, 37.
73. "These are a particular favorite of young boys": Jennings, *Brainiac*, 113–14.
75. Born in Alton, Indiana, on February 22, 1918, Robert Pershing Wadlow: Claire Folkard, managing ed., *Guinness World Records 2005* (London: Guinness World Records Ltd., 2004), 6–17.
76. by the fiftieth anniversary 2005 edition: Ibid.
76. flagship museum in London's Trocadero, the synthetic Wadlow: *Times* (London), Jan. 12, 1985, 14.
76. Amazingly, Wadlow was still growing fast: Folkard, *Guinness World Records 2005*, 16–17.
76. After his death, Wadlow's brother Howard recalled: Ibid.
77. Chris Sheedy, Guinness World Records's representative in Australia: *The Age* (Melbourne), Aug. 25, 2007, 3.
77. "He had to duck to go through all doorways": Folkard, *Guinness World Records 2005*, 16–17.
77. Given that he also held the records for having: Ibid.
77. led the renowned Italian director Fellini: Norris McWhirter et al., *Guinness: The Stories Behind the Records*, (Salt Lake City: Sterling Press, 1981), 100.
77. The *New York Times*: *New York Times*, Aug. 7, 1978, D9.
77. Bao saved the lives of two dolphins: *New York Times*, Dec. 15, 2006, A10.
78. "After searching high and low": CNN.com, Mar. 28, 2007.
78. "The best part of the job for me": *Edmonton Journal* (Alberta), Sept. 1, 2006, F5.
79. "It gives you a place in the world": *Times* (London) Aug. 29, 2004, C8.
81. "One of the marvelous things about doing this job": *Scotsman*, Nov. 17, 2004, 16.

81. David Boehm, the publisher of the American edition, had Izumi : *New York Times*, June 14, 1980, 29.

81. McWhirter was very proud of the self-proclaimed fact: *Scotsman*, Nov. 17, 2004, 16.

81. "It was very fascinating—she remembers Vincent van Gogh": *Herald* (Glasgow), Oct. 4, 1996, 11.

81. In France, they have a creepy: *Washington Post*, Feb. 21, 1995, D1.

82. Remarkably, for a period of time in 2007: *Yahoo News*, www.yahoo.com, June 18, 2007.

83. "Records are used there": *Newsweek*, Sept. 15, 1975, 81.

84. "The old Guinness looked more like a psalm book": Ibid.

85. "Nothing, however, points up the book's success more dramatically": *Sports Illustrated*, July 30, 1979, 60.

86. *Shortcuts: How to get into the record books*: CNN.com, Sept. 22, 2006.

96. a new record for "Demolition Work": Ross and Norris McWhirter, *The Guinness Book of Records* (London: Superlatives Ltd., 1972), 277.

96. This record would stand for more than a decade: N. McWhirter, *The Guinness Book of World Records 1984* (London: Superlatives Ltd., 1984), 186.

98. when he lit the fuse of an 720-pound firework: *New York Times*, June 29, 1980, SM6.

100. By 1999, the *Wall Street Journal* reported: *Wall Street Journal*, July 30, 1999, B1.

101. "Except that it's not that kind of book anymore": *Independent* (London), Oct. 29, 2004, 37.

105. *The Guinness Book of Records* got its first American airtime: Boehm, *Fascination of Book Publishing*, 17.

106. *Smithsonian* magazine reported: *Smithsonian*, Aug. 2005.

106. By 2005, fully half the records in the book were held by humans: Ibid.

107. a ten-year-old Guinnessport aspirant from Texas: *Wall Street Journal*, Sept. 21, 1988, 1.

107. "We get claims from people who have worn a pair of socks" *Smithsonian*, Aug. 2005.

108. Chris Sheedy, a former vice president of Guinness World Records: *The Age* (Melbourne), Aug. 25, 2007, 3.

108. "What made the four-minute mile special": *Sports Illustrated*, July 30, 1979, 70.

CHAPTER 5 15 MINUTES OF FAME

109. *his object was not*: Ben Schott, *Schott's Sporting Gaming & Idling Miscellany* (London: Bloomsbury, 2004), 44.

109. In his moving prologue: *Independent* (London), Oct. 29, 2004, 37.

110. One swimmer even seized the mantle: Schott, 59.

112. "People tell us it's a dream": *Washington Times*, Sept. 28, 2007, A12.

112. "For most of these people, the motivation is all about": *Edmonton Journal* (Alberta), Sept. 1, 2006, F5.

112. "people seeking their fifteen minutes of fame": *USA Today*, Jan. 9, 2003.

112. Norris McWhirter saw the appeal of notoriety: *Newsweek*, Nov. 12, 1979, 131.

113. He told England's *Guardian* newspaper: *Guardian* (London), Dec. 11, 2000.

113. he put them up for sale on the Internet: *Guardian* (London), Dec. 11, 2000.

115. Born in war-torn Sri Lanka: *Toronto Sun*, July 15, 2007, 8.

117. what *Newsweek* dubbed "Guinnessitis": *Newsweek*, Sept. 15, 1975, 81.

118. In *Sports Illustrated*'s landmark 1979 magazine feature: *Sports Illustrated*, July 30, 1979, 56.

118. "Why do people break Guinness World Records?": Promotional trailer for *Guinness World Record Breakers Week* on the *Food Network*, USA, 2006.

118. The *Times* of London even coined a term: *Times* (London) Sept. 21, 1983, 12.

119. Take Lucky Diamond Rich: *The Age* (Melbourne), Aug. 25, 2007, 3T.
123. "The scorch of fame can be brutal": Maureen Orth, *The Importance of Being Famous* (New York: Henry Holt, 2004), 25.
123. "Since I started reporting": Ibid., 303.
124. Carey Low, the book's spokesperson for Canada: *Toronto Sun*, July 15, 2007, 8.
125. According to Professor Elizabeth Vandiver: Elizabeth Vandiver et al., *Great Authors of the Western Literary Tradition, Course Guidebook* (Chantilly, VA: The Teaching Company, Ltd., 2004), pt. 1, 34.
125. Vandiver defines the concept of *kleos aphthiton*: Ibid., 36.
126. consider the case of Philip Rabinowitz: Transcript, *All Things Considered*, July 6, 2004.
127. The same 2007 edition welcomes: Craig Glenday, ed., *Guinness World Records 2007* (London: Guinness World Records Ltd., 2006), 6.
127. Likewise, on the first page of the 2006 edition: Glenday, ed., *Guinness World Records 2006* (London: Guinness World Records Ltd., 2005), 6.
128. "Celebrity Secrets," described as: Glenday, *Guinness World Records 2007*, 160–62.
129. As Stephen Moss wrote: *Guardian* (London), Apr. 22, 2004, 6.
129. McWhirter did indeed object to the wholesale changes: *Guardian* (London), Mar. 23, 2001, 25.
131. Without the promise of fame, would John Evans ever have: *Telegraph* (London), Nov. 21, 2004, 7.
132. This may be what led twenty-eight-year-old Christopher and his friends: *Wall Street Journal*, June 21, 1989, A14.
132. "The motivations for mastering certain fields": McWhirter et al., *Guinness: The Stories*, 3.
132. Boehm himself interviewed world record stilt walker: Ibid., 9.

133. what is believed to be the ONLY anonymous record holder: Ross and Norris McWhirter, *The Guinness Book of Records* (London: Superlatives Ltd., 1971), 175.

CHAPTER 6 SEVENTY-TWO HOURS IN HELL: GETTING BACK INTO GUINNESS
134. "If it was easy": *Wall Street Journal*, June 21, 1989, A14.

CHAPTER 7 THE CHEESE DOES NOT STAND ALONE: GIANT FOOD AND GUINNESS
159. At the 1962 Seattle Worlds Fair: *Guinness Time* (no copyright), vol. 20, no. 2, Spring 1967.
161. To date, the largest haggis on record: *Herald* (Glasgow), Aug. 18, 1997, 10.
162. The record-setting attempt: *Reed Business Information Ltd. Hospitality* (Australia), Feb. 17, 2005.
162. the attempt required a custom-made pan: AAP Newswire (Sydney), Nov. 26, 2004, 1.
163. *Guinness World Records* officials sometimes: Associated Press State & Local Wire, May 25, 2007.
163. The biscuit still had to be canine edible under Guinness rules: *Telegram & Gazette* (Worcester, MA), June 25, 2007.
167. To mark the re-launch of its Vanilla Coke last year: Associated Press State & Local Wire, May 25, 2007.
168. The 2003 record breaker was a Hershey's Rich Dark Kiss: *Professional Candy Buyer*, Sept. 2003, 86.
168. July 7, 2007 was the 100th birthday of the iconic Kiss: *Confectioner*; July 2007, 6.
169. Eepybird Perfetti Van Melle: *Candy Industry*, June 2007, 15–16.
170. Krispy Kreme, who supplied the hardware for the tower: *Evening Mail* (Birmingham, England), Nov. 10, 2005.
170. As *PR Week*, a trade publication . . . wryly noted: *PR Week* (U.S.), June 27, 2005, 2.

171. "He explained that the attempt was": *Times* (London), Mar. 4, 2007.

172. "Claims We Don't Want to See,": Glenday, *Guinness World Records 2008*, 13.

172. "We also disappointed the Hungarian village": *Telegraph* (London), Nov. 21, 2004, 7.

CHAPTER 8 RECORDS GO GLOBAL

173. *"Is there a record for the nation with too much free time"*: *Time*, Jan. 20, 2006, 26.

174. it has been translated into thirty-seven languages: *London Daily Mail*, Oct. 30, 2006.

175. In pure world record bulk: Associated Press, Sept. 4, 2007.

175. Actually, India is only tenth on the list: Associated Press, Sept. 4, 2007.

175. In the 1990s, record mania in India: Associated Press, May 6, 1993.

175. a seventeen-month-old toddler who ate: Indo-Asian News Service, July 10, 2007.

176. "India is a land obsessed with superlatives": Associated Press, Sept. 4, 2007.

176. Guinness Rishi, sixty-six years old, whose business card: Associated Press, Sept. 4, 2007.

177. Rishi has served as the president of the Guinness World Record Holder Club of India: Associated Press, May 6, 1993.

178. Titled the *Limca Record Book*, it was created: (http:// en.wikipedia.org/wiki/Limca_Book_of_Records).

180. He is not alone. Toronto stuntman: *Toronto Sun*, June 24, 2001.

181. Not to be outdone, the CN Tower: *Toronto Sun*, Nov. 10, 2006.

181. "Most building staff are stuffy about what they let people do: *Toronto Sun*, June 24, 2001.

181. That could explain a lot of things: *Toronto Sun*, July 15, 2007.

182. "For good or ill, Canada has made its mark": *Ottawa Citizen*, Sept. 10, 2006.
182. The nation is among the world's top five: *Toronto Star*, Aug. 26, 2007.
182. with the nation of just 33 million snapping up: *Ottawa Citizen*, Sept. 10, 2006.
182. Four times the population of Singapore, Chile submitted: Financial Times Information, Global News Wire, Nov. 12, 1999.
183. According to Wu Xiaohong: *Daily Telegraph*, Feb. 20, 2005.
184. the *Irish News*, *Irish Independent*, and *Daily Mail* have all done stories: *Irish News*, Sept. 29, 2006; *Irish Independent*, Oct. 30, 2006; *London Daily Mail*, Oct. 30, 2006.
184. "the most consistent chart artist ever in Britain: *London Daily Mail*, Oct. 30, 2006.
185. Ireland's greatest claim: *Irish Independent*, Oct. 30, 2006.
185. "That's a staggering amount of tea.": *Irish Independent*, Oct. 30, 2006.

CHAPTER 9 THE DARK SIDE: GUINNESS RECORDS GONE BAD

188. The Vienna pub owner was a passionate skydiver.: *Washington Post*, Feb. 8, 1998, F1.
189. the only record left up for grabs at the polar extremes: Ibid.
189. According to the *Washington Post*, Rezac partnered: Ibid.
190. Kearns could not explain: Ibid.
192. Boonreung Buachan, known as "the Snake Man": *Independent*, Mar. 23, 2004.
192. reported that Guinness banned all endurance-based records: *Independent*, Mar. 23, 2001, 10.
193. "Now that it is officially acknowledged that eating can seriously damage your health": *Times*, May 23, 1989.
194. ... the Grenoble native has consumed an impressive diet: *Edmonton Journal*, Sept. 1, 2006, F5.

194. "I believe he was the only man to ever have a coffin: Ibid.

195. "problem is, we've got copycats: Ben Sherwood, *The Man Who Ate the 747* (Bantam, New York, 2000), 155.

196. Bennet D'Angelo, when he made ice cream history: McWhirter et al., *Guinness: The Stories,* 52–53.

197. "This gentleman regurgitates what he has drunk halfway through": *Times*, Aug. 12, 1971, 6.

197. "Some of the records have got to such extremes": Ibid.

197. His rationale? The goldfish being used: *New York Times,* Feb. 10, 2000, B10.

198. Guinness staffer Carole Jones told . . . that gluttony: *Los Angeles Times*, Feb. 19, 1996, E1.

200. Master Chi, whose real name was Ronald Chamberlain . . .: *New York Times,* Jan. 3, 1977, 24.

201. when seven-year-old Jessica Dubroff was killed: *Washington Post,* Apr. 13, 1996, B1.

201. The same goes for helicopters: *Telegraph,* Dec. 21, 2003, 6.

203. 1974, when sailors of the Royal Navy attempted to break: *Times,* Sept. 27, 1974, 7.

203. In 1995, a boy was crushed to death in Germany: *Los Angeles Times,* Feb. 19, 1996, E1.

203. Eastport, Maryland's John DiPietro learned: *Washington Post,* Nov. 4, 2006, 61.

204. "One of the many disagreements I had": Boehm, *Fascination of Book Publishing,* 24–25.

204. "We just don't want to encourage": *Los Angeles Times,* Feb. 19, 1996, E1.

204. yet the book creatively gets around this by allowing: *People,* May 14, 2007.

205. the unfortunate consequences that befell: *Daily Mail,* June 25, 2007.

206. In 2007, Hong Kong civil servant Barry Kwok: *Birmingham Post,* Sept. 10, 2005.

206. Guinness World Records officials told the *Times: Times,* Jan. 21, 2007.

206. The unofficial record for a bizarre case: *Times*, June 22, 2007, 45.
208. The book's officials said they had been contacted: *Evening Times* (Glasgow), Sept. 5, 2003.
209. "People will do dangerous things: *Financial Times*, Jan. 21, 2006, 1.

EPILOGUE
219. The spur-wing goose: *Calgary Herald*, Apr. 25, 2004, B6.
219. while the absolute winner, according to the McWhirters: *Smithsonian*, Aug. 2005.

APPENDIX 1: THE STORIES OF
MY FAVORITE RECORDS
222. organizers were able to add a bona fide celebrity element: *Washington Post*, Mar. 15, 2007.
223. . . . the Smiths in all this?: *The Guinness Book of Records* (London: Superlatives Ltd., 1955), 77.
223. *Accidental Hero*: Boehm, *Fascination of Book Publishing*, 24.
224. But despite its passionate reputation: *Time*, Nov. 20, 2006, 26.
224. stuntman Eric Scott flew: *Popular Science*, Mar., 2006, 44.
224. Since Berg set his first record in 1992: CNN.com, Nov. 14, 2007.
225. The repeat and multiple record holder built: *Weekly Reader*, Apr. 8, 2005.
225. seized a second Guinness World Record: CNN.com, Nov. 14, 2007.
225. This mini-city required 178,000 cards: *Weekly Reader*, Apr. 8, 2005.
225. At the 2007 Texas State Fair: CNN.com, Nov. 14, 2007.
226. Kontrimas also earned a spot on the "Strength Feats" list: *Joe Weider's Muscle & Fitness*, Dec. 2004, 92.
226. Josh the Wonder Dog: *Washington Post*, July 29, 1997.
227. *Hungry for Breasts*: U.S. Federal News Service (HT Media Ltd.), July 31, 2006.

228. *Pub Trivia—Without the Trivia*: Australian Associated Press, Oct. 19, 2006.
229. *There is no "I" in Team*: Business Wire, Sept. 28, 2006.
230. "This walk is something I *must* do: Steven M. Newman, *Worldwalk* (New York: William Morrow, 1989), 2–3.
231. "So from canned baked beans and peanut butter sandwiches: Ibid., 82.

APPENDIX 2: THE LONG WAY INTO GUINNESS: AN ODE TO DRUDGERY

233. "The main thing that record holders share": *Newsweek*, Nov. 12, 1979.
233. After spending 147 days buried in a coffin: *Outside*, June 2004.
235. But the mileage was not the only challenge: *Express* (London), May 21, 2002.
235. But there is no quit in Blessitt: *Outside*, June 2004.
235. "Having outrun everyone in the history of mankind": *Daily Mail*, Apr. 2, 2007.
236. Along the way, his diary describes: *Guardian*, Mar. 28, 2007.
236. These smoking guns have inspired many doubters: *Daily Mail*, Apr. 2, 2007.
237. Guinness stuck by him: *Daily Mail*, Feb. 18, 2008.
237. Eric Peters's tale: *Times*, Sept. 21, 1983.
237. George Meegan, a British merchant seaman: *Times*, July 31, 1984.
238. When he finally reached the Beaufort Sea: *Times*, Sept. 20, 1983.
238. Few road warriors, even the most harried: *Telegraph*, Mar. 8, 2004.
239. Hertrich has kept the streak alive: *Oregon Mail Tribune*, Sept. 1, 2006.
240. Dale Webster, who was featured: *Washington Post*, Nov. 21, 2006.

240. "Great day, snow, and fun!!!: *Oregon Mail Tribune*, Sept. 1, 2006.

240. "I could stop and end the damn thing tomorrow: *Washington Post*, Nov. 21, 2006.

240. they were moved to include: *Express* (London), Nov. 9, 2006.

APPENDIX 4: A RECORD-BREAKING TIMELINE

254. 1960: Sir Hugh Beaver retires: *Times*, Dec. 31, 1960, 14.

254. 1962: Boehm licenses paperback rights to Bantam: Boehm, *Fascination of Book Publishing*, 17.

254. April 1970: The first U.S. television special: Ibid.
1973: Guinness PLC signs updated contracts with Sterling Publishing and Bantam: Ibid.

254. 1975: the *Guinness Book of World Records* "has set a record as the largest selling book": *Newsweek*, Sept. 15, 1975, 81.

254. 1995: Irwin tells the *Wall Street Journal*: *Wall Street Journal*, July 30, 1999.

255. 1995: Guinness Publishing sells two museums: *Business Week*, Mar. 13, 1995.

255. 1997: "We're called Guinness World Records now," says Alistair Richards: *Financial Times*, Jan. 21, 2006, 1.

255. 1995–98: Sales triple: *Wall Street Journal*, July 30, 1999.

255. 1999: *Guinness World Records: Primetime* is replicated in Britain, Germany, and Scandinavia: *Wall Street Journal*, July 30, 1999.

256. 1999: The official target reader switches: *Wall Street Journal*, July 30, 1999.

257. 2008: Guinness World Records Ltd. is purchased by Jim Pattison Group: Reuters, Feb. 15, 2008.

Index

About the Author

Larry Olmsted is a prolific freelance writer who has published thousands of articles in national publications, including *Outside, Playboy, USA Today,* and *Inc.,* is a contributing editor to numerous publications, and was a longtime columnist for *Investor's Business Daily.* He lives in Vermont.